The New Wellness Revolution

Second Edition

How to Make A Fortune
in the Next Trillion Dollar Industry

PAUL ZANE PILZER

John Wiley & Sons, Inc.

To J. I. Rodale (1898–1971)

CONTENTS

The Revolution Continues

What's New in *The New Wellness Revolution*

*T*he *Wellness Revolution* (Wiley, 2002) was the "shot heard round the world" for the wellness industry. It defined wellness as an industry—linking hundreds of thousands of disparate service and product suppliers with a single cause. It showed like-minded scientists, fitness providers, businesspeople, food manufacturers, restaurant owners, wellness product distributors, doctors, and others focused on disease prevention and anti-aging that they were part of a worldwide revolution—not just lone iconoclasts inside their chosen profession or industry.

Following the publication of *The Wellness Revolution,* I was called the "economist turned wellness guru" by the *New York Times.* I received an honorary doctorate for the role played by the book in helping Congress pass Health Savings Accounts (HSAs) and other healthcare financial reforms—reforms that now allow wellness-oriented consumers to save money on their health insurance and finance their wellness. And my book was published in 12 languages and became the focal point for an international wellness community—thousands of people contacted me to share their wellness experiences and/or to tell me about new business opportunities in this exciting, soon-to-be $1 trillion industry.

As a restless writer and economist, I've always preferred to move on to new frontiers after each book or project. But in this case, my publisher and editor convinced me to write this revised edition, because so much has happened in wellness in the past five years. Some of these events happened as I predicted, and some I missed back in 2002.

The Wellness Revolution foresaw the meteoric rise of wellness from $200 billion in 2002 to $500 billion today, and that Health Savings

Accounts (HSAs), which began in South Africa and were spreading worldwide, would soon become universally allowed for U.S. citizens. However, I missed how quickly governments around the world would embrace wellness food standards, and I miscalculated the voluntary conversion of many sickness and food industry providers (including, to some extent, McDonald's and Wal-Mart) to wellness and healthy food offerings. I also missed the extent to which the bifurcation of the United States and the other developed nations would continue into wellness "haves" and "have-nots." While millions of people embraced wellness during the past five years, millions more turned the opposite direction—the percentage of overweight Americans alone rose from 61 to 65 percent and the increase in diet-related diseases like Type 2 diabetes now make the United States look medically like a third world nation.

These trends have kept us on track to meet or exceed my original $1 trillion prediction for the wellness industry, and have greatly accelerated the need and opportunity for more wellness entrepreneurs.

Sir Isaac Newton said, "If I have seen further than others it is by standing on the shoulders of giants."[1] Since I began tracking the wellness industry back in 1996, my giants have been the wellness revolutionaries I first began profiling in *The Wellness Revolution*—men and women pioneers in wellness who had already made a major difference by 2002. People like:

- Frank Yanowitz, the wellness cardiologist who created a business specializing in preventing heart disease versus just treating it;
- Jill Kinney, the fitness expert who built a $100 million fitness club business that delivers exercise at the workplace; and
- Steve Demos, the "soy wonder" who founded SILK soymilk and assembled the first billion dollar national wellness brand.

Their stories, along with an update on where they are today, are in *The New Wellness Revolution*.

But, equally significant, since 2002 I have become aware of hundreds more wellness revolutionaries—people who have also made a difference in the wellness industry, and in doing so, have greatly enriched our world. Some of these wellness revolutionaries include:

- Peter and Kathie Davis, cofounders of IDEA and ACE, who organized 20,000 fitness professionals into a cohesive international force that brought professionalism, standards, and accreditation to the fitness industry;

- Information pioneers like Tod Cooperman and Joseph Mercola, who built enormous web-based businesses by simply supplying wellness information to tens of millions of consumers worldwide;

- Chiropractors like Fabrizio Mancini and Bob Hoffman who, along with other leaders in this 100-year-old international profession, are returning the chiropractic industry back to its wellness origins;

- Entrepreneurs like Patrick Gentempo, who are using the franchise and distribution methods of fast-food companies to build national wellness franchise businesses;

- Medical doctors who are trying to put themselves out of business, like Russ Reiss, a heart surgeon who seeks to eliminate the need for heart surgery through stem cell research; and

- Nonprofit professionals like Geoff Tabin, who has taken the most popular operation in the world, a $3,500 antiaging cataract surgery, and made it available to millions of people in the third world by using contemporary technology to reduce the price to $20 per surgery. As the wellness revolution enters its next stage, similar opportunities to make wellness affordable to the masses, just as Henry Ford did with the automobile, are appearing in all parts of the wellness industry.

Since 2002, the list of wellness revolutionaries, my "giants," has expanded one hundred-fold. As I stand on their collective shoulders I am able to see clearer into our wellness future. I wish I had room to tell you all of their stories, and I apologize to the many whose stories did not survive the editing process into this book.

These wellness revolutionaries are the true heroes of the wellness revolution. Whether you are an experienced wellness professional looking to grow your business, or you are reading this book in search of a new business opportunity, their stories will provide you the inspiration and the information you need to capitalize on the great opportunity ahead:

The opportunity to make an incredible fortune by doing incredible good in the greatest industry on earth—wellness.

The Next Millionaires—
Wellness Entrepreneurs

If you are an entrepreneur, or are considering becoming one in wellness, there has never been a better time in history to own your own business.

When I was growing up in the 1950s, millionaires were fictional characters in television shows like *The Millionaire* or in comic strips like *Little Orphan Annie*. Nobody actually knew or saw a millionaire. Even on *The Millionaire* the "millionaire" John Beresford Tipton never appeared on camera. I remember asking my dad to go out to dinner and hearing his reply: "What do you think we are, millionaires?"

But by 1991, the amazing U.S. economy had produced 3.6 million U.S. households that had a net worth of $1 million or more. Then, in just the next 10 years, the number of millionaire households doubled to 7.2 million. It took the U.S. economy 215 years to create the first 3.6 million millionaire households, and then just 10 years to create 3.6 million more.

As explained and predicted in my 1991 book *Unlimited Wealth*, what happened in the 1990s was the beginning of a 40-year period of international economic growth. From 1991 to 2001 U.S. household wealth tripled—from $13 trillion to $40 trillion—and a similar expansion occurred in every developed nation except Japan.

There have always been periods of economic growth and wealth accumulation, but in the past this often meant that the rich got richer and the ordinary person didn't stand a chance. What was so unique about the 1990s was the enormous number of new households that shared in this wealth. But the 1990s were only the beginning:

The 1990s were the beginning of a period that will be known one day as The Democratization of Wealth, not just in the United States, but in every nation from China to Europe.

As you will see in this book, because of fundamental changes in the world economy, in technology, and in new legislation favoring the individual over the organization, we are just beginning a period of democratization of wealth that would make Karl Marx stand up and cheer. But even Marx couldn't have fathomed what is happening today—for we are not taking from the rich and giving to the poor, we are creating new wealth in which everyone who chooses to can share.

Today, more than 10 million U.S. households have a net worth of $1 million or more. By 2016, there will be 20 million U.S. millionaire households. Each household represents approximately 2.5 people, meaning that 50 million Americans will soon live in a household with a net worth of $1 million or more.

Number of U.S. Millionaires, 1991–2016

	1991	2001	2006	2016 (predicted)
Number of millionaire households	3.6 million	7.2 million	10 million	20 million
Number of Americans living in a millionaire household	9 million	18 million	25 million	50 million
U.S. household wealth	$13 trillion	$40 trillion	$60 trillion	$100 trillion

Millionaires are the fastest growing minority in the United States and the developed world today.

And as you will see throughout this book, as people become millionaires, or just increase their wealth on the way to becoming one, the most important thing they desire with their newfound wealth is wellness.

The more people increase their wealth, the greater proportion of their income they spend on wellness.

Is It Nature, or Nurture?—It's Neither

One of the most fascinating parts of my research is discovering who is becoming a millionaire today—becoming a millionaire seems to have less correlation each year with your race, religion, country of origin, or even your parents or your education.

When the Forbes 400 list of the richest 400 Americans was first published in 1981, it contained 12 Rockefellers, 10 Morgans, 6 Astors, and other family names that had become synonyms for American wealth. Twenty-four years later only 40 of the original 400 (or their children) remain on the list, and none of these family names are in the top 10. The top 10 today possess 32 percent of the total wealth of the top 400 richest Americans.

But, rather than the rich getting richer, all of the top 10 on the Forbes 400 list were born poor or middle class, and only two of the top 10 finished college. Having an Ivy League education and/or being born into great wealth may even have a negative correlation for great financial success.

Moreover, it appears that many if not most of the people on the Forbes 400 list have something else in common—a brother or sister who is as great a failure in life as they are a success.

Several recent U.S. Presidents have a degree from Yale and a brother who has been to jail (or close to it). Donald Nixon, Billy Carter, Roger Clinton, Neil Bush—none of these people were either nurtured or natured to fail, and most had the same family upbringing and educational opportunities as their successful sibling.

Achieving great success today is no longer mostly determined by the color of your skin, your country of origin, or even your individual parents. Great success is now, more than ever before in human history, about making a choice. Of course your education, your parents, and other factors outside your control play a role, but the largest determinants of success today are the choices you make.

If you have read this far, you have already made your choice—the choice to either become one of, or help create more of, the next 10 million millionaire households that will be created in the next 10 years.

There are many paths to success you can choose. It is my hope that you will choose a business or career in the emerging wellness industry. For as you will soon see, starting or building a wellness business creates the perfect storm of opportunity to make a lot of money and to do incredible good.

What Are Some of the New Wellness Trends Highlighted in *The New Wellness Revolution?*

As expected in a revised edition written by an economist, the numbers and projections have been updated. But there is more to this revised edition than just updated forecasts. Here are a few of the new trends in wellness:

1. The wellness revolution began in the United States, but is growing even faster internationally.

The Wellness Revolution, published in 2002, was focused solely on the U.S. domestic market, where the modern wellness movement began. Yet this book has been published in 12 languages, and unit sales overseas, particularly in Asia, have exceeded sales in the United States. While the modern wellness industry may have begun in the United States, like so many other new products and industries originally made in America, it is now growing even faster outside the United States.

The New Wellness Revolution *is written for people around the world.*

2. Wellness today is primarily a grass-roots movement driven by individual entrepreneurs and small businesses.

In 2002, I wrote mostly about the larger $100 million wellness companies, since that is how I originally became acquainted with the wellness industry. Yet the majority of wellness sales, then and today, are made collectively by individual entrepreneurs, direct selling professionals, chiropractors, osteopaths, other health professionals, and small businesses. This is because becoming a wellness customer requires a paradigm shift on the part of the consumer, and direct person-to-person contact is the best way, and sometimes the only way, to make this paradigm shift in a person's thinking take place.

The New Wellness Revolution *explains why the majority of opportunities in wellness still await the individual entrepreneur or health professional, and how new management techniques and forms of business organization (like direct selling and franchising) can allow such individuals even better technology than if they were part of a large corporation. This will continue for at least another decade, until wellness is a mature industry and the majority of wellness consumers are not new to wellness.*

3. Some large sickness-oriented food companies have switched sides and joined the wellness revolution.

When I wrote *The Wellness Revolution,* in 2002, some of the worst sickness-oriented food businesses were milk dairies. Following the book's publication, the world's largest dairy, Dean Foods (U.S. sales $10 billion), purchased one of the best wellness food companies in the world; Steve Demos's $300 million WhiteWave, Inc., the maker of SILK soymilk. Yet, as explained in Chapter 4, rather than destroying SILK and its quality wellness product line, it looks like WhiteWave and its wellness philosophy have taken over at Dean Foods.

> The New Wellness Revolution *explains how this turnaround in thinking at Dean Foods and other large food companies is only the beginning, and how this phenomenon is increasing rather than decreasing wellness opportunities for everyone, particularly wellness entrepreneurs. As explained in Chapter 2, once a consumer has his or her first wellness experience (like drinking soymilk), he or she typically becomes a voracious consumer of more and more wellness products and services.*

4. Retailers and restaurants, formerly known for only sickness-industry products, have similarly switched sides and joined the wellness revolution.

In 2002, most wellness food retail sales were through designated wellness outlets like health food stores and wellness restaurants. While the number and sales of these wellness outlets have increased, the majority of wellness food sales is shifting to traditional retail food and restaurant outlets.

In 2005, McDonald's began selling a fruit and walnut salad, and overnight it became the country's largest food-service consumer of apples, requiring an estimated 54 million pounds of apples per year. McDonald's has a great tradition of solving social problems, and now this worst offender (e.g., "Super Size Me") is poised to become a major wellness contributor. In the 1970s, McDonald's become the first major employer to embrace hiring and training inner city youth, after many in America had given up on them. In the 1980s, McDonald's reengineered its operations to be able to hire senior citizens in selected markets through innovations such as flexible hours and large-button cash registers. This slumbering giant, which feeds more than 46 million people every day, has been awakened to wellness.

At the beginning of 2006, Whole Foods Market (sales of $7 billion) was the largest wellness food market. But on March 26, 2006, Wal-Mart (sales of $275 billion) opened its first organic foods Supercenter in Plano, Texas, and simultaneously began featuring wellness products in all of its stores. By the time you read this, Wal-Mart may be the world's largest wellness food retailer.

> *All of this bodes well for the wellness industry, and particularly for wellness entrepreneurs, because this greatly increases the acceptance of well-*

ness products and distribution outlets for mass-market wellness pro-
duce. Despite the recent growth of wellness to a $500 billion industry,
most consumers have still yet to have their first wellness experience, and
the numbers of overweight and obese have continued to rise.

5. This switching sides phenomenon is generally not taking place among sickness-industry (e.g., traditional medical) providers.

Unlike the $1.3 trillion food industry, the $2 trillion medical industry has not embraced wellness and shows few signs of doing so. While there are exceptions, for the most part U.S. hospitals, pharmaceutical companies, and health professional organizations are either ignoring wellness or fighting it whenever it crosses into their territory.

The traditional medical or sickness industry is fighting a losing battle. Like the railroads at the beginning of the 20th century, which saw their industry as trains versus transportation (and subsequently lost out to trucks and automobiles), the sickness industry is poised to lose out to wellness.

When the automobile first came out 100 years ago, most people saw it as just a carriage without a horse or a train that didn't require rails. A select few realized that the horseless carriage was not like a carriage or a train, but represented a new industry that would fundamentally change almost every aspect of American life—people like Henry Ford (autos), John D. Rockefeller (gasoline), Ray Croc (drive-in restaurants), Howard Johnson (roadside motels), and thousands more became the billionaires of their day and the leaders of our society. A similar opportunity awaits entrepreneurs and health professionals who realize that wellness is a new movement, a revolution, rather than a single healthier item of food or alternative medical treatment.

While everyone reading this book might personally wish that traditional
medicine would return to its Hippocratic roots and embrace wellness,
the stubbornness and shortsightedness of many traditional medical pro-
viders has created an enormous business opportunity for wellness entre-
preneurs and professionals.

6. Thousands of new wellness products and services have come to market, some of which I predicted back in 2002, but, frankly, many of which I didn't expect to occur until at least 2012.

In 2002, I expected that in about 10 years DNA- and other scientifically-based tests for targeted nutritional supplementation would become universal, adding legitimacy to the then-$80 billion vitamin business. But I far underestimated how fast legitimacy would come to the wellness diagnostic industry. In 2004, a DNA-based swab kit to identify vitamin deficiencies became available for $10 per test. In 2005, a $10 million, room-sized, fingertip-reading light scanner that reads antioxidant levels was redesigned into a booksized unit and made widely available for less than the cost of a laptop computer—already 10 million people have had their antioxidant levels measured with this portable device.

Moreover, as also explained in Chapter 10, another new development, stem cell research, holds great promise for wellness. Although scientists still don't know exactly how stem cells work, medical professionals are using them to rebuild damaged organs and to slow down the aging process.

The New Wellness Revolution *explains how these and many other new products are legitimizing the wellness industry by applying medical testing techniques and pharmaceutical-grade manufacturing standards to wellness products and services.*

7. In the United States, from 2004 to 2007, enormous changes occurred in health insurance that now allow employees and individuals to invest in their own wellness, and to keep what they don't spend on sickness today for their future wellness (or retirement) tomorrow.

In 2002, I correctly forecast that Congress would have to make Health Savings Accounts (HSAs) universally available for all Americans—but I didn't expect it to happen so quickly, nor did I expect that my work would play a role in helping convince Congress to take action.

The New Wellness Revolution explains how and why three million Americans have already opened HSAs, and how more than 11 million Americans are now covered by employer-provided Health Reimbursement Arrangements (HRAs). HSAs and HRAs allow employees a 100 percent income tax deduction for many of their wellness expenditures, and they allow people to keep for their future wellness tomorrow what they don't spend on sickness today.

HSAs, HRAs, and other Consumer Directed Healthcare (CDH) vehicles allow consumers to choose their own health providers—putting chiropractors, osteopaths, naturopaths, and other wellness-oriented providers on an equal basis with traditional sickness-industry medical providers.

This leveling of the playing field between sickness and wellness providers began in South Africa, and is now taking root in every developed nation—because governments finally recognize that preventing disease and supporting antiaging are the only solutions to the rising medical costs that threaten their economies.

8. In 2005, the cost of providing U.S. employees sickness-industry health benefits exceeded profits for the Fortune 500 largest corporations—and stockholders worldwide are questioning whether to continue funding many once-viable corporations, like General Motors.

While everyone has talked about the rising cost of employer sickness-industry expenses for decades, 2005 was the watershed year—the year in which rising sickness-industry expenses went beyond just reducing profits to actually threatening the very existence of major U.S. employers. Employers en masse have realized that the only long-term solution to rising sickness-industry expenses is wellness—programs that increase fitness and prevent disease from occurring in the first place.

The New Wellness Revolution *explains the enormous opportunity for local wellness entrepreneurs to provide workplace wellness programs in their own communities, starting with weight loss and smoking cessation programs for employers powered by HRAs.*

9. Despite the growth of the wellness industry from $200 billion to $500 billion in just five years, and the resulting millions of new wellness industry consumers, the untapped market for wellness has actually increased in size. In the United States alone, the number of overweight adults increased from 61 to 65 percent during the past five years, and childhood obesity grew 10 percent, from 27 to 30 percent of children.

When I began writing about obesity and overweightness in 1996, I never thought this epidemic would be even larger more than ten years later. Although millions of new consumers every day embrace wellness, millions more remain outside the reach of the current wellness industry and become more overweight, malnourished, exercise less and/or continue to smoke.

The New Wellness Revolution explains how the population of every developed nation continues to divide itself into two opposing socioeconomic groups—those who are fit and healthy and take care of their wellness, and those who don't. This terrible phenomenon has catastrophic economic and social consequences.

The contractual sickness-industry obligations to solely former employees now threatens the viability of many U.S. school systems and the ability of local and national government to provide basic human services. In the United States alone, this unfunded local and state government obligation to provide unlimited sickness care to former employees now exceeds $1 trillion, and the resulting scandal will make the $300 billion S&L scandal of the 1980s pale by comparison. The scandal may even be worse in Europe and other developed nations.

10. I've joined the wellness revolution as an entrepreneur.

In 1999, I founded a company to spread wellness by reforming health insurance. This company became part of Steve Case's *Revolution Health Group* in 2005, and today supplies wellness-oriented health benefits to millions of people through their employers or through Wal-Mart's Sam's Club stores.

In 2006, I founded a similar company focused on distributing similar wellness-oriented health benefits through wellness entrepreneurs and financial services professionals. This new company, Zane Benefits LLC (www.zanebenefits.com), is already making a difference on hundreds of college campuses and with thousands of entrepreneurs and employers, by getting consumers better, safer, and cheaper wellness-oriented health insurance.

Action Plan for Entrepreneurs and Wellness/Health Professionals

At the end of each chapter you will find a section called *Action Plan for Entrepreneurs and Wellness/Health Professionals*. This is meant for new entrepreneurs or for people currently employed who are contemplating striking out on their own. I do not want to imply that my suggested *Action Plan* is the only one you should follow. My objective is to illustrate how great an opportunity there is in wellness, and to stimulate your mind to apply your own background, education, and life experiences to becoming an entrepreneur in the wellness industry.

Paul Zane Pilzer
Park City, Utah

Why Wellness Is the Next Big Thing

In the twentieth century, our lives were revolutionized by things like the automobile, airline travel, the personal computer, and family planning. In those cases, initial discoveries led to the birth of empires and to unprecedented individual wealth for those entrepreneurs and investors who got in first. The next big thing of the twenty-first century has begun, and it promises to similarly revolutionize our lives and offer opportunities for tremendous wealth building over the next 10 years.

This book is not about a fad or a trend—it's about a new and infinite need infusing itself into the way we eat, exercise, sleep, work, save, age, and almost every other aspect of our lives.

This next big thing is the *wellness revolution.*

The desire for wellness already pervades our decisions, from which toothpaste and shampoo we use in the morning to what we eat throughout the day to the type of bedding and cosmetics we use at night. We demand more safety from our products; we want more prevention from them, too. And yet we are only at the beginning of the public consciousness of this growing need—because most people still aren't aware of how simple choices affect their wellness, and many wellness products and services aren't yet widely available in the marketplace.

This book explains the emerging wellness industry, so as to arm you with the information that you need in order to profit from it, both financially and personally.

I show you how to stake your claim in this huge opportunity—how to find your place in this new total-life industry that not only can bring you riches, but also does incredible good.

The Next Big Thing

When Henry Ford first invented a mass-produced automobile that was affordable to the common person, many scoffed at the thought that people would buy it. There were few paved roads on which to travel, gasoline stations were nonexistent, and most people lived within walking distance of their workplaces. But the need grew along with the proliferation of the product. People moved to suburbia and needed cars. At the same time, gasoline stations sprang up. Soon the car became necessary just to get to work or shop for daily necessities.

What if you had been told back then that Henry Ford's Model T wasn't just another new product, but the beginning of a whole new trillion dollar sector of the world economy—that in 100 years there would be 500 million cars on the road, necessitating ancillary trillion dollar industries in gas stations, road construction, replacement tires, motels, suburban homes, and fast-food restaurants?

Would you have accepted this notion? In addition to the limitations of no roads, no gasoline stations, and conveniently nearby workplaces, people typically worked six days a week for little pay, with little time off for Sunday drives in the country. To accept this concept you would also have had to foresee the coming five-day, 40-hour workweek and the rise in discretionary income.

But suppose you overcame your skepticism and saw the new self-powered vehicles of Henry Ford and others as the beginning of a trillion dollar industry. As an entrepreneur or an investor, where would you have placed your bet? Would it have been on gasoline-powered cars or on electric or diesel ones? Would it have been on road construction, on replacement parts like tires, or on residential land development? And just as significantly, once you picked one of these areas, what specifically would you have done to stake your claim?

More recently—in 1981—a surprise mega-industry was born from the newly minted personal computer, the IBM PC, along with competitive models by Apple and RadioShack. Perhaps most people were similarly unable to predict that these were not just new products, but the harbingers of another trillion dollar sector of the world economy—a sector growing so fast that personal computer sales would surpass U.S. automobile sales in only 10 years, by 1991.

In our modern economy, changes that used to take place over the span of 100 years or more now take place in 10 years or less. Had you been able to foresee the rise of the trillion dollar personal computer business like Bill Gates (Microsoft, software), Michael Dell (Dell Computer, hardware), Jeff Bezos (Amazon, distribution), and countless others, in what part of the personal computer industry would you have placed your bet?

Historically, pivotal new products became available because of scientific breakthroughs that allowed their invention and affordable manufacture.

The self-powered vehicle and the personal computer were the oxymora of their times. After all, in the days of the horse and buggy, the public had a difficult time accepting that a vehicle could be self-powered. Similarly, in the days of roomsize mainframe computers, who could easily visualize that a computer could be personal?

People didn't need the automobile and the personal computer before they became available—any more than today we need interplanetary travel. Yet once they became available, they quickly went from simply being new products to becoming absolute necessities for daily work and life.

What was it about these two new products, and several others, that made them so immediately successful? Was there something self-evident about them that foreshadowed how pervasive they were about to become in almost every aspect of our lives? Knowing those traits could perhaps help you predict other new industries from which to profit.

There are actually five distinct characteristics of emerging pervasive industries, which I will tell you about in a moment. But first I want to share with you a crucial way of thinking about wellness and understanding the causes of its inevitable growth.

Defining the Trillion Dollar Wellness Industry

We are now at the beginning of the next trillion dollar industry—an industry that will impact almost every aspect of our lives and achieve $1 trillion in sales in just five more years, but one that is as unknown today as the automobile industry was in 1908 or the personal computer industry was in 1981.

The automobile industry was spawned by scientific breakthroughs in chemistry, metallurgy, and mechanics. The personal computer industry was spawned by scientific breakthroughs in physics and binary mathematics.

This next trillion dollar industry is being spawned by scientific breakthroughs in biology and cellular biochemistry.

The wellness industry is tackling one of the most profound issues of life, solving one of the few remaining mysteries of human existence—age and vitality—on which technology has yet to make its mark. In order to define the wellness industry and identify its opportunities, we must first distinguish it from a related industry based on some of the same technology—the current $2.0 trillion (U.S.) healthcare industry.

Approximately one-sixth of the U.S. economy, about $2.0 trillion, is devoted to what is erroneously called the "healthcare" business. *Healthcare* is a misnomer, as this one-sixth of the economy is really devoted to the *sickness* business—defined in the dictionary as "ill health, illness, a disordered, weakened, or unsound condition, or a specific disease."[1]

The sickness business is *reactive*. Despite its enormous size, people become customers only when they are stricken by and react to a specific condition or ailment. No one really wants to be a customer.

In the next 5 years, an additional $500 billion of the U.S. economy will be devoted to the still relatively unknown already-$500 billion *wellness* business—defined in the dictionary as "the quality or state of being in good health *especially as an actively sought goal* [emphasis added]."[2]

The wellness business is *proactive*. People *voluntarily* become customers—to feel healthier, to reduce the effects of aging, and to avoid becoming customers of the sickness business. Everyone wants to be a customer of this earlier-stage approach to health.

From this point forward I use the following definitions:

Sickness industry products and services provided reactively to people with an existing disease, ranging from a common cold to existing cancerous tumors. These products and services seek to either treat the symptoms of a disease or eliminate the disease.

Wellness industry products and services provided proactively to healthy people (those without an existing disease) to make them feel even healthier and look better, to slow the effects of aging, and/or to prevent diseases from developing in the first place.

How to Read This Book

Throughout this book I highlight important points you need to know in order to explain the importance of this new industry to your family, associates, clients, customers, investors, and partners.

I also highlight points essential to helping you stake your claim through entrepreneurship, investment, distribution, and/or by using this information to change your existing business today.

In Chapter 1, I share with you my vision for the wellness industry. When I began to write the first edition of *The Wellness Revolution* (2002), I thought the existing items in the wellness industry—fitness clubs, vitamins, and the like—might already total a few billion dollars in U.S. sales. I was very surprised to find that sales in 2002 had already reached approximately $200 billion—they rose to approximately $500 billion by 2007. Yet still only a small percentage of the population know about wellness. Imagine what will happen as more people understand the potential that wellness can add to the quality and longevity of their lives!

In Chapter 2, I explain the notion of demand, how it operates in relation to wellness, and how controlled growth of demand can occur. I show why the $500 billion in proven demand today is still only the tip of the iceberg, and why these new products and services represent the beginning of a *new* $1 trillion sector of our economy (as opposed to offshoot products in existing industries like agribusiness or medicine).

In Chapter 3, you learn how our $1.3 trillion existing agribusiness and food industry targets overweight and obese consumers for ever-

increasing consumption—causing a health crisis in the United
States that finds 65 percent of the population currently overweight
and 30 percent clinically obese. These numbers have doubled in the
past two decades and have increased seven percent in the last five
years. Other developed nations, especially in the EU, Japan, and Taiwan, are not far behind.

Then, in Chapter 4, you learn how this has created one of the greatest business opportunities of our time—educating consumers and
providing healthy food and the necessary vitamins and supplements
that are no longer contained in our modern food supply.

In the past, a significant part of the health and sickness industry
was concerned with wellness. At the beginning of the last century,
technological breakthroughs in inoculation and antibiotics allowed
medicine to develop preventive measures for many diseases (smallpox, typhoid, tuberculosis, polio) that had been the scourge of
humankind for millennia.

That was the past.

**Most of the one-sixth of the U.S. adult working popula-
tion that work in the healthcare industry today focus on
treating the symptoms of disease rather than on preventing disease. This is because it is more profitable for medical companies to research and develop products that
create customers for life.**

It is also because the third parties paying for most medical treatments—insurance companies and ultimately employers—have less
of a long-term financial stake in the health of their employees. If you
are among this one-sixth of the workforce in the healthcare field,
Chapter 5 examines some of the entrepreneurial opportunities aris-
ing in the wellness industry for medical professionals. Providing wellness products and services that people will voluntarily purchase with
their own funds works better than providing bureaucratic procedures
to unhappy consumers without choice who are financed by distant
third parties.

In Chapter 6 you learn why our existing employer-based healthcare insurance system is on the verge of collapse and what you can
do to protect yourself and your family. Despite a rising economy
since the beginning of the 1990s, U.S. personal bankruptcy filings
tripled—from approximately 750,000 in 1990 to 2,000,000 in
2005—with much of the increase resulting from family medical

catastrophes. One million middle and upper-class U.S. families are now forced into bankruptcy every year by the sickness industry.

In Chapter 7 you learn how opting out of the existing sickness-based system (i.e., getting permanent, renewable, wellness-oriented health insurance today) can save you thousands of dollars a year and pay for the wellness products and services you need to invest in your long-term health and vitality.

The entrepreneurial opportunity to convert households from employer-based sickness-only health insurance to wellness-oriented individual and family health insurance is one of the greatest opportunities within the wellness industry.

As exciting as some of these developments may seem today, they all pale in comparison to the coming new wellness products and services. As with automobiles in 1908 and personal computers in 1981, the best new products and services are still in the laboratory and will be coming onto the market in the next few years. Already today, it is possible to examine a person's DNA and predict his or her probability of developing certain diseases. It is now possible, using a portable laser-based device, to take an indirect reading of antioxidant and other vitamin levels. Using this information, a wellness entrepreneur can now target specific exercise, food, vitamin, and supplement-based therapies—adding years in both quantity and quality to the life of a customer. And these breakthroughs of the past few years are just the beginning.

Even these immediate opportunities pale in comparison to what is coming next—for we are getting close to cracking the genetic code for aging itself, and once we do, the wellness industry will be at the forefront in distributing the resultant products and services.

In any industry based on new technology, the greatest entrepreneurial fortunes are consistently made by those who distribute products and services rather than by those who make them. This is partly because, in any area of rapidly advancing technology, today's CD-ROM disc is tomorrow's eight-track tape, and only distributors unbeholden to a specific technology are able to quickly shift to new and more efficacious products. But it is mostly because of the following, as you learn in Chapter 8:

Today, 70 to 80 percent of the cost of most retail products is in distribution—which explains why the world's greatest individual fortunes are now being made by people focused on distributing things rather than on making things.

You also learn in Chapter 8 how the nature of the opportunity within distribution has recently changed—from the physical distribution of products themselves to the intellectual distribution of information about them. Sam Walton (Wal-Mart) became the richest man in the world 20 years ago by physically distributing to customers what they already knew they wanted; however, more recently Jeff Bezos (Amazon.com) became *Time* magazine's Person-of-the-Year by teaching customers about products that they didn't know even existed. Nowhere is this more true than in the emerging wellness industry—an industry in which most of the costs of products and services lie in their distribution and in which the overwhelming majority of future customers do not yet know that the products even exist.

Some readers who are not doctors, health professionals, or experienced businesspeople may be asking themselves what is the best place to get started in wellness without putting their savings or job at risk? For most of these people, as well as for experienced businesspeople, the Direct Selling industry is a great place to find their wellness fortune. As explained in Chapter 9, you can get started for less than $100 and work part-time until your business takes off. Even if you discover that Direct Selling is not for you, you can still win in the long run by applying the skills and leadership you learn in another field.

Suppose I told you in 1845 about the gold rush that would be coming to California in 1849. No matter how motivated you were to get rich and no matter how hard you worked once you got to California, you wouldn't have made a dime unless you knew where to stake your claim once you got there. In reality, very few of the wannabe miners who spent their lives searching for gold actually made it. Many of the fortunes of the California gold rush were made by individuals using skills and relationships they had already developed elsewhere to provide products and services for the gold rush industry—men like Henry Wells (1805–1878) and George Fargo (1818–1881), who formed the Wells Fargo Company to provide banking and express transport services for miners.

Each of us has generic abilities, functional skills, and personal relationships based on what we have done in our lives until now. In Chapter 10 you learn where you should stake your claim to your share of this emerging $1 trillion wellness industry.

From providing services to distributing products to investing in wellness companies, there are numerous opportunities, but the best ones for each of us are the ones that best utilize the assets we already have.

The Five Distinct Characteristics of Pervasive Industries

The most successful investors and entrepreneurs know how to distinguish between a passing fad and a long-term trend—the five distinct characteristics of pervasive industries that I promised to tell you about. Let's take a look at these characteristics and analyze each one with respect to the emerging wellness industry.

Most people think of Henry Ford as the inventor of the automobile in 1908 with his Model T. However, cars were actually around for decades earlier as recreational toys for the wealthy.* Ford's real invention was to use various new technologies to produce, in his own words, a car "so low in price that no man making a good salary will be unable to own one."[3]

A similar story can be told about radios, televisions, restaurants, airplane travel, VCRs, DVDs, fax machines, personal computers, PDAs, e-mail, and many other inventions that have become ubiquitous and changed the way we live.

All of these products, like the automobile, started out as products for the rich. Then, once technology advanced to the point where they could be produced at a price affordable to working people, they became ubiquitous. Why did they become so popular? What else did these products or services have going for them in addition to being first enjoyed by the rich?

---

*Ford, like most entrepreneurs, at first did not succeed. He founded his first motor company in 1899—it flopped. He founded a second one in 1901, which also failed. And the firm we know today as Ford Motor Company, which he started in 1903, almost failed in 1906 because he went too far upscale before deciding to make the affordable Model T.

Each of these now-ubiquitous products or services had five distinct characteristics at the time they traveled from the classes to the masses.

Experienced entrepreneurs and investors look for all five of the following characteristics to be present before they launch a new mass-market business.

1. **Affordability**
2. **Legs**
3. **Continual consumption**
4. **Universal appeal**
5. **Low consumption time**

---

1. *Affordability.* When the VCR first came out in 1976, every household wanted one, but few could afford the $1,500 price. As advancing technology lowered the price to less than $100, so many VCRs were sold that by 1990 there were 121 million VCRs in 110 million U.S. households. The same phenomenon happened more recently with DVD players, iPod music players, satellite GPS devices—except in some of these cases what took place in 14 years with VCRs during the last century took place in our century in 14 months. In some cases, such as with the automobile or single-family homes, rapidly advancing technology couldn't make them cheap enough to be affordable—but then another new industry, consumer finance, emerged to spread out the cost on an affordable monthly basis.

2. *Legs.* No amount of marketing will make a product or service ubiquitous unless it has legs—the ability to walk off the shelf without promotion once a critical mass of people own it. Cars, televisions, and PCs are all products that consumers immediately want once they see them being enjoyed by others. Marketing graveyards are filled with products that stopped selling the minute their promotion had stopped.

3. *Continual consumption.* It costs more than $100 today in promotion and advertising expenses to get consumers to try a new product, and that's just to see if they like it. If they do like it, to succeed it must be part of a business with products or services that they will continue to purchase. With television or radio, continual use leads to more advertising sales, which leads to more shows, which leads to more televisions and radios. While

a consumer might purchase a VCR or DVD player for $100 only once every five years, each VCR or DVD creates hundreds of dollars in annual sales and rentals of prerecorded movies. Once people buy a new PC, they typically then want a new printer, a better monitor, a faster Internet connection, and so on. Ubiquitous products must be continually consumed in order to succeed.

4. *Universal appeal.* In order to become a mass-market business that changes the way in which we live, especially with the high cost today of customer education, the product or service must be one wanted by virtually everyone who learns about it. Virtually everyone today wants a car, a radio, or a PC—but not everyone wants a kayak, a mountain bike, or a luxury cruise. However, just because a business has universal appeal doesn't mean that there is such a thing as a universal product—each consumer has different needs that must be served within the same product family. Henry Ford initially made his Model T affordable by making a single universal model, often boasting that he would sell you a car "in any color you want, so long as it's black." Yet Ford lost out in the 1920s to General Motors when GM appealed to the Model T owner who wanted to trade up to a higher-quality model with a wide choice of colors and with annual model changes to stimulate recurring demand.

5. *Low consumption time.* This is the greatest challenge today for new products and services seeking to become ubiquitous— busy consumers must have time to enjoy them. At the time they became widespread, most of today's ubiquitous products, in addition to being enjoyable, actually saved the consumer time. The automobile and jet plane got them there faster, the VCR or DVD let them watch a movie in less time than it took to go to the theater (or gave them more time with their families while they watched their favorite show over dinner), and the PC produced finished letters in a fraction of the time it took using a typewriter.

Wellness Is a Pervasive Industry That Won't Go Away

Until recently, many wellness products and services were available only to the rich. I first became aware that such products and services existed in the late 1990s, when we built our family beach house in Pacific Palisades, California, and I noticed how my wealthy and celebrity neighbors approached the subject of food and health. After I became a wellness consumer, I found it difficult to obtain many of the products and services I wanted when I traveled outside of my up-scale community—from restaurants serving healthy food to exercise facilities at hotels.

Today things are changing. Every day more restaurants serve healthy food, new exercise facilities open, and more vitamins and supplements are being touted in mainstream advertising. But have things changed enough for the wellness industry to be ready to jump from the classes to the masses? To answer that question, let's take a closer look at the five characteristics of ubiquitous products and how the wellness industry relates to each of them.

First, are wellness products and services affordable? It used to be that the only way to get fresh, healthy food was to make it yourself. Restaurants served either expensive, heavy cuisine or prepackaged processed food. Today, healthy food is available not only in health food restaurants, but in most eating establishments, as they add af-fordable, healthy alternatives to their menus. As we examine later in more detail, a similar lowering of prices is occurring in other wellness areas: Personal trainers now work by the hour for dozens at one loca-tion, rather than for only one celebrity at a private home, and quality vitamins and supplements are now readily available without having to grow or mix them up yourself. Moreover, as we discuss in Chapter 7, when it comes to making wellness affordable, new health insurance plans have emerged that give healthy consumers and employees thousands each year to invest in their wellness, or save for future sickness or wellness expenses.

Second, do wellness industry products have legs to "walk off the shelf on their own" without continued promotion? Every time suc-cessful wellness consumers mention their age, adeptly perform some physical activity, or lose weight, their friends and associates ask what they are doing to look so young, become so strong, or get into such good shape. Invariably, their response leads to the purchase of a similar item by the person asking the question.

Wellness industry products and services have perhaps the strongest legs of any product or service, as people imme-diately notice when someone has a wellness experience and are anxious to duplicate the results.

Third, are wellness industry products and services continually con-sumed? By their very nature, vitamins, exercise, food, and other wellness products and services are perhaps the most continually con-sumed products and services in our economy. When wellness con-sumers find something that works for them, they typically become enthusiastic consumers of that product or service and become open to trying other wellness items. For example, once people start exer-cising to lose weight, they often start taking dietary supplements and seeking out healthier cuisine.

Fourth, do wellness products and services have universal appeal? Every human being, no matter how healthy or fit, wants to be even healthier and more fit. This is partly because there is no limit to how well and strong we can feel, but mostly because only the wellness in-dustry offers solutions to the universal problem of human aging, rather than just telling aging consumers to meekly accept their dete-riorating physical condition.

Last, and perhaps most important in assessing both the short- and long-term prospects for the wellness industry, do consumers have available the time it takes to consume most wellness products and services? The answer to this question bodes well for our entire econ-omy as well as for the wellness industry.

As explained in Chapter 2, the growth of our modern economy de-pends on consumers spending their increasing disposable income on luxury goods that soon become necessities—often on new products and services that didn't exist when they were born. However, a close examination of some of these new products and services yields a par-adox that could limit this growth in the future.

Most new luxury products, from Harley-Davidson motorcycles to home garden tractors, have one major drawback: they take time to enjoy. This is one of the great paradoxes of modern life. Each year, consumers seem to have more and more disposable income but less and less time to enjoy it. In contrast to the "idle rich" and "working poor" stereotypes of the past, disposable income today is inversely proportional to leisure time for almost every class level. When you asked people years ago why they hadn't bought a particular new item, a typical response might have been that they couldn't afford it. Today, a more likely response might be that they haven't had time to play with the new item they bought a week or month ago.

Moreover, an increasing amount of the growth in consumer de-mand today is for entertainment and services rather than for physi-cal products. These time-consuming purchases, ranging from massages to luxury cruises to opera tickets, have their own limitation on demand—the 24-hour day and the 365-day year. Some con-sumers report that their main time constraint today comes from other leisure activities rather than from their work.

Our modern economy could grind to a halt because of such a non-monetary limit to consumer demand—unless, of course, technology could come up with products and services desired by consumers that do not take time to enjoy.

Wellness products and services represent perhaps the only sector of consumer spending that does not take time to enjoy. Money spent to make a person feel stronger, smile better, look younger, or feel healthier yields rewards that are enjoyed every moment of every day—on the job, at home, and at every moment in between.

It is clear that wellness is about to change our lives as much as did the automobile or the personal computer. Before I explain how you, the entrepreneur, can benefit from this pervasive and eternal industry with tremendous growth potential, let's examine how the wellness industry got started and how pervasive it is about to become.

CHAPTER 1

Why We Need a Revolution

First, let's check out the definition:
rev·o·lu·tion[1]
I   *a: a sudden, radical, or complete change*
  b: a fundamental change in political organization
  c: activity or movement designed to effect fundamental changes in the socioeconomic situation
  d: a fundamental change in the way of thinking about or visualizing something: a change of paradigm <the Copernican revolution>
  e: a changeover in use or preference esp. in technology <the computer revolution> <the foreign car revolution>

The seventeenth-century English writer John Milton saw revolution as the right of society to defend itself against abusive tyrants—creating a new order that reflected the needs of the people. To Milton, revolution was the means of accomplishing freedom.[2]

The eighteenth-century German philosopher Immanuel Kant believed in revolution as a force for the advancement of humankind—a natural step in the realization of a higher ethical foundation for society.[3]

The nineteenth-century German philosopher G. W. F. Hegel saw revolutions as the fulfillment of human destiny, and he saw revolutionary leaders as necessary to instigate and implement reforms.[4]

These insights aptly apply to the wellness revolution.

Entrepreneurs and revolutionaries are really the same kinds of people born into different circumstances. Both see the status quo in need of change, and both are willing to take the risks, and reap the rewards, of changing it.

The emerging wellness industry is as much a reaction to the tyranny of the sickness and the food industries as it is to every person's desire for the freedom wellness offers. Wellness is the next natural step forward in our destiny and in the advancement of humankind. By extending your years of strength and wellness, you can accomplish those things you want to accomplish.

The revolutionary leaders in wellness are the entrepreneurs who grow and procreate wellness, the inventors who instigate wellness services and products, and the practitioners and distributors who carry the wellness message throughout society. Take your pick of how you want to be a leader of this new industry.

Revolutions and entrepreneurial journeys often begin with an epiphany—an illuminating discovery by an individual that typically sets him or her out on a quest. For everyone, this trigger will be different. For you, it could be what you learn from this book, or it could be a sickness experience—your own or that of a loved one—that could have been prevented. My epiphany occurred during a speech I was giving in 1996.

How Wellness Became My Cause

When I was growing up in the 1950s, economic issues seemed to dominate 95 percent of our waking lives. My father left for work at 5:30 A.M. and returned home after dinner, just as my mother was putting my brothers and me to bed. He did this six days a week. All our neighbors and relatives lived a similar existence, except those unlucky enough to be out of work. And, although everyone talked mostly about economic issues (how to make money, where to find work, etc.), no one seemed to have solutions for how to achieve economic success. This is why I became an economist: to find these solutions—solutions to what then seemed to be the most important problems facing my immediate society—my parents, relatives, and close friends.*

---

*In 1971, when I began college and chose to study economics, half the world lived under communism, and world leaders freely debated the merits of capitalist versus communist systems. In the United States, people were divided over whether the government or the private sector should be the exclusive provider of services, from mail delivery to phone service to train travel.

Twenty-five years later, while giving a speech in the Midwest, I realized that I was in the wrong profession, given the original reason I had chosen to become an economist.

It was Saturday, September 7, 1996, at the RCA Dome in Indianapolis. I was getting ready to go onstage as the keynote speaker before 45,000 people to discuss my latest book, *God Wants You to Be Rich*. My speaking fee had just been handed to me in a sealed envelope—more money for a 45-minute speech than I used to make in a full year when I graduated from Wharton and started working at Citibank.

I should have been elated. But instead I felt guilty. As I watched the audience file into the stadium and began my speech, I felt as if I were about to rip them off.

Like much of America, half of the audience was unhealthy and overweight, a direct consequence of diet and lifestyle evidenced by the fatigued look on their faces and the size of their waistlines. Nothing I was about to say about economics was going to improve the quality of their lives until they first learned how to take care of their bodies.

A strange urge seized me—to scrap my prepared speech and tell my audience that good health was more important than any riches they might acquire— but I chickened out. I didn't want to offend my hosts. And truthfully, I didn't know back then what actions would allow most people to take control of their health.

On the flight home early the next morning I began to wrestle with this question: Why would intelligent people spend time and money to improve their lives in every area *except* the one in which they most obviously needed improvement? And, more significant, what should a person who is unhealthy and overweight do to begin taking control of his or her life?

Why We Need a Revolution: Two Nations Divided by Great Want*

I arrived in Los Angeles around 10 A.M. that Sunday morning and rushed to Pacific Palisades to meet the contractor who was renovating our family beach house. As we stood outside discussing the construction, neighbors jogged or biked by on their way to the beach. I was struck by how fit and healthy everyone appeared. Compared to

---

*In 1845, Benjamin Disraeli, the future prime minister of England, warned of the danger of his country disintegrating into two nations, as though they were dwellers in different zones or inhabitants of different planets.

some of the people I had just seen in Indianapolis, these neighbors seemed to be inhabitants of a different planet.

That week, as I began the research that led to this book, I became excited about why an economist needed to write about health and weight.

I quickly discovered that the major reason so many people are unhealthy and obese has more to do with economics than with biology.

Incredibly powerful economic forces are preventing people from taking control of their health and are actually *encouraging* them to gain weight—forces so powerful that nothing short of a revolution will be able to stop them.

For many individuals, it may be impossible to take control of their health until they first understand the $1.3 trillion food and $2.0 trillion medical industries that represent a quarter of our national economy.

I discovered that the effects of obesity and poor health go far beyond a person's mere appearance. In our new millennium we have replaced racial and gender discrimination with a new kind of discrimination, based on a person's weight and appearance. Whereas in the past poverty was associated with thinness and obesity with wealth, most people who are overweight today occupy the lower rungs of the economic ladder.

***Rich fat man* has become an oxymoron, and *poor* and *fat* have become synonymous.**

Incredibly, despite the fact that we are enjoying the greatest economic prosperity ever known to humankind, 65 percent of the U.S. population is overweight, and a staggering 30 percent are clinically obese. These figures increased 7–10 percent in just five years since I wrote the first edition of this book (2002 to 2007).[5]

Weight and appearance now define social and economic opportunities, just as family name and birth did in the nineteenth century.

When a person is fat—not just 15 pounds overweight, but clinically obese—it is hard to find a job, a relationship, or the energy to stay on top of the everyday demands of even a simple life.

Even most people of normal weight are unhealthy, although they often don't know it. Modern medicine tells them to accept headaches, stomach distress, body pain, fatigue, arthritis, and thousands of other common ailments as inevitable symptoms that afflict an aging population. Yet these ailments, like being overweight and obese, are the direct result of a terrible diet.

How Economics Perpetuates Obesity and Malnutrition

Economics is largely to blame for this state of affairs. A powerful trillion dollar food industry bombards us with messages calculated to make us eat more and more of the worst possible food.

Understanding how the food industry works today is critically important for entrepreneurs wanting to lead and/or participate in the wellness revolution.

Packaged food companies, such as General Foods and Procter & Gamble, employ some of the best and brightest minds to study consumer psychology and demographics. In trying to decide what sorts of foods to sell us, they invariably apply one of the great unwritten laws of marketing: it is easier to sell more product to an existing customer than to sell that same product to a new customer. In other words, it is easier to influence a regular customer to eat four additional bags of potato chips per month than it is to persuade a new customer, who may never have tasted potato chips, to buy even one bag of this exotic new substance.

Most processed food sales, products such as Hostess Twinkies, Oreo cookies, and McDonald's Happy Meals,[6] are governed by what those in the business call a "potato chip marketing equation." According to this law, more than 90 percent of product sales are made to less than 10 percent of their customers. In the case of processed foods, that coveted 10 percent consists largely of people weighing more than 200 pounds and earning less than $35,000 per year. The targeting of overweight customers is especially lucrative since these unfortunate individuals typically consume twice the amount per serving as a person of normal weight.

Each company studies its 10 percent, known as the *target market,* like rats in a laboratory. Customer surveys reveal their likes, dislikes, hopes, dreams, heroes, and desires. High-consumption customers are recruited to take part in focus groups, where they are asked to sample new products, view advertising, and offer opinions.

No expense is spared to hit every psychological button that matters to the target market. If people in that market like a particular actor or singer, that very celebrity will soon appear on radio or television, praising the product. If a certain look, feel, or lifestyle appeals to people in that market, legions of stylists and designers will descend on the studio to simulate it. Like a deer caught in the scope of a hunter at close range, the target never has a chance.

At times, the ruthlessness of the process troubles the consciences of the $200,000-per-year marketing executives in charge of it. Some actually refuse to attend their own focus groups. Rather than confront their future victims in person, they prefer to review transcripts in the safety of their offices. Imagine the table talk in the homes of such executives. "Today, I met ten 200-pound women who barely had the energy to participate in the group," they might report to their families over dinner. "If my team can get each of them up to 210 pounds by April by increasing their consumption of our potato chips, we'll make our first-quarter sales numbers and I'll get the bonus we need to take that vacation in Barbados."

This executive is probably eating a healthy meal, even as he speaks these words.

One of the great scandals of the junk-food culture is the extent to which its most enthusiastic promoters personally avoid the very products they are pushing.

Moreover, many of the emotional and medical challenges some people face today, from controlling one's temper to depression to cancer, are as much products of these junk-food companies as are frozen pizza and low-fat cookies.

These food companies do something even worse than targeting lower-income, unhealthy, overweight consumers for their products. Once the target actually tries the product and becomes a customer, company chemists ensure they will never be satisfied with eating just a healthy amount of it.

Say, for example, I give you an apple, a banana, a stalk of asparagus, or almost any food in its natural state. After eating two or three apples or bananas, your body begins craving a different type of food, as the pleasure you feel in your taste buds lessens with each bite. But if I give you a chocolate bar, a McDonald's french fry, a can of cola, or almost any other item of processed food, you almost always crave more and more of the same item, because the chemical flavorings have been altered to ensure that "nobody can eat just one" of them. This chemical alteration causes great overconsumption, promoting obesity and destroying the natural tendency of our taste buds to seek variety in what we eat.*

The human body requires a daily intake of 13 essential vitamins,** most of which the body cannot manufacture on its own. These vitamins, along with certain minerals, are necessary to sustain the millions of chemical reactions our bodies perform each day. Eating a variety of fresh fruits and vegetables throughout the day gives us all of what we need, and our bodies are naturally programmed to seek out the different types of natural foods we require. But the majority of Americans are not getting the minimum amount of these vitamins and minerals that their bodies require because of the chemical alteration of the processed and fast foods they consume.***

> **Over the short term, these vitamin and mineral deficiencies manifest themselves as mood swings, lack of energy, joint pain, failing eyesight, hearing loss, and thousands of other ailments that medical science tells us to accept with advancing age. Over the long term, these deficiencies cause major illnesses like cancer and heart disease.**

In the twentieth century, U.S. tobacco companies altered the chemical composition of their products to increase consumption—creating lifelong customers by getting children addicted to specific brands of processed tobacco. Recent legislation has forced Big Tobacco to curb some of these activities when it comes to promoting cigarettes, but they are not letting their acquired expertise go to waste—they have been purchasing the major brands of addictive processed foods. Philip Morris, the world's largest tobacco company,

---

*In family still photos, our four young children often have a vegetable or fruit in their hands. In reality they have a different fruit or vegetable in their hands, as their taste buds (and attention) tire of whatever natural food they have just been eating.
**The term *vitamin* was coined in 1912 by biochemist Casimir Funk. Funk discovered that these substances were vital for life, and he originally thought that they were all ammonia-based products—hence the term *vital amine* or *vitamin*. Later, as scientists identified the critical 13 vitamins required for human life, they discovered that they were not all ammonia-based substances.
***Another reason for these deficiencies is that the more we process foods from their natural state—mostly to differentiate them as distinct brands and to retard spoilage—the less efficacious their vitamins become. In addition, some vitamins should be taken with certain foods in order to be digested properly.

now owns some of the most popular children's processed-food brands, including Oreo cookies, Ritz crackers, and Life Savers candies.[7] This makes Philip Morris, which produces everything from Oscar Mayer bacon to Post cereals to Philadelphia cream cheese, the world's second largest food company after Nestlé, Inc.[8] In 2003, Philip Morris changed its name to Altria to keep more consumers from finding out that Kraft Foods and its other children's food brands are from the same company that is bringing their children Marlboros and Virginia Slims.

How Economics Perpetuates Sickness

As my research led me to the medical industry, I encountered large multinational companies whose nefarious practices made those of the food companies pale by comparison. It quickly became apparent to me why an economist needed to write about obtaining good medical care along with how to obtain food for a healthy lifestyle.

Understanding how the medical (i.e., sickness) industry works today is critically important for entrepreneurs wanting to lead and/or participate in the wellness revolution.

When patients go to see a physician, they believe they are receiving a prescription for the best drug or treatment available for their specific ailment. Not likely.

Just as obese consumers are the target market of the food companies, physicians are the target market of the medical and pharmaceutical companies. Patients receive the drug or treatment that is most profitable for the supplier of the treatment, the health insurance company, and, in some cases, even the individual physician. This may or may not represent the best medical treatment available. In the United States, doctors typically prescribe completely different treatments for the same ailment, depending on which drug company has the dominant market share in their region.

Medical technology and pharmaceuticals change so fast today that what physicians learn in medical school is often obsolete by the time they graduate. In practice, doctors learn about new drugs and treatments from a special type of salesperson, called a *detail person* in the medical industry. Detail person is actually a euphemism for "a very attractive, highly paid young person of the opposite sex." Detail people lavishly hand out free samples and handsomely reward physicians and their staff in proportion to the amount of prescriptions they write for their company's product. Physicians and their families receive expensive dinners, cruises, and tax-free trips to resorts, where they "learn" more about such products at taxpayers' expense.

Although the ethical (prescription) pharmaceutical companies around the world justify the very high prices of their drugs by citing the high cost of research and development, drug companies actually spend much more money marketing drugs than they do on research and development. Moreover, a considerable amount of the research and development that leads to the creation of new drugs is funded by the federal government through grants to nonprofit entities such as research labs at universities, medical schools, and the National Institutes of Health.

When your wellness customers pay staggering prices for prescription drugs, they are also paying for the marketing campaign that successfully induced the doctor to check the box on the prescription form that reads "DAW"—*dispense as written,* meaning the prescription will be the more expensive name brand rather than the cheaper generic that is available for about 90 percent of all prescriptions. Drug company profits often come from outdated name brand drugs taken on an ongoing basis by patients prescribed years before when they first developed the condition. Prescription drug companies limit informing customers and physicians of improved products in cases where they could lose existing customers to competitive brands when patients visit their doctors for revised prescriptions. Generic drugs are sometimes safer or better than the brand-name products they replace because they have been prescribed more recently and thus contain improved formulas.

There are enormous business opportunities in educating consumers about the prescription drugs they are already taking: how to obtain alternative prescription drugs that are more effective, less expensive, have fewer side effects, or all three. See Chapter 7 for how to save 10 to 75 percent on prescription drugs, and see Appendix B for how to save 100 percent—by getting off prescription pharmaceuticals entirely.

In recent years the pharmaceutical companies have hired the same advertising firms as the food companies and have begun direct image-based advertising to consumers. In these advertisements for prescription-only items that may be legally dispensed only on the written recommendation of a doctor, the patient is *directly* urged to demand the product and told to "ask your doctor" for a DAW prescription—with the knowledge that if the doctor refuses to write the prescription, the presold patient will simply find another doctor who will.

Sadly, most physicians have become technology dispensers for the products and services of the large multinational medical companies—companies that always seem to tip the scale between profits and patients in favor of profits.

These practices have pushed the price for U.S. drugs so high that patients cannot afford to fill approximately 22 percent of the prescriptions written each year. Prescription drugs now represent the single largest monthly expense for most over-65 U.S. citizens—approximately $300 per month—and millions of people are forced to make the terrible choice of purchasing food or medicine. Medicare pays for doctor visits but generally does not pay for prescriptions.[9]

This and hundreds of other examples are symptoms of the two underlying problems with medical care in the developed world today—both of which are almost entirely economic rather than scientific.

---

1. **It is more profitable for medical suppliers to produce products consumers use for the rest of their lives than to make products that a consumer might use only once. Invariably, *this means spending research and development funds on products that treat the symptoms of diseases rather than the causes or the cures.***
2. **The third parties paying for most medical treatments—insurance companies and, ultimately, employers—do not have a long-term financial stake in the health of their employees. Most individuals bear little or no direct responsibility for their medical expenses, and almost all expenses to prevent illness (e.g., exercise, vitamins, nutritional supplements) are disallowed for reimbursement.**

As I discuss in Chapter 6, the American health insurance system is really a disguised payment and discounting mechanism designed to extract the most out of those who can often afford the least.

No Solution in Sight

The more I pursued my research, the more distressed I became that there might not be a solution to this plague of obesity and ill health that afflicts the majority of our population.

Although there was obviously no direct conspiracy between the $1.3 trillion food industry (which causes most of the problems) and the $2.0 trillion medical industry (which treats just enough of the symptoms to get the target consumers back to work and consumption), the economic effect was the same as if these two industries were conspiring against the American consumer in the most sinister fashion.

> **The thousands of companies that comprise the $1.3 trillion U.S. food industry and the $2.0 trillion U.S. medical industry are governed by universal laws of economics that cause them to act in concert, as though they were part of a vast, nefarious conspiracy.**

On a microeconomic level, each time consumers got real information that could help them take control of their health, the food and medical industries, acting in their own economic self-interest, manipulated this information against them.

For example, prior to 1990, consumers were told that eating too many calories was the primary cause of obesity. In the 1990s, when the public became aware that the amount of fat in their diets was a major cause of obesity, the food industry reacted with enticing low- and nonfat foods, advertising that consumers could now eat as much as they want without gaining weight. The food industry went so far as to repackage many products that *never* had fat in them, like sugar-coated candies and pretzels, to suggest that they had created new, healthy, nonfat versions of these products.

What their massive advertising didn't tell consumers was that these low- and nonfat products had extremely high levels of sugar and carbohydrates, which turn to fat once ingested into the body, not to mention more addictive chemicals that made them worse in the long run than the "fattening" products they replaced. Since the 1990s obesity, as well as the sales of low- and nonfat foods, have steadily increased.

On a macroeconomic level, it seemed as if there would be no escape.

> **When it comes to attempting to control our federal, state, and local governments, the food and medical companies follow their own Golden Rule: He with the gold makes the rules.**

Lobbyists for the food industries have created mandatory school lunch and milk programs that hook children on addictive processed foods. Pharmaceutical companies have helped create government-sponsored programs that put millions of children on dangerous drugs to combat the effects of their terrible diets. In some cases, such as when Ritalin is used to control hyperactive children, parents are threatened with losing custody of their own children if they refuse to force them to take such drugs for alleged disorders.[10]

The U.S. Food and Drug Administration, originally designed to protect consumers from unhealthy products, now often protects the very companies it is supposed to regulate by keeping out competition and prolonging the economic life of the drug companies' government-sanctioned patents.

Typically the news media, acting in its own self-interest for publicity and ratings, leads society in exposing such heinous activities. But in this area the media are all too often ineffective. As consumers themselves, members of the media are subject to the same disinformation and thus are largely unaware of the problem. Moreover, a major funding source for the media—especially network television advertising revenue—comes from food and drug companies.

For example, the detrimental health effects of drinking cow milk have been widely known for years in the medical community but have rarely been covered by the media, which reaps fortunes each year by running ads for the American Dairy Association. Imagine the hypocrisy of celebrities who sport milk mustaches in paid advertisements but themselves drink only soy-based milk products.

The scandal of these celebrities goes even deeper than endorsing products that they would never consume themselves. Leading actors, singers, and models make literally millions of dollars each year on their looks. Most of them lean toward vegetarian diets lacking in processed and addictive fast foods. Yet these societal role models for fitness and beauty are cautioned by their managers not to let their elite dining habits become known to the press, lest they be boycotted by television producers in an industry where most of the revenue comes from advertisements for processed foods and fast-food restaurants.

Despite the fact that many young people admire them for more than just their professional talents, celebrities today have learned not to take positions on controversial issues that could affect their careers. As one Hollywood manager once told me, no one wants to become the "Jane Fonda of healthy eating"—referring to the talented actress who was boycotted by some theatergoers in the 1970s because of her controversial left-wing political views.*

In a free enterprise system, when people want something that can't be provided by profit-seeking entities, they typically turn to government (the provider of last resort) for assistance. This worked well in the last few decades, when consumers demanded that government restrict the actions of businesses that were destroying the environment.

But in this case, government seems helpless. Like the media, our elected officials are consumers who are subject to the same disinformation and thus are unaware of the health issues.

Take a look at the waistlines and the diets of most politicians if you want to know what they think of food and health! Our politicians have been effectively controlled by the food and drug companies for so long that our government is now a large part of the problem, rather than being poised to be part of a solution.

It seems incredible to me that although we won the cold war and democratic ideals are more universally cherished than ever before in history, we also must admit that half of our people have become personally enslaved to a lifestyle that limits their daily lives, dreams, and happiness as much as would any autocratic government or dictatorship.

While I was conducting my original research into wellness, between 1996 and 2002, the percentage of the U.S. population that is overweight and obese increased by 10 percent, to 27 percent obese and 61 percent overweight. These figures rose from 2002–2007 to 30 percent obese and 65 percent overweight today.

Equally significant, the resultant medical (sickness) industry costs had reached $1 trillion by 2000. The sickness industry's sales doubled to $2 trillion in 2006, and now occupies almost one sixth of

---

*One notable exception is the talented Alicia Silverstone (born in 1976), star of *Clueless* (1995), *Batman & Robin* (1997), and 13 other major films. Although there are many famous vegetarian actors (Brad Pitt, Kim Basinger, Richard Gere, Alec Baldwin, Drew Barrymore, Paul Newman, Liv Tyler, William Shatner, David Duchovny, Daryl Hannah, Dustin Hoffman), Ms. Silverstone, to the detriment of her career, is one who consistently uses her celebrity status against the dairy and processed food lobbies in trying to teach healthy eating to her young fans.

our economy—and sickness medical expenses are the leading cause of bankruptcy among U.S. families.

It became depressing to me to think of these numbers in terms of human suffering—90 million Americans clinically obese and 195 million overweight and unhealthy because they lacked the resources, information, and motivation to safeguard their most precious asset: their wellness.

It seemed only a question of time before virtually everyone in the United States would be overweight, and more than half of the population would be obese and unhealthy. I decided to take a closer look at the healthy, nonoverweight 39 percent of the U.S. population to see how much time we had left.

When I began examining the 39 percent of our population that was not overweight, I stumbled across the seeds of the revolution about to take place.

An Economic Solution to an Economic Problem

When I looked closer at the nonoverweight 39 percent of the population, I found a growing group of millions of Americans who are eating and living healthier than ever before in history. This wellness-based group includes most of the movers and shakers in our society as well as celebrities who literally make their living on how they look. This group has quietly embraced a revolutionary new approach—to diet, to exercise, to vitamins, to nutritional supplements, to medical care, and, most important, to the aging process itself.

In ancient Greece, physical strength, health, and beauty were just as central to one's *arete,* or excellence, as were creative talents, intellect, industriousness, or moral character. Indeed, outward beauty was believed to reflect the beauty within. For obvious reasons, the people today most dedicated to *arete* are the professionally beautiful, those people who economically depend on maintaining their health and appearance. Movie stars, talk show hosts, entertainment professionals, and many leading business executives inhabit a secretive world in which the physical fundamentals of life (food, exercise, vitamins, nutritional supplements, medical care, and aging) are seen from a perspective radically different from that of most human beings.

> To the wellness elite, each act of apparent pain or denial,
> from sessions with their personal trainers to navigating
> through menus at exclusive restaurants, is a positive, al-
> most religious experience.

These people focus on how they will feel hours later *because* of
each laborious exercise, or they focus on how much stronger they will
feel that evening *because* of what they are not eating for lunch or dinner. Thus, what may seem painful to others becomes to them a eu-
phoric experience with its own almost immediate rewards.

> At first I thought that this revolutionary way of forward
> thinking about the impact of food on your health might be
> only a Hollywood or West Los Angeles phenomenon. But
> further research quickly showed this to be a worldwide
> movement with revolutionaries around the globe.

The reason is simple. Everyone, no matter how healthy or fit, wants
to be even healthier and more fit. Everyone wants to look and feel
more youthful. However, until recently, there was very little anyone
could do to obtain efficacious wellness services and products. Until
now, the few wellness products and services available were affordable
only by the very rich. Now that they are becoming widely available
and affordable, entrepreneurs are rushing in to provide wellness
products and services to a delighted public—creating an economic
solution to what is essentially an economic problem.

When I was growing up, mealtime conversation seemed to center
around personal economic issues. Today, mealtime conversation is
becoming more and more centered around wellness issues—which
foods to eat, which supplements to take, how to exercise, and how to
avoid getting sick and to limit the effects of age. This is only the beginning of a huge new wave of wellness.

The First $200 Billion (2002)

When I began the research that led to this book, I had two objectives
in mind: (1) exposing the nefarious practices of the food and medical industries and (2) teaching people the correct choices to make in
order to be healthy and obtain good medical care. Explaining a new
business opportunity that would allow people to make money was
not one of my objectives.

The more my research progressed into obesity and sickness, the more upset I became with the status quo. The more upset I became, the more I felt that nothing short of a revolution was needed in the way we think about health, eating, and the practice of medicine. I could see that this revolution might eventually take place, but the most surprising part of my initial research was how far the revolution had already progressed.

The nascent wellness industry today encompasses some of the following businesses:

Vitamins

Nutritional supplements

Skin care products and services

Cosmetic plastic surgery

Voluntary eye surgery (LASIK, radial keratotomy)

Cosmetic dermatology

Genetic engineering (sex selection and fertility enhancement)

Cosmetic and reconstructive dentistry (caps, implants)

Preventative medicine

Health Savings Accounts

High-deductible (wellness) health insurance

Fitness clubs (including trainers)

Fitness and athletic equipment

Voluntary pharmacy: Viagra (for impotence), Rogaine (for hair growth)

Health food products

Health food restaurants

Weight loss products

Although most of these businesses did not exist at an economically significant level just two or three decades ago, by 2002 they already totaled approximately $200 billion in annual sales, about half the amount then spent to purchase new U.S. automobiles.[11]

When I saw that wellness had already achieved sales of this magnitude, I knew that the wellness industry had already jumped far beyond being products for only the wealthy or the professionally beautiful. I began to focus on which segments of our society were consuming most of this $200 billion and on the potential demand for future consumption.

> **It became apparent that wellness would reach sales of $1 trillion or more over the next 10 years and that wellness would be the industry in which the greatest fortunes of the new century would be created—fortunes eclipsing even those of the Internet billionaires of the late 1990s.**

However, before we examine why this is so (in the next chapter), and where the wellness industry is headed, it is important to understand where the wellness industry has been and why the concept of wellness has come so late to our food and medical industries. The wellness industry really began when entrepreneurs were legally allowed to explain the benefits of their products and services in the late 1970s.

Our wellness industry today exists in large part thanks to a historic battle won in the 1970s by the greatest wellness revolutionary of our time: the late J. I. Rodale, founder of *Prevention* magazine and Rodale Press (*Men's Health, Runners World*).

How Rodale Paved the Way for the Wellness Revolution

In 1954, entrepreneur and author J. I. Rodale had a lot to lose. His company, Rodale Press, was just getting his fledgling *Prevention* magazine off the ground. *Prevention* was dedicated to teaching readers how to prevent disease versus just treating the symptoms of disease.

Rodale had concluded that eating large quantities of red meat and dairy products dramatically increased the risk of heart disease and that physical activity actually decreased the risk of having a heart attack. This was at a time when the U.S. government was spending millions encouraging Americans to eat more red meat and dairy products at every meal, three meals a day. Doctors were telling patients with heart disease to reduce or eliminate physical activity entirely. No wonder heart disease was the leading cause of death in the United States!

Rodale wrote about his new findings in two books: *How to Eat for a Healthy Heart* and *This Pace Is Not Killing Us*. He was convinced that this information could save millions of lives. But, like many writers in the 1950s, he was not on an approved list drawn up by Senator Joseph McCarthy's House Un-American Activities Committee, so his publisher refused to publish his new books.

This situation forced Rodale to print the books himself and try to sell them through bookstores along with his other Rodale publications. But many booksellers refused to distribute his new books. Undaunted, and convinced that the public needed this information as soon as possible, Rodale took out full-page advertisements in national publications and offered his new books via mail order at a special price.

The Federal Trade Commission ordered Rodale to stop advertising and selling the books, claiming that the medical advice given in his books was unsubstantiated. The FTC had successfully taken similar action against other publishers who had promulgated then unconventional medical advice.[12]

Rodale was furious! He felt that the FTC action was a blatant violation of the First Amendment guarantees of freedom of the press.

The FTC scheduled hearings in 1955, at which Rodale was ordered to present proof that people who purchased the books and followed their advice would, indeed, reduce their risk of heart disease. Rodale refused to attend, claiming that the First Amendment gave him the right to publish any information he wanted, regardless of its efficacy.*

At these hearings, the nation's most respected medical professionals testified that (1) there was no correlation between heart disease and eating large quantities of red meat and dairy products, and (2) following Rodale's advice on increasing physical activity to avoid heart disease could be injurious, if not fatal. The FTC ordered Rodale to cease and desist from claiming, directly or indirectly, that readers of any of his publications would improve their health.**

Rodale appealed the case, mainly on the grounds that the First Amendment prohibited the FTC from regulating information-based products. His legal battles with the federal government dragged on for almost two decades, at times putting his entire personal net worth

---

*At the original hearing on this case before the FTC, dissenting FTC commissioner Philip Elman foreshadowed the path that the FTC was to take when he wrote: "Congress did not create this Commission to act as a censor of unorthodox ideas and theories in books, whether they deal with politics or health. We should not forget that, in both fields, today's heresy may become tomorrow's dogma."[13]

**FTC commissioner Elman wrote in his dissenting opinion: "It is the glory of a free society that a man can write a book contending that the earth is flat, or that the moon is made of green cheese, or that God is dead, without having to 'substantiate' or 'prove' his claims to the satisfaction of some public official or agency. It is arrogance to presume that in any field of knowledge, whether dealing with health or otherwise, all the answers are now in."[14]

at risk. Over the years, the FTC, fearing that they would lose their case on constitutional grounds, attempted to settle with Rodale. But despite financial hardship, Rodale refused to back down unless the FTC agreed to acknowledge that the First Amendment prohibited them from regulating books and printed material.

In the later years of the case, Rodale's lawyers introduced new testimony from some of the same leading medical experts that the government originally used at the initial FTC hearings almost 20 years earlier. One by one, these experts refuted their original testimony, claiming they "didn't know back then," and admitted that many of Rodale's original claims had since become established medical facts. Rodale felt that there could never be a better example of what our Founding Fathers had in mind when they made freedom of the press the very first item in the Bill of Rights.

Then, in 1971, while describing his legal problems with the federal government on national television, J. I. Rodale dropped dead. Until he actually stopped breathing and turned blue, everyone watching the taping of *The Dick Cavett Show* thought Rodale was facetiously faking a heart attack in order to make a point about his troubles with the FTC.

The case never reached the Supreme Court.

Soon after wellness pioneer J. I. Rodale passed away, the U.S. government reversed its position, stating that the FTC would no longer require advertisers of information-based products to establish the efficacy of their claims. This policy change opened the door for the free flow of wellness information, allowing the vitamin, nutritional supplement, fitness, and alternative medicine industries to grow to their current level, laying the foundation for the wellness revolution.

Today *Prevention* magazine has 12 million readers, and Rodale Press is the largest health-oriented publisher in the world, publishing over 100 new wellness titles each year that sell a combined 20 million copies per annum.

One of the greatest challenges facing Rodale, and facing many entrepreneurs like you today who base their businesses on a new technology, is human rejection of the new or unknown, especially when the new technology forces people to rethink established beliefs.

Why We Often Reject New Ideas

Understanding the cause of this phenomenon, and how to surmount it, is crucial for the entrepreneur seeking success.

The human quest for knowledge, in both religion and science, is really the quest for order in our lives. Once people believe they have found such order, they will often risk heaven and hell to preserve their beliefs, even in the face of irrefutable evidence to the contrary. For example, until roughly the fourth century B.C., it was commonly believed that the mysterious lights in the sky were gods wandering about the heavens. In fact, the word *planet* comes from the Greek word for "wanderer." This is how most people explained the disorder in their daily lives. The gods (planets) wandered about the heavens, and their wanderings caused the crops to grow, the rain to fall, and the tragedies and joys of a disorderly human existence.

The Greek philosopher Aristotle refuted this belief. Aristotle believed that there was an order to things that people could understand and use to bring order to their lives—particularly in the area of understanding the seasons and their effect on agricultural production. In 340 B.C., Aristotle theorized that the planets and every other object in the heavens were not gods, but were simply spheres that revolved in fixed paths on a schedule around a stationary earth.

The Aristotelian geocentric view of the world, although wrong in its fundamental assumption that the earth, rather than the sun, was at the center of our solar system, became the bedrock of civilization for the next 1,800 years. Looking back, we can see that its endurance was hardly surprising, as it agreed with the evidence of one's senses. After all, from our vantage point on earth, it certainly looks as if everything revolves around us.

But the Aristotelian-Ptolemaic calendar was not accurate, because it incorrectly placed the earth at the center of the universe. Every 100 years or so it would snow in Rome in July, and the pope would have to set the calendar back about six months. This led to a great quest among astronomers to discover a working model of the universe that could more accurately track the months and predict the beginning of the seasons—the use of which could greatly increase agricultural and economic output.

It wasn't until the early sixteenth century that the Polish astronomer Nicolaus Copernicus succeeded in this quest. By manipulating mathematical equations, Copernicus determined that the sun was at the center of the solar system and that the heavenly bodies—including the earth—revolved around it. Fortunately for Copernicus, his *De Revolutionibus Orbium Coelestium* was not published until he was on his deathbed in 1543, and his heliocentric view of the universe did not become known for over half a century.

In 1609 the Italian mathematician and physicist Galileo Galilei began observing the heavens through his new invention, the telescope. He was able to see that the sun rather than the earth was at the center of our universe, and he wrote a treatise about Copernicus's theory in colloquial Italian, which could be read by the masses, rather than in the traditional Latin of academia. This treatise soon attracted widespread support for the heliocentric model of the universe.

The bulk of that support, however, came from outside the establishment. The reaction from inside was quite different. Galileo was bitterly attacked by both scholars and theologians, and in 1616 the Church commanded him, under penalty of death, never again to "hold, teach, or defend the Copernican system in any way whatsoever."

Nine years later, in 1623, Galileo's childhood friend Maffeo Barberini became Pope Urban VIII. Emboldened by his friendship with the pope, Galileo again began to write about the heliocentric theory. The reaction from the Church was swift. Galileo was forced to kneel in front of the Inquisition and recant his belief in the Copernican system. While his friendship with the pope probably saved him from being burned at the stake, Galileo was condemned to life in prison for having disobeyed the 1616 order. His works were placed on the pope's *Index of Prohibited Books,* and only in 1992 did the Roman Catholic Church formally reexamine the case and admit its mistake.

Looking back, it seems difficult to understand why the pope thought it was his duty, as God's emissary on earth, to so vigorously defend the geocentric model of the universe. After all, what does believing in Jesus Christ have to do with whether God put the earth or the sun at the center of our universe? Yet surprisingly, and perhaps on a different scale, most people today behave similarly in clinging to their established beliefs.

As children, people are typically taught beliefs about religion by their parents, then spend their adult lives looking for reinforcement of those beliefs—including outright rejection and avoidance of anything that might challenge them. When was the last time you visited a different church, synagogue, or mosque than the one you were brought up to believe in, to see what they had to offer? When was the last time you read a book by someone you knew held political opinions opposite from yours?

> **The reason we do not embrace opposing views is that our human mind fears disorder—and automatically avoids or rejects new ideas that challenge the existing order.**

A lawyer friend of mine who tries death row cases believes that some trials are decided the very instant that the jury first sees the accused. Individual jurors, particularly in high-profile capital crime cases, are anxious to solve their own personal "disorder" problem of guilt or innocence as soon as possible. To do so, they sometimes make up their minds on first seeing the accused enter the courtroom. Then, throughout the trial, they nod and listen attentively to evidence that supports their prejudicial decision, rolling their eyes when a conflicting view is being presented.

> **When presenting a new hypothesis that might challenge the status quo, it is important to be able to explain the history behind an established belief and to be able to explain where our society may have gone wrong when such a belief was first established.**

Here's how most people developed incorrect views of many wellness treatments.

How Traditional Western Medicine Rejected Wellness

Throughout history, people, especially the very rich, have sought wellness. In every civilization from ancient Egypt to medieval Europe, alchemists believed that gold dissolved in *aqua regia* was the elixir of life, and they consumed fortunes trying to discover the correct formula.* In the sixteenth through the nineteenth centuries, monarchs backed expeditions like those of Ponce de León to find the mythical Fountain of Youth.** While some of these quests proved

---

*While the alchemists failed in their quest to make gold and discover the elixir of life, many laid the foundation for modern science (pharmacy, medicine, metallurgy, physics, chemistry, etc.), which today has accomplished exactly what the alchemists hoped to achieve: pharmacy and medicine along with the potential for unlimited prosperity.

**Although Ponce de León failed in his quest to find the Fountain of Youth on the island of Bimini in the Bahamas, he more than paid for his expedition by accidentally discovering Florida in March 1513—much as the alchemists themselves ultimately succeeded by discovering not gold, but chemistry.

fruitful in other areas (like the alchemists' discovery of chemistry or Ponce de León's discovery of Florida), they all failed miserably in their quest for wellness, and wellness practitioners were often characterized as charlatans.

Then, in the twentieth century, scientific discoveries linked disease and aging to food and exercise. In 1908, Polish-born biochemist Casimir Funk discovered that there were four ammonia-based substances vital for life, which he called "vital amines," or *vitamins*.[15] Studies of longshoremen and other labor-intensive occupations showed that physical exercise was beneficial to overall health and to the avoidance of chronic disease. But for the most part, these and other now-accepted wellness discoveries were rejected by the Western medical community.* Here's why.

Prior to the nineteenth century, doctors administered the few medicines that existed, and by trial and error observed which medicines cured which diseases. Medical knowledge was accumulated like this over centuries and was occasionally diffused between cultures.[16]

But when a medicine or treatment worked, doctors didn't know *why* it worked. The underlying theories that explain infections, and the inoculations and antibiotics that these theories produced, had to await the widespread use of the compound optical microscope (which was invented at the beginning of the seventeenth century but didn't become ubiquitous until the late nineteenth century). The microscope led to the discovery of cells and bacteria and allowed scientists to actually see how they worked.

In the late nineteenth and early twentieth centuries, scientists became international heroes as they eliminated, one after another, the major diseases that had been the scourge of humankind (e.g., smallpox, tuberculosis, typhus, polio).

Emboldened by this success, and partly to distinguish themselves from charlatans who were practicing magic more than medicine, Western medical science began arrogantly rejecting age-old treatments and cures whose function could not be scientifically explained by the then-current level of technology.

---

*This also explains why direct selling (person-to-person versus television-to-person or store-to-person) is often the best way to explain a new product or service that challenges an established belief. When most people are confronted with such a challenge, they simply change the channel or continue to walk down the aisle—something that politeness prevents when listening to a friend or acquaintance.

The basic unit in biology, the cell, is about 20 micrometers in diameter. It takes about 10,000 human cells to cover the head of a pin. For physical reasons, an optical microscope cannot resolve two points that are closer together than approximately one-half of the wavelength of the illuminating light—and an individual bacterial cell, for example, is approximately one-tenth the wavelength of visible light.[17]

> **Today we know that the critical biochemical functions performed by exercise, vitamins, minerals, and nutritional supplements take place on a molecular versus a cellular level. And because each cell is composed of trillions of molecules, these functions cannot even be detected with an optical microscope.**

Until the relatively recent invention of the electron microscope, which is still not as widespread as the optical microscope was in the 1800s, scientists were unable to study the molecular structure of cells and how they function.

> **This led most Western medical school training to virtually ignore, to this day, the importance of nutrition and the effect of vitamins, minerals, and natural supplements.**

Meanwhile, during the twentieth century, while Western medicine was ignoring the importance of diet and exercise in preventing disease and aging, the amount of exercise performed by individuals declined due to labor-saving devices in the home and to machines in the workplace. The quantity and variety of vitamins and minerals in our diets declined as food became more processed and less varied. And the percentage of fat in our diets increased by 75 percent—from about 20 percent of our calories in 1910 to about 35 percent of our calories today. These and other factors contributed to the epidemic in obesity and ill health we have today in the United States, sowing the seeds for the wellness revolution that is about to take place.

The Wellness Revolution Is about More than Just Making Money

In the rest of this book we will examine the increasing size of the wellness industry and the thousands of fortunes that will be created through wellness.

As you read ahead and start to think about your place in this emerging industry, keep in mind that there is something even more important than your personal economic reward—your impact on the world in which we live.

Economically, we live in halcyon days that have far surpassed the wildest dreams of our forebears, who fought so hard and lost so much to create what we have today. Yet due to our plague of obesity and ill health, we begin this millennium with more human unhappiness than at any time in our history.

Fully 65 percent of Americans are trapped within their own prison of being malnourished and overweight, and almost half of those, about 30 percent, are clinically obese—overweight to a point where they are hopeless and have no idea where to turn for help.

These Americans are malnourished to the point that they live with constant headaches, body pain, stomach distress, heartburn, fatigue, arthritis, and hundreds of other ailments—ailments that contemporary medicine wrongly tells them to accept as symptoms of advancing age. Medical companies sell consumers billions of dollars worth of products (e.g., aspirin, laxatives) that treat only their symptoms while ignoring their cause. A similar situation exists in Western Europe, Taiwan, and most other developed nations, and it is emerging in China as chronic fatigue syndrome.

However, this is about to change, thanks to the wellness revolution. Never before in history has a business opportunity had the potential to have such an incredibly positive impact on the lives of its customers.

Before Proceeding to the Next Chapter

*Action Plan for Entrepreneurs and
Wellness/Health Professionals*

1. Make a list of 10 potential wellness businesses that interest you.

2. Assess how you could participate in each of these areas:

   a. Entrepreneur

   b. Investor

   c. Distributor

3. Analyze each business area with respect to the five characteristics of pervasive industries (outlined in the introduction).

4. Choose the three best areas for you to pursue, based on your prior skills and experiences.

5. Analyze why each of these three areas of wellness business opportunity does or does not yet exist. For those that do exist, analyze your potential competition and the opportunity for growth in each area.

6. Rethink your choices of your three best areas of wellness business opportunity, and perhaps choose a different three based on your analysis thus far.

Now read chapters 2 through 9, and at the end of each chapter, think about dropping and replacing any or all three of your chosen areas of wellness business opportunity.

CHAPTER 2

The Baby Boom Generation: Understanding and Controlling the Demand for Wellness

The current boom in wellness products and services is being driven by another boom that occurred between 1946 and 1964—the baby boom—that represents about 28 percent of the U.S. population, but accounts for about 50 percent of our nearly $14 trillion economy. Boomers are just discovering the potential of the wellness industry to preserve what they hold dearest: their youth. But even this is only the beginning, thanks to the nature of demand in our modern economy, to our current economic expansion due to advancing technologies, and to our unlimited propensity to consume more wellness products and services once we have had a positive wellness experience.

Practice What You Preach

Like many people of my generation, I barely knew what wellness was when I turned age 40 in 1994. Managing my health then used to consist only of skipping meals when I felt I was putting on weight—often with disastrous results.*

Since then, I have spent thousands of dollars a year, and part of every day, consuming wellness products and services. I choose my

---

*Prior to age 40 I typically reduced my caloric intake by skipping meals, without ensuring that my body was receiving the minimum daily required amount of vitamins and minerals. This led to my having colds on a regular basis, winter respiratory infections, and not functioning at my optimum level. Worst of all, since I had done this all of my adult life, I had no idea what I was missing until I began eating healthy food throughout the day, exercising regularly, and taking vitamins and supplements.

food based on how I will feel afterward rather than on my immediate sensory gratification. I take vitamins, minerals, and supplements on a daily basis. My family has a health insurance program that allows us $5,450 per year for wellness expenses and lets us put an additional $5,450 per year into our IRA-type Health Savings Account (HSA) for our future healthcare needs. I work out by lifting weights or doing pilates twice a week, and depending on the weather, I mountain bike, surf, or snowboard for one to two hours almost every day. When I first began writing this book, I thought that the U.S. market of individuals like me, who were already practicing wellness, might amount to a few billion dollars a year.

As noted earlier, I was very surprised to find out that wellness spending had already reached $200 billion a year by 2000. And I was even more surprised to discover that this $200 billion represented just the tip of the iceberg for the wellness industry over the next decade. Here's why.

The Baby Boom Generation Is the First Wellness Generation

The birthrate of American citizens increased dramatically after World War II. Between 1946 and 1964, approximately 78 million children were born in the United States. In contrast, in the same amount of years just prior to 1946 only 50 million births were recorded. And in the same amount of years immediately following 1964, despite a much larger population base, only 66 million births were recorded.

This huge bulge in the U.S. population is generally referred to as the *baby boom,* or the baby boom generation. We define it as a *boom* because birth rates rapidly declined after 1964; had this not occurred, the postwar birth rate increase would simply have represented a long-term trend rather than a distinct population group.

The significance of this fact cannot be overstated.

In any society, there is a limit to the number of topics that can occupy public concern at a specific period in time. With a normally expanding population, these topics are typically dominated by the concerns and tastes of the younger members of the society, since there are simply more (and more) of them. However, the bulge in the U.S. population of those born between 1946 and 1964 has

> **caused our topics of concern to be dominated by this**
> **group rather than by the concerns of the next generation.** *

This phenomenon initially manifested itself in the late 1960s and early 1970s when certain oldies radio stations became more popular than contemporary ones—as the first baby boomers entering adulthood continued to listen to the music of their youth.

Beginning in the 1970s we saw boomers increasingly returning to the fashions of their youth in clothing, automobiles, housing, furniture, industrial design, and commercial architecture. A new word was coined to define this phenomenon, *retro,* which entered our vernacular (and our dictionary) in 1974.[1]

Now, as the baby boom generation (currently ages 43 to 61) is in its most economically productive years, this phenomenon of catering to their concerns will accelerate even more. Their economic dominance will continue until sometime after 2010, when the first boomers turn 65 and their economic power and social influence begin to wane.

The economic impact of the baby boomers on wellness is even stronger than their numbers suggest—because this group is behaving differently than any prior generation. Boomers are refusing to passively accept the aging process.

A recent book by Cheryl Russell explains it best from a marketing perspective:

> One of the most important truths about boomers is that they are still the youth market. In their teens and twenties . . . boomers created the youth market. As they enter their forties and fifties . . . boomers are proving the youth market to be a state of mind rather than a stage of life. Most boomers still live in that state, refusing to adopt the attitudes and lifestyles of their parents. . . . Businesses savvy enough to determine what boomers want will catch a wave of consumer demand that will be the ride of a lifetime.[2]

Boomers are already responsible for the largest stock market rise in history, the housing boom, the rise of international airlines, the personal computer, the Internet, the sport utility vehicle—in short,

---

*A similar phenomenon exists in Western Europe, where there is a bulge in the population of those born between 1946 and 1964, although there it is related more to a severe decline in the birthrate that began in the late 1960s rather than a dramatic increase in the birthrate following World War II.

boomers are responsible for roughly $7 trillion of our near $14 trillion national economy. But it is even more important to know which consumer products boomers are purchasing most. From the current T-Bird convertible that looks like the 1956 model, to retro furniture and clothes, boomers flock to purchase products and services that remind them of their youth.

> If baby boomers are spending all this money on things that simply remind them of when they were young, think of how much these boomers will soon spend on wellness products and services that actually make them young or slow the effects of aging. It's easy to see why boomers are driving wellness to a $1 trillion sector of our economy as they seek to preserve what they hold dearest.

Moreover, most of our current $500 billion in wellness sales are to boomers born closer to 1946 than to those born closer to 1964—the ones in their 50s versus those in their 40s. Over the next five years alone, boomers will drive sales of wellness-based services from approximately $500 billion to $1 trillion or more. This growth will come partly from the demographic expansion of the market (age range of boomers shifting from ages 43 to 61 to ages 48 to 66) and partly from sales growth due to improvements and new efficacious wellness-based products and services.

> Hundreds if not thousands of better wellness-based products and services are coming out of the laboratory during the next five years. This list includes improved types of vitamins and minerals, supplements that ward off colds and diseases, and natural hormones and soy-based antiaging creams that truly retard wrinkles and impart youthful vitality to the cells they touch.

And this five-year doubling of the market is only the beginning. Just as boomers now set the pace for the desires of the next generation, from retro tastes in music to housing and independent lifestyles, boomers will set the pace for the wellness industry for generations to come. Moreover, as we examine in more detail in Chapter 7, the current sickness-based health insurance system is being replaced by many Americans with a new wellness-based system that is shifting sickness dollars to weight reduction, exercise plans, nutritional advice, vitamins, minerals, smoking cessation, and hundreds of other wellness-related or preventative treatments.

By 2012, Generation X—those born between 1965 and 1982—will be entering their most productive and highest-spending years. This, and subsequent generations, will take the boomer-established proactive approach to wellness and aging as standard medical procedure.

But the main reason that wellness sales are growing so fast is because of what happens once consumers of any age have their first wellness experience—they typically become voracious customers with an unlimited appetite for more wellness products and services. Before we examine these powerful developments, which will take the U.S. wellness industry to $1 trillion and beyond by 2012, it is important to understand the nature of demand in our modern economy, and to understand what is fueling the economic expansion of both the past and the current decade that will allow us to afford this new $1 trillion industry.

The Mistake Many People Make: Misunderstanding Consumer Demand

During the Depression of the 1930s, the economist John Maynard Keynes foresaw that advancing U.S. technology would one day be able to supply the American people with everything they could want.

Lord Keynes made the optimistic prediction to President Franklin D. Roosevelt that one day soon most American families would have a telephone, an automobile, and a four-bedroom, one-bathroom house with indoor plumbing. However, the economist warned the President, once people had fulfilled this American dream, they would lose their incentive to work. These productive Americans would stop spending their increasing income and start saving it, bringing the economy to a halt—a victim, as it were, of its own success.

Therefore, Keynes suggested that the U.S. government adopt progressive income taxation, to keep the most productive people in society from hoarding more and more of their earnings as their income increased.

This was radical thinking back then. When the (flat rate) federal personal income tax was first established, in 1913, many people thought it unfair that a person earning $100,000 a year should pay

10 times the amount of federal taxes as a person earning $10,000 a year—yet both had equally only one vote. Now Keynes was advocating raising federal income tax rates on a progressive scale, so that the more a person was earning, the higher (and higher) his or her percentage income tax rate would be.

Thanks to Keynes and the U.S. policymakers who followed his advice, individual federal income tax rates rose throughout the twentieth century, reaching peak marginal rates of 92 to 94 percent by 1964 before stabilizing at 70 percent until the 1980s.[3]

As Chapter 6 shows in detail, to avoid these insidious rates of taxation, and also to get around government wage and price controls, employers and unions lobbied Congress for the right to pay employees with nontaxable perks such as company-provided medical care for them and their immediate families. This, more than any other single economic factor, has led to the problems we face in the United States today in regard to escalating medical costs.

We can sometimes learn more by studying the mistakes of history's greatest minds than by studying their successes. Although Keynes's theory that increasing affluence breeds complacency and that oversaving seems logical, today we know that it is incorrect. The very opposite of what Keynes predicted has come to pass.

Looking back at the time when Keynes developed his landmark theory of oversaving, it is easy to see where he went wrong. During the 1930s, an insufficiency of consumer demand was the root cause of the continued depression—nothing the government did seemed to get consumers spending again. Keynes was convinced that doom was inevitable unless the government established graduated income tax rates on personal income and then injected this money back into the economy through increased government spending.

Most people think that Keynes had a greater impact during his time than he actually did. Many of the government programs of the 1930s and 1940s attributed to Keynes's recommendations were actually part of a larger phenomenon—active government involvement in the economy—and Keynes's *General Theory* was merely used after the fact to justify their continued existence. The actual New Deal programs of the 1930s preceded the *General Theory* by several years.

Over the past century, and especially the past two decades, upscale consumer demand has proven itself insatiable. The more we earn, the more we spend; the more we spend, the more we get; the more we get, the more we want; and

the more we want, the harder we seem to be willing to work to earn it.

If any segment of our society has lost the incentive to work, it is the very poor, whom we seem unable to help over the hurdles of purchasing their first cars or their first houses—purchases that lead to the never-ending cycle of unlimited consumer demand.

In the world we live in today, advancing technology has been able to meet the basic primary needs for most Americans.

Advancing technology is constantly creating its own demand—offering new products and services that, before too long, become considered basic primary needs by the majority of the population.

Before the invention of the first electric washing machine, around the time of World War I, few Americans cared how many times they wore a shirt before they washed it, and clothing was constructed to require a minimum number of washings. Shirts, for example, came with detachable collars and cuffs—the parts that got dirty most quickly. Once the washing machine became available on a widespread basis, every American had to wear a clean shirt every day—and detachable collars and cuffs went the way of the horse and buggy.

When Henry Ford first invented a mass-produced automobile that was affordable to nearly everyone, people scoffed at the thought that anyone would buy it—there were few paved roads available, gasoline stations were nonexistent, and most people lived within walking distance of where they worked. Then, thanks to the automobile, most people actually moved to suburbia—gasoline stations proliferated, and the automobile soon became a necessity, just to get to work or shop for daily necessities.

When the telephone first became available to businesses, most businesspeople communicated through hand-delivered written messages that they originated by dictating to their secretaries. Many were convinced that using the telephone was a waste of time. After all, who wanted to dictate a message to a secretary, have it transcribed, then read by the secretary over the telephone to the recipient's secretary, then transcribed by the recipient's secretary into a written message for the recipient. Of course, before long the telephone changed the way that businesspeople communicated: speaking directly to one another, rather than through notes transcribed by their secretaries.

Inevitably, the telephone, like the fax machine in the 1970s and e-mail in the 1990s, became an absolute necessity for every business.

The story of how the telephone was initially rejected by businesspeople contains an important lesson for us today. Most people use computers and other new inventions merely to modify existing, obsolete ways of doing things, rather than reengineerimg the work itself to fit the ability of newly available tools. Many entrepreneurs launching new wellness products and services will inevitably make this same mistake.

Today, almost 95 percent of the things we spend our money on—which most of us think of as necessities—were not even around when many of us were born: television sets, airline travel, Disneyland vacations, high-fashion clothing, stereos, DVDs, air conditioners, personal computers, day care, movies, fast-food restaurants, dry cleaning, Internet access, to name a few. The same will happen with wellness.

Even basic necessities like food, clothing, and housing are no longer necessities in the traditional sense, because we consume quantities of them that are far in excess of our basic needs. In 1935 the average American lived in 136 square feet of living space; today, it's in excess of 750 square feet per person.

The reason that consumer demand is so unlimited has to do with the nature of the two types of demand in our technological society: *quantity demand* and *quality demand.* This is critically important for the entrepreneur to understand, especially an entrepreneur with a long-term plan for success.

Quantity Demand and *Quality Demand*

Quantity demand is the consumer's desire for more of what he or she has already purchased: another television set, a second car, a bigger house, an extra suit of clothing—even if he or she has just made their first purchase of such an item.

Consider a young person entering the workforce after graduation, possibly for the first time in his or her life needing business attire to wear to work. He or she proudly goes to the store and purchases a first suit. But on the first day of work it becomes clear that what's needed is more suits, so they don't have to wear the same thing every day—not to mention ties, scarves, shirts, and shoes to match.

Or think of a young couple buying their first automobile. The automobile changes everything for them: where they work, how they travel, where they dine, and so on. But they soon realize their new need for something they hadn't even dreamed of before: a second car, so they can each independently get to work and go shopping. Similarly, a couple might purchase a second television set for their bedroom, only to quickly discover the need for a third set in a child's room or the kitchen.

A first house may seem to be the ultimate purchase for many young people starting out, yet it's actually just the beginning, as the home acquisition ignites a never-ending demand for furniture, kitchen appliances, entertainment equipment, and so on. New home construction is the most important indicator in forecasting most types of retail sales.

Savvy retailers of every product or service know that a purchase by a satisfied customer is just the beginning, rather than the ending, of their relationship.

A men's clothing store might sell 100 suits a year to first-time purchasers just entering the workforce, but 2,000 suits a year to consumers who already own one or more. The most important marketing information to an automobile dealer is what type of car the potential consumer already owns. And for every first-time homebuyer in the United States each year there are at least five homes sold to existing homeowners moving on to (typically) larger ones.[3]

But at some point, a classical economist like Keynes might argue, demand must be sated. After all, how many new suits, cars, homes, and televisions can a consumer own? The seemingly obvious answer to this question has confounded many merchants.

When *quantity demand* is satiated (as it is these days among a majority of people in the developed nations), *quality demand* kicks in. When you have all the food, clothing, and TVs you need—you start wanting *better* food, *better* clothing, and *better* TVs.

Whereas *quantity demand* reflects the consumer's demand for a larger supply of an existing product, *quality demand* reflects the appetite for a different or improved kind of product.

In the case of TV sets, *quality demand* reflects a consumer's more sophisticated yearning for a *better* TV (say, a high-definition color receiver with picture-in-picture capability and six-channel sound) as well as for related but otherwise entirely new products (such as TIVO, satellite receiver, or a DVD player). A typical middle-class couple would probably have little if any interest in buying a third sedan to add to the two they already own. But they might jump at the chance to get rid of one of the sedans and upgrade to a new sport utility vehicle (SUV). A young executive whose closet is filled with eight $200 suits would probably have little interest in purchasing a ninth one. But he or she might jump at the chance to purchase a new $400 designer suit.

Moreover, this flip in the nature of demand goes both ways. As the consumer begins to satisfy his or her desire for higher quality, *quantity demand* once again begins to work its magic. Now the couple wants *two* SUVs so they don't argue over who has to drive the sedan. Now the young executive wants *seven* $400 designer suits because he or she no longer "feels right" wearing the older $200 ones. Theoretically, of course, the demand for more and better goods will be satiated when the consumer finally owns a sufficiently large number of the best cars or best suits on the market. But as long as technology continues to advance, there will never be a best car or a best suit—at least not for very long. Each year a better one will be developed, and the process will start all over again.

The more emotionally detached you are from your entrepreneurial marketplace, the easier it can sometimes be for you to understand *quantity demand* and *quality demand* and how to navigate between them to create constant, ongoing demand.

For example, when it comes to riding the shift between *quantity demand* and *quality demand* for American and European consumers, no one has been able to do it better than the Japanese. In the 1960s, the Japanese overwhelmed many of the world's markets with inexpensive products—in effect, satiating *quantity demand.* But in the early 1970s, they turned their attention to increasing the quality of their goods, riding the shift from *quantity demand* to *quality demand* (leaving the now unprofitable market for cheaper goods to their imitators). In less than 20 years, they went from being known as the lowest-cost producer of almost everything consumers could want to being known as the highest-quality (and usually the highest-priced) producer of almost everything.

In the 1990s Japanese industries also dumped many of their traditional brand names, like Datsun and Toyota, in favor of new ones like Nissan and Lexus. And they left General Motors in the dust, wondering why GM's satisfied Chevrolet customers weren't buying any more Chevrolets.

Ignoring *quality demand* is one of the biggest mistakes made by new entrepreneurs, particularly in areas of new technology like wellness. Many entrepreneurs begin with a lower-quality item—hoping to improve the quality and increase the price as they build their business. This is shortsighted.

If you begin with a lower-quality item, it may be difficult or impossible for you to retain clients when your once-satisfied customers begin demanding a higher-quality product or service. When a business or distributor becomes known for having lower prices, which is often correctly equated with lower quality by the consumer, it is sometimes impossible to change this perception.

The most successful wellness companies today manufacture or distribute the highest-quality (which often means the highest-priced) wellness products and services.

The consumer's continual desire for higher-quality items is so incorporated into our marketplace that it is often transparent. Each year, as advancing technologies lower the cost of products and services, smart producers and providers recognize that they want to maintain existing customer relationships. To do so, they automatically improve the quality of their products rather than lowering the price.

Suppose you spent $600 on a 27-inch color television in 1997 and went out in 2007 to buy its replacement at the same store. You would have found that virtually the same television now costs only $300 (actually $231 in 1997 dollars after adjusting for inflation). But rather than purchase the same television, you would probably elect to spend $600 again ($462 in 1997 dollars) to purchase a 36-inch model—or perhaps $1,000 ($777 in 1997 dollars) on a superdeluxe high-definition flat-screen LCD model with six-channel sound and picture-in-picture channel displays. Moreover, you probably won't even find the $300 model at your local store, as your merchant, aware that satisfied customers want increasing quality rather than lower prices, no longer carries the (now) lower-end CRT tube-type models.

Or suppose in 2000 you entered medical school hoping to purchase a new $45,000 convertible automobile on completing your residency in 2007. When you go to the dealer in 2007, you find that the car with all the features you wanted back then now costs only $25,000. But rather than purchasing this car and pocketing the $20,000 savings, you decide to "trade up" to a $45,000 car that has twice the features of the car you wanted back in 2000.

This consumer-driven phenomenon of choosing increasing quality over lower price is so prevalent today that most people don't realize how much the material quality of their lives has steadily increased—thanks to the improved quality, safety, and lower prices of their products. Whether you are talking about TVs or toys, automobiles or air conditioners, blue jeans or bedding, digital cameras or convertible sofas, refrigerators or MP3-recorded music, people today invariably enjoy better-quality goods at a lower real cost than they did at any time in history.

Wellness *Quantity* and *Quality Demand*

All of this has great implications for the wellness industry.

The majority of consumers today are not even aware that there *is* a wellness industry. Yet each of us knows someone who has recently had a wellness experience:

1. A single mother who changed her diet and lost 35 pounds.

2. A boy with a new vitamin regimen who now focuses twice as hard in school.

3. A father using magnetic therapy who has eliminated chronic pain.

4. A girl taking echinacea who no longer misses school because of colds.

5. A former athlete using glucosamine who has returned to bicycling without knee problems.

6. A patient with an enlarged prostate who avoided painful surgery by taking saw palmetto.

The list goes on and on.

Now think for a moment what else may happen in this person's life after an initial wellness experience:

1. The single mother probably has a new schedule that includes regular athletic activity like jogging.
2. The boy is trying out for sports since his academics are under control.
3. The father wants something to develop more energy to keep up with his children since pain no longer dominates his thoughts.
4. The girl's parents want to know what supplements they should be giving their other children.
5. The former athlete wants products to improve his memory since he now believes in nutritional supplementation.
6. The former prostate patient has completely changed his diet and now wants to learn everything about alternative medical treatments.

For each of these people, the initial purchase of a single wellness product or service ignited *quantity demand*—the demand for more of what they had just purchased—even though they were unaware such a product existed before they purchased it. Even more important, when the wellness product or service had worked its magic, it ignited *quality demand*—the demand for different and/or better wellness products and services.

Thanks to *quantity demand* and *quality demand,* satisfied wellness customers are beginning a lifetime consumption of products and services that have the potential to improve every aspect of their lives for every moment of their lives. More than any other factor, this unlimited propensity to consume wellness products and services will take the industry to $1 trillion and beyond by 2012.

How Some Prospective Entrepreneurs Misunderstand Our Economy

It wasn't too long ago that the most common culprits of being late for a meeting would be either a flat tire or a flooded carburetor—problems that advancing technology (radial tires and electronic fuel injection) have eliminated from our daily concerns.

Sometimes, potential entrepreneurs are dissuaded by economic indicators that regularly appear in our media, particularly in times of recession or economic contraction. But because of advancing technology, these economic indicators are often misinterpreted as reasons *not* to start a business, when in reality they are actually *good news* for the budding entrepreneur.

For example, lower prices and better-quality products are sometimes reported in our media as a decrease rather than an increase in our material wealth. This is because our most common economic indicators, such as gross domestic product (GDP) and retail sales, are not indexed for either increasing quality or for price deflation caused by the ability of technology to lower prices. When the medical student purchased his $45,000 car with twice the features of the one he originally wanted, he experienced a $20,000 unreported increase in his material lifestyle. If he had purchased his $45,000 original dream car for $25,000, it would have been reported in the media as a $20,000 decrease in GDP or retail sales.

Similarly, when the average cost of a new home is reported by the U.S. government, this figure is not indexed for the fact that it is more than twice the size of the average new home in the 1960s, or that it contains features and appliances that alone make it worth twice as much to the consumer. Most of us were raised in a typical middle-class home of 1960—about 900 square feet, without a dishwasher or air conditioning, which today could be considered a fairly primitive standard of living compared to a new home in 2007, which averages about 2,300 square feet and contains a host of modern appliances and conveniences.

Yet probably the most misunderstood economic indicator in our society is unemployment—particularly the type of unemployment we mostly experience today, which comes from technological change, or what economists sometimes call *structural unemployment.*

As we will see in a moment, such unemployment, caused by the substitution of technology for labor, is actually the first sign of true economic growth. And as we shall also see, it is because of structural unemployment that the labor force is available to develop and grow new industries.

This brings us to our next topic underlying the growth of the next $1 trillion industry: what has been fueling the economic expansion of the past and current decades that allows us to afford all of these new products and services, and is it going to continue?

How Unemployment Leads to Economic Growth

Imagine a self-sufficient island with 10 men, all of whom make their living by fishing with poles from a communal boat. One day, a missionary shows the men a new, technologically better way of fishing—using a large net instead of 10 individual lines. Two fishermen, one to pilot the boat and one to throw the net, can now catch the same number of fish as 10 fishermen could with lines.

On the surface, unemployment on the island has risen from 0 to 80 percent, since 8 of the 10 fishermen are now out of a job. Yet, although eight of the men are no longer working, the island society as a whole remains just as prosperous, because two fishermen using the net catch as many fish as ten did with lines.

Now the island society must decide what to do with the eight unemployed fishermen and their families. They have three options: (1) they can pass a law making the use of fishing nets illegal; (2) they can tax the two working fishermen 80 percent of their earnings and redistribute this 80 percent to the unemployed; or (3) they can help the eight unemployed fishermen develop new jobs in new industries (e.g., education, medicine, food preparation) that will add to the wealth of the entire community.

What civilized society would deliberately stunt economic growth by limiting the use of new technology? What society would tax 80 percent of the earnings of their best producers (i.e., the ones with the nets)? Yet these have been the traditional responses when the implementation of technology made certain people richer than their neighbors.

Throughout the nineteenth and twentieth centuries, governments passed prounion legislation limiting the ability of private companies to substitute technology for labor. Between 1913 and 1960, the United States and Western Europe instituted highly progressive income taxes, increasing the personal marginal income tax rate to 91 percent and more on their most efficient citizens (i.e., the ones with the nets). Eastern Europe and China chose communism (effectively 100 percent taxation), removing the individual's incentive to implement new technological methods and devastating their economies.

In the United States, in 1930, there were approximately 30 million farmers, producing just enough food to feed a population of about 100 million people. Technological breakthroughs in agriculture over the next 50 years made farming so efficient that by 1980 only 3 million farmers produced enough food for a population of more than 300 million*—and the displaced 27 million farmers, or their children, moved on to producing new products and services that added to the total wealth in the economy. This is how our economy has evolved since the beginning of civilization.

New technology makes workers more efficient, which causes structural unemployment, but over time, the displaced workers end up producing new products and services that add to society's overall wealth. The only thing new about this process today is the speed with which it is occurring.

Changes that used to take place over millennia or centuries now take place in years, months, or even days—as was the case in our island example with the fishing net. This increased speed underlies our employment challenges today, as individuals must often change careers and/or professions several times within a single lifetime, rather than slowly over several generations.

The 27 million farmers who were displaced were relatively fortunate. They had 50 years to grow old, retire, and watch their children develop new careers as carburetor mechanics or vinyl record manufacturers—careers that were then on the cutting edge of new technologies. Their children, who left the family farm to pursue these new careers, weren't nearly as fortunate, as they had only five years or less to adjust to similar changes.

In 1980, approximately 300,000 people in the United States were employed in the manufacture and repair of mechanical carburetors. In just five years, by 1985, virtually all of these jobs disappeared, as automakers replaced $300 mechanical carburetors with much more efficient $25 computerized electronic fuel injectors. The rest of society greatly benefited from fuel injectors, which effectively halved fuel cost (by doubling fuel economy) and halved harmful automobile emissions.

---

*Unfortunately, as we will see in Chapter 4, as this occurred, the profit opportunity in agriculture shifted from producing healthy foodstuffs (e.g., wheat, milk, fruit) to manufacturing these foodstuffs into terribly unhealthy name-brand foods with long shelf lives (e.g., cereals, condiments, processed cheeses, canned foods, frozen foods, junk, or snack foods).

In 1985, approximately 100,000 people in the United States were employed in the manufacture of vinyl records. In just five years, by 1990, these jobs disappeared, when the music industry replaced the vinyl record, costing $2.50, with the digital compact disc, costing 25 cents. (Today it's the music industry's turn to cry, as consumers burn their own CDs and download free music from the Internet via MP3 files.)

Similar examples in the past century made total economic growth in the United States the envy of the world—so much so that the cold war ended in the 1990s when the people of Eastern Europe and China democratically decided to become free-market economies.

Today, most leaders worldwide realize that they cannot stop structural unemployment without devastating their economies. This is especially true in a free trade environment, where multinational employers can simply take jobs overseas if they wish. While this has resulted in much greater total economic output and greater overall prosperity, it has made employment much less stable for individuals, who must now be ready to retrain themselves on short notice.

Economic Implications for the Wellness Industry

Because of misunderstood economic indicators, our economy is actually growing at a higher rate than is reported. Despite some media reports to the contrary, most of the unemployment we are experiencing is *structural unemployment,* which is actually the first sign of true economic growth. These facts bode well for the wellness industry.

There is more than enough growth in the economy to support a new $1 trillion industry.

Just as U.S. GDP increased from roughly $7 trillion to almost $14 trillion between 1997 and 2007, even the most conservative growth estimates forecast U.S. GDP hitting $17 trillion by 2012.

Despite the existence of relatively low levels of unemployment, the labor force is available today to support a new $1 trillion industry.

Economic growth almost invariably starts with structural unemployment, as technology displaces productive individuals and frees them for new jobs in new areas of the economy.

The main question for us, as businesspeople and entrepreneurs, is "Which sectors of the economy will attract the greatest share of this growth and employ these displaced employees?" The wellness industry is poised to become the next $1 trillion sector of our economy because everyone, no matter how fit or how healthy they are, wants to be more healthy and more fit. The wellness industry is poised to become the next $1 trillion sector of our economy because it contains the five distinct characteristics of pervasive industries:

1. **Affordability;**
2. **Legs;**
3. **Continual consumption;**
4. **Universal appeal; and, most important,**
5. **Low consumption time.**

Wellness products and services represent perhaps the only sector of consumer spending that does not take time to enjoy.

This may seem obvious when stated, but it is often overlooked, because consumers have only recently had the option to purchase wellness products and services. Until now, *most people were told to accept their wellness deficiencies as part of the aging process, as though there was nothing they could do about them.*

How the Vitamin Business Shifted from Sickness to Wellness

One of the fastest-growing sectors of the wellness industry today is the vitamin and nutritional supplement business. But until very recently this business was limited almost entirely to treating sickness.

Scurvy, or vitamin C deficiency, is one of the oldest known nutritional disorders, and its symptoms were written about in Crusader history. It was the major cause of disability and mortality among British sailors until the Scottish physician James Lind noted that the Dutch employed citrus fruits to eliminate scurvy. In 1795 the consumption of lime juice became mandatory on all British naval vessels—and people of British descent are still called "limeys" to this day.

Rickets, or vitamin D deficiency, was noted throughout history, and caused skeletal deformities, especially in children. Beginning in the eighteenth century it was treated with cod-liver oil and sunlight.[4]

Beriberi, or vitamin B1 deficiency, is caused by the unnatural removal of this vitamin from processed rice and other grains. Beriberi literally means "extreme weakness" in Sinhalese, and has been noted in Asian countries since polished white rice became a staple more than 1,000 years ago.[5] In all of these cases, scientists recognized these nutritional deficiencies only when they manifested themselves as terrible sickness.

In the twentieth century it was discovered that there are 13 essential vitamins required to maintain good health that generally cannot be manufactured in the body.* More recently, it has been discovered that these same vitamins can prevent disease from developing, make us feel better than well, and even slow the aging process itself.[6]

Today, almost 50 percent of Americans take some sort of nutritional supplement, and industry sales for these products exceed $100 billion. Yet the vitamin and mineral industry has barely scratched the surface of what is possible, for we are just beginning to understand the biochemistry that explains how vitamins, minerals, and other supplements work.

As explained in Chapter 1, when it comes to understanding how our cells function on a molecular level, we are where the sickness industry was prior to the nineteenth century—we know that many wellness products and services work, but we do not yet fully understand *why* many of them work. Yet medicine established itself as a major science long before the microscope was able to explain so many of its mysteries, and wellness will do the same.

Similarly, we have already seen the wellness industry garner about $500 billion in U.S. annual sales, even though science does not yet understand the molecular secrets behind much of its efficacy. Even if

---

*Vitamins contain no energy directly, but are required catalysts in order to produce the hundreds of chemical reactions required for sustaining life. Since they generally cannot be manufactured by the body, they must be obtained elsewhere on a daily basis.

we don't uncover these secrets in the near future, this $500 billion is just the beginning.

Many potential customers have never even heard of wellness products and services, let alone tried them. As we have seen, customers who try a wellness product or service and have a positive experience usually open their minds to trying other wellness products and services.

In my case, between the ages of 35 and 43 I had pain in my left knee—the result of years of competitively racing down mogul-laden ski slopes. Each orthopedic surgeon I visited came to the same conclusion—surgery. One young orthopedic surgeon even joked that he expected my left knee to finance his grandchildren's college education as, even after the surgery, I would probably be his patient for life. At age 43, I was finally considering scheduling the surgery.

I started taking glucosamine and the pain in my knee disappeared within two months. One year later the same orthopedic surgeon asked me who had operated on my knee. When I told him about the glucosamine, he took some X rays and asked me not to publicize my experience, as it could put him out of business—only this time he wasn't joking. I was amazed that I, an economist, was teaching an orthopedic surgeon about glucosamine.

This experience opened my mind to thinking about what else the medical practitioners in my life might not know. After completing some research, I started taking the daily vitamins and mineral supplements I take today, and I became open to taking other dietary supplements in the future.

For too long, medical science has told people to expect and accept chronic pain, declining health, and reduced energy levels as they age—partly because many doctors have only rudimentary training in nutrition and partly because the ultimate payors or providers of medical services (employers) do not have the proper financial incentives to pay for wellness. We examine both of these phenomena in Chapters 5 and 6.

But first, let's examine in Chapter 3 the changes in our food supply that created most of the sickness problems we have today and, in Chapter 4, the opportunity to fix these problems, using the same entrepreneurial skills that created them.

Before Proceeding to the Next Chapter

Action Plan for Entrepreneurs and Wellness/Health Professionals

1. Make a list of what you and your family currently spend on wellness that you weren't spending 10 years ago. Your own personal accounts of wellness activity are powerful tools when explaining the emerging wellness industry to others.

2. Analyze the items on this list with respect to your current areas of potential wellness businesses. Are you already a customer of any of these areas? Why or why not?

3. Analyze your current areas of potential wellness businesses with respect to the baby boom market (customers born between 1946 and 1964).

4. Analyze your current areas of potential wellness businesses with respect to the Generation X market (customers born after 1964).

5. For each of your current areas of potential wellness businesses, make a list of products that you would offer to satiate *quantity demand*—the initial customer demand for more of each product.

6. Now analyze each product to see how you can make the eventual transition to *quality demand*—the demand for a different or higher-quality product.

7. What areas in your region of the world are experiencing structural unemployment (displacement due to technology), and how could these displaced people work in each of your three areas of wellness business opportunity?

Based on your answers to these questions, think about dropping and replacing any or all of your individual areas of wellness business opportunity.

CHAPTER 3

What You Need to Know about Food and Diet

Most of the immediate demand for wellness, and most wellness products themselves, exist today because of two major problems with food. To understand the wellness industry, you are going to have to understand why we need food and the origin of these two major problems with our supply of food.

Once you start your wellness business, you will need to go beyond simply understanding the problems with our food supply—you will have to be able to explain and teach the origins of these problems to your customers, your associates, and your investors. Thus, you will probably read this chapter more than once.

If you are still choosing which wellness business opportunity to pursue, you should carefully read this chapter, noting each of the problems with food and my personal suggestions for improving your own diet— then analyze how you might be able to turn one or more of these suggestions into a profitable wellness business opportunity.

What Is Food and Why Do We Need It?

Adam and Eve didn't worry too much about food. According to the Bible, the Garden of Eden freely contained "every tree that is pleasant to the sight, and good for food."[1] Then, because Eve tasted the apple, the ground was cursed so that it would yield food only with hard labor.

Ever since then, the search for food has dominated our existence. But what is food, and why is it so necessary for human existence?

In addition to enjoying food because it tastes good, human beings require food for three purposes:

1. *Energy.* Fuel (calories), necessary to perform external work and to simply allow the heart, lungs, and other organs to function.

2. *Building blocks.* Raw materials (e.g., proteins, most minerals), used to manufacture blood, skin, bones, hair, and internal organs; the human body is constantly replacing and renewing every cell on a daily to monthly basis.

3. *Catalysts.* Chemical compounds (e.g., vitamins, enzymes, and some minerals), necessary to facilitate the chemical reactions that convert food into energy and into the body's organs.

Human beings require food for energy every few hours and require specific foods that function as building blocks and catalysts on a daily or semidaily basis. Our bodies are biologically programmed to immediately sense when energy is needed—we experience hunger pain. Unfortunately, we usually become aware of missing building blocks or catalysts only when our bodies become ill from these deficiencies.

Our bodies are also biologically programmed to seek out foods containing the highest amounts of energy. Foods containing the highest amounts of energy (e.g., sugar, fat) taste the best.

The successful exploitation of our biological programming by the entrepreneurs and commercial providers of our food supply is the major cause of obesity and ill health in the developed world today.

The United States is the poorest of the developed nations when it comes to health—U.S. citizens are the unhealthiest and spend three times more money on medical care than their European or Asian counterparts. This massive difference, not just in the cost of medical care but also in the unhappiness caused by poor health, is mostly the result of our having a terrible diet.

The Two Major Problems with Our Food Supply

There are two major problems with the diet of most people in the United States and many people in other developed nations:

1. We eat too much. Fully 65 percent of U.S. citizens are over-weight.
2. Most of us are not getting the minimum amounts of building blocks and/or catalysts that our bodies need.

To understand how these two problems of overeating and poor nutrition were created, and to understand the entrepreneurial opportunity to cure these problems (Chapter 4), it is first necessary to understand how our bodies process food into energy and living matter.

How Our Bodies Process Food into Energy and Living Matter

All food consists of one or more of six nutrient categories:

1. **Water**
2. **Carbohydrates (contained in sugars, breads, etc.)**
3. **Lipids (contained in fats, oils, etc.)**
4. **Proteins (contained in meat, fish, eggs, vegetables, etc.)**
5. **Vitamins (contained in fruits, vegetables, etc.)**
6. **Minerals (contained in fruits, vegetables, etc.)**

Digestion begins when food enters your mouth and starts being broken down by your teeth and the enzymes in your saliva. Then chemicals in your stomach go to work digesting the food into its six nutrient categories.

The Opportunity in Water

The human body is composed of about 60 percent water and requires a minimum of two quarts of fresh water per day. It is estimated that 75 percent of Americans are chronically dehydrated and that 37 percent mistake thirst for hunger. A mere 2 percent drop in body water can trigger fatigue and mental dysfunction. As a preventative measure, drinking five glasses of water daily decreases the risk of colon cancer by 45 percent, the risk of breast cancer by 79 percent, and the risk of bladder cancer by 50 percent.

If possible, and if it will not interfere with getting your minimum daily water requirement, you should try to avoid drinking this water during mealtimes. The chemicals in your stomach become less effi-cacious when diluted, and this can cause valuable nutrients to wash through versus being absorbed by your body.

To ensure that I drink enough water each day, and especially not just at mealtimes, I travel with a small, soft backpack called a Camel-bak. My Camelbak contains three liters of distilled drinking water in a refillable plastic sack attached to a plastic tube. This lets me drink safely while biking, driving, walking, or in almost any situation. In my home and office, I make sure there is a water filter or reverse osmo-sis unit at every sink, so that clean drinking water is always available and in sight.

One of the simplest wellness business opportunities is providing consumers with clean, healthy water at con-venient times and locations throughout their day.

How We Obtain and Burn Calories

The energy contained in specific portions of food and the energy needs of the body are both measured in units called *calories*. The number of calories in a particular food can be measured by burning a weighed portion of the food and measuring the amount of heat pro-duced. It is also possible to measure the number of calories burned by a particular physical activity, from sleeping to jogging up a steep hill.

Of the six nutrient categories, only carbohydrates (4 calories per gram), lipids or fats (9 calories per gram), and proteins (4 calories per gram) provide energy.*

The human body requires approximately 2,200 calories of energy per day for a woman and 2,900 calories per day for a man. A person doing daily athletic exercise requires more calories per day than a sedentary person. The following chart shows the amount of calories burned per half hour by different types of activities. At any level of ac-tivity, the human body uses about 65 percent of its energy for basal metabolic functions like breathing and pumping blood.

When your daily intake of calories exceeds your daily bodily re-quirements, the body converts these excess calories into fat, which is

---

*Proteins are typically not digested into energy because they are the most difficult to digest and because the body needs these building blocks to constantly replace its organs.

Calories Burned per 30 Minutes of Activity[2]

Activity (30 minutes)	120-lb. person	175-lb. person
Bicycling 14–16 mph	288	420
Skiing, downhill	238	346
Bicycling, mountain	230	336
Jogging	191	278
Swimming, moderate	166	242
Tennis, singles	166	242
Golf, carrying clubs	166	242
Walking 4 mph	140	205
Weight lifting, general	94	136
Golf, using a cart	94	136
Sitting	29	42
Sleeping	25	37

then stored throughout the body. A normal amount of fat, typically between 15 and 25 percent of body mass, is important for hundreds of bodily functions. These functions range from maintaining temperature to absorbing fat-soluble vitamins to cushioning vital organs. If you have too little fat in your system, the body will begin destructively breaking down muscles and internal organs to meet its requirements for energy.

However, when you consume more calories than the body uses over a period of time, your body starts to store excess fat in visible places. This excess fat often first appears in the stomach on a man and in the thighs on a woman. Excess fat is associated with fatigue, heart disease, cancer, and hundreds of other life-threatening diseases.

Four Reasons It's Difficult to Lose Fat

Excess stored fat should be converted back into calories when the body next requires more energy. This does not typically occur today for four main reasons:

1. We consume available carbohydrate calories before fat calories.
2. Our bodies tell us to look for more food before using stored reserves.
3. Readily available food causes our metabolism to stabilize at the higher fat level.
4. The type of food we eat today is different than it was when our biological formula for energy storage was developed.

First, just as a hungry person consumes the most readily available source of food, the human body always consumes the most easily convertible source of energy. Of the nutrients containing calories, molecules of carbohydrates are the simplest in form and thus are the easiest for the body to quickly convert into energy. This is why people crave carbohydrates when they haven't eaten for a while or immediately after performing strenuous exercise.

In contrast, molecules of fat are more complex and require additional energy and additional time to be converted into energy (or burned). The body always looks to available carbohydrates first for energy before it begins to break down ingested and then stored molecules of fat.

Second, when a person needs energy, he or she experiences hunger (typically for more carbohydrates) long before the body turns to its stores of excess fat. This biological programming served us well in prehistoric times—telling prehistoric humans to keep eating (and eating and eating) when food was plentiful before drawing on their stored reserves.

We are biologically programmed to eat each meal as though it were the last one we are going to get for a long time—and in many cases it was, before humankind learned how to preserve foods, to farm, and to domesticate animals.

The ability to make conscious choices contrary to our biological programming is what separates us from most of the animal kingdom. Humans and animals have virtually the same biologically driven appetites and desires, which yield pleasure when satisfied, with one all-important difference: Humans have a mind and soul that is superior to and can control their biological desires. Unfortunately, this seems true for most people today in every area except their dining habits.

Some animals have learned how to supersede their biological programming in our world of abundant food. Many people with pets today use dried food and leave it out to be consumed on a leisurely basis rather than waiting until their pet begs for its next meal. Veterinarians and pet owners have learned that if you feed your pet only when it gets very hungry, it will eat the full amount given even if its body no longer requires it. However, if food is continuously available, most pets will adjust their appetites and eat only what they need for optimum health. Sadly, this is a lesson that most doctors and U.S. citizens have yet to learn for themselves and their own children.

We also eat much faster today than our parents did—when people often sat around the table for long time periods to share conversation.

It typically takes 10 to 15 minutes from the time we ingest food until our hunger becomes sated—this is why you are sometimes no longer hungry at a restaurant when an entrée arrives late.

When you take time between courses or bites to digest your food, your hunger becomes satisfied with only the amount of calories you require. But when you eat quickly at your desk between appointments or at fast-food restaurants, you often think you are hungry and keep eating even though you have already ingested more than enough calories.

Third, when people put on additional fat, say 15 pounds of weight during a vacation with lavish meals, their daily basal metabolic requirement for calories increases. Where their hunger used to be sated with 2,500 calories per day, these people now require approximately 3,000 calories in order not to feel hungry—their body and appetite having reached a new equilibrium at the heavier, 15-pounds-extra, level. As long as food is readily available and people listen to their stomachs (hunger) regarding how much to eat, their increased amount of weight will remain.

Once a person puts on excess weight he or she will most likely have to take proactive measures (e.g., diet) to lose it.

And fourth, the main reason that this stored excess fat may not be converted into energy calories is because our food today is very different than food was when our biological program for storing energy was developed—it contains much more fat. When our biological programming for food was developed, our ancestors ate mostly a low-fat vegetarian diet, with some game meats. And even those foods that contained fat had much *less* fat than they do today—game meats contain about 5 percent fat by weight versus the 30 percent fat by weight contained today in commercially produced and hormonally treated domesticated animals.

Back then, fat was so rare and so useful that our taste buds evolved to crave it and the parts of the animals that contained most of it. Today, unfortunately, this sensory craving has been exploited by our food suppliers. Like the first victim in the movie *Seven,* which is about the monastic seven deadly sins, we are literally eating ourselves to death.

In just the past century we have almost doubled the percent of fat in our diets—from 20 percent of our calories in 1910 to about 35 percent today.[3]

This 35 percent average number belies the fact that our nation is divided when it comes to health: millions of upscale Americans eat diets that have 20 percent or less of their calories from fat, and millions more eat diets that have 50 percent or more of their calories from life-threatening fat. Most experts agree that our bodies are biologically programmed for a diet requiring about 20 percent of our calories from fat.

The Critical Importance of Proteins, Vitamins, and Minerals

The second major problem with the diet of most U.S. citizens is that they are not getting the minimum amounts of building blocks and/or catalysts that their bodies require.

The first book of the Bible, Genesis, which is common to Judaism, Christianity, and Islam, speaks of the Garden of Eden, where God made "every tree that is pleasant to the sight, and good for food."[4] This reference to a wide variety of food has more than just aesthetic significance.

Although most adults think of their bodies as fully grown, the individual cells that comprise their organs actually replace themselves on a daily to monthly schedule.

Our bodies manufacture 200 billion red blood cells each day, replacing all the blood in our body every 120 days. Skin is completely replaced every 1 to 3 months. It takes 90 days for old bone to be broken down and replaced by new bone.

The cells that comprise these replacement organs contain over 100,000 different proteins made up of 20 different amino acids. Food supplies us with plant and animal proteins containing the

amino acids that our bodies require as the building blocks of this living tissue.

> **Without a daily supply of proteins, vitamins, and miner-
> als, no matter how much energy we get in the form of calo-
> ries, our bodies and minds deteriorate because we are not
> able to fully replace the dying cells in our internal and ex-
> ternal organs.**

Food also supplies us with certain minerals we require as building
blocks to repair and regenerate our living matter. There are 14 essential minerals, some of which are required as catalysts rather than
as building blocks. Seven of these are *major minerals,* defined as
those of which we need more than 100 milligrams per day—calcium,
chloride, magnesium, phosphorus, potassium, sodium, and sulfur.

The remaining seven are called *trace minerals,* such as iron and
zinc. In addition to supplying proteins and minerals as building
blocks, food contains the 13 essential vitamins our bodies require as
catalysts to convert food into energy and to convert amino acids into
bodily tissue. A catalyst is a substance that must be present, typically
in a very small quantity, for a specific chemical reaction to occur.*
For example, without vitamin B3, which is contained in green leafy
vegetables and unprocessed grains, our bodies cannot break down
plant and animal proteins into basic amino acids. It doesn't matter
how much protein you eat if your body can't convert it into the building blocks of your living tissue.

> **When we don't get enough protein, vitamins, and minerals,
> our initial symptoms include mood swings, fatigue, nerv-
> ousness, headaches, confusion, and muscle weakness. Over
> the longer term, such poor nutrition can cause cancer, hy-
> pertension, Alzheimer's disease, and many other diseases
> that we used to just accept as part of our aging process.**

Modern medicine typically treats these problems with drugs that
focus on each symptom rather than on the underlying problem,

---

*The chemical composition of a catalyst is not altered by the reaction, and thus a single cata-
lyst molecule can be used over and over again. This explains why we need only a small quantity of each vitamin—although we do need to ingest these small quantities daily, because
most vitamins do not remain in the digestive system.

which is what we eat, or more correctly in the case of poor nutrition, what we don't eat.

Before you become alarmed that you're never going to get enough of all these critical nutrients, here is some good news. Our bodies require only a small amount of protein and a minuscule amount of minerals and vitamins on a daily basis.

The human body requires approximately 46 grams (1.6 ounces) of protein per day for women and 58 grams (2.0 ounces) of protein per day for men. This is less than most people believe they need, thanks to successful but misleading advertising campaigns by the beef and cattle industry. Ironically, meat and milk products are actually a poor source of protein because they contain high amounts of harmful fats compared to other protein sources such as fish, nuts, breads, and vegetables.

The human body requires 13 essential vitamins in dosages ranging from 60 milligrams per day for vitamin C to 200 micrograms per day for vitamin B8 (folic acid). These quantities are naturally abundant in commonly available fresh foods.

Similarly, the 14 minerals we require are contained in fresh foods in more than adequate quantities—100 milligrams is only 3/1,000 of an ounce.

Now here's the bad news.

Despite the relatively small amounts of proteins, vitamins, and minerals we require on a daily basis, and despite their abundance in natural foods, our biologically programmed need for these substances is not being met by our modern food supply.

How the Green Revolution Changed the Economic Opportunity within Food Production

When our ancestors were hunter-gatherers they subsisted on a plant-rich diet of nuts, fruits, beans, grains, and roots, with some game meats. Because no single type of food was found in abundance, while they searched primarily for calories they automatically consumed the variety of foods containing the different proteins, vitamins, and minerals that their bodies required. (Conversely, their bodies adapted to the nutrients in the variety of foods they consumed.)

Over time, these hunter-gatherers became farmers. Using human ingenuity and the economic abundance that results from specialization, they learned how to efficiently produce large quantities of specific foods that they could then trade for other foods. They learned how to produce the foods that naturally tasted the best and could last the longest—foods rich in fat like dried meats and aged cheeses. World population rose steadily from around 200 million at the time of Jesus Christ to about 1 billion by the end of the nineteenth century.

In the twentieth century, rising agricultural technology finally eliminated the age-old problem of food scarcity—with a vengeance. Thanks to the green revolution, India and China went from starvation economies to net exporters of food. World population rose from 1 billion to almost 6 billion. Thanks to advances in agrarian technology, led by the United States, between 1930 and 1980 the United States went from 30 million farmers, barely producing enough food for a domestic population of 100 million people, to 3 million farmers producing more than enough food for 300 million people. Farm production became more and more efficient, with no end in sight.

The U.S. Department of Agriculture (USDA) was originally created to safeguard the economic interests of farmers, particularly in times of drought and famine. During this period of rising agricultural efficiency, the USDA budget was shifted to government "farm income stabilization" programs that paid farmers billions of dollars each year *not* to grow more food, thus keeping food prices higher, thus safeguarding the farmers' economic interests. Today, in addition to forcing consumers to pay higher prices for food, these subsidies keep many farmers from learning how to use new technology and from switching to crops that consumers really want. Worst of all, this subsidy encourages many young people to become farmers even though our economy no longer needs more farmers.

Yet despite efforts to the contrary by the USDA, the relative prices for farm produce fell steadily throughout the second half of the twentieth century as supply far exceeded demand.

As the price farmers received for basic food fell, the profit opportunity in agriculture shifted from producing raw foodstuffs (e.g., wheat, milk, fruit, cattle) to manufacturing these foodstuffs into name-brand foods with long shelf lives (e.g., cereals, condiments, processed cheeses, canned foods, frozen foods, and junk or snack foods).

It became particularly profitable to make junk or snack foods, products that initially consumers didn't know they wanted, but which they developed a seemingly unlimited propensity to consume.

> Additionally, in the postwar U.S. economy, the supply
> and demand for a new type of food arose—a food type de-
> fined not by its taste, price, or availability, but by its long
> shelf life and speed of service: *fast food.*

How Food Economics Created the Wellness Food Opportunity

During this period of great technological advances in our food
supply, our knowledge of basic nutrition was just evolving. Many of
our food scientists and engineers, let alone the consuming public,
didn't know enough about the need for proteins, vitamins, and minerals. Each food company concentrated on making each product
taste better than that of the competition, last longer, and be safe from
contamination by microorganisms.

Looking back, they did an admirable job in fulfilling their mission.
Processed and fast foods effectively didn't exist for most Americans
at the end of World War II. By the end of the twentieth century,
processed and fast-food sales had risen to dominate the U.S. $1 tril-
lion food industry.

Despite making basic calories affordable for everyone, our food
industry unwittingly injured the health of much of the nation. In
order to make their products taste better, they added fat. The better
it tasted, the more customers ate their products. The more customers
ate their products, the fatter they became. The fatter customers became, the more food products they were able to consume on a daily
basis—and so on, and so on, and so on.

In order to make their products safe from contamination, they pasteurized and/or heated them.[5] Today, all canned foods and virtually
all milk and juices are pasteurized. Unfortunately, the application of
heat to food, as well as its storage over time in cans and other airtight
containers, destroys many of the vitamins and some of the minerals.
In general, canning and most other types of food processing do not
affect proteins, fats, and carbohydrates.

In order to increase the shelf life of their products (as well as to add
to their safety), food producers added preservatives, ranging from
enormous amounts of sodium to a dizzying array of chemical compounds in supposedly safe amounts. While a typical adult requires
about 500 milligrams a day of sodium, which is found naturally in
common foods, salt is so widely added to most processed foods that
the typical U.S. adult consumes 10 to 14 times this amount per day.

In addition to desensitizing our taste buds so that natural, un-processed foods no longer taste good, salt is the primary cause of high blood pressure, which leads to increased risk of stroke, heart disease, and kidney failure.

In order to get people to consume more of their product, produc-ers chemically altered the flavorings so that people would continually crave more and more of their single product rather than naturally seeking the variety in foods that their bodies require.

Empty Calories: The Core of the Food Supply Problem

The end result is that today the U.S. food supply is dominated by what nutritional experts call *empty calories*—food containing high amounts of caloric energy but low (or empty) in essential vitamins, minerals, and proteins.

The human body can consume only 2,200 to 2,900 calories per day for energy without becoming obese, but it must get the required amounts of protein, vitamins, minerals, and healthy fats along with these calories. Just a quick glance at the nutritional facts printed on any processed food label shows us what we are *not* getting along with our calories.

A typical can of soda contains 140 empty calories (38 grams of sugar, 70 milligrams of sodium, added caffeine, various preserva-tives, and 0 milligrams of proteins, vitamins, and minerals). A typical fast-food meal contains an incredible 1,000 calories or more with few essential vitamins or minerals. One 1-ounce serving of Lay's potato chips ("Betcha Can't Eat Just One")[6] contains 230 empty calories (plus 270 milligrams of sodium).

But these foods are even worse for what they *do* contain than for what they are missing: most empty-calorie foods have incredibly high levels of fat, which is added to make them taste better. A healthy food should yield about 20 percent of its calories from fat (each gram of fat contains 9 calories) and the rest from carbohydrates and proteins. Just one deluxe McDonald's burger contains 810 calories, with an in-credible 490 calories (55 grams, or 61 percent) from fat. Even with-out the medium-size french fries (containing 450 additional calories and 22 grams of additional fat), *55 grams of fat is the full amount you should consume in an entire day, not the amount you should consume from a single item of food.*[7] The typical American now eats three ham-burgers and four orders of french fries each week.[8]

In contrast, foods in their natural (unprocessed) state are packed with caloric energy, vitamins, minerals, and low levels of fat.

Fruits are high in carbohydrates, vitamins, and minerals and contain virtually no fat. A banana contains 103 calories of energy with 0 grams of fat. Fresh vegetables contain enormous quantities of vitamins, some protein, and almost no fat. A single stalk of broccoli contains 5 grams of protein with no fat, and a single medium-size potato containing 100 calories has 6 grams of protein and no fat. Moreover, when eating a natural food, people typically tire of its taste and automatically seek out different natural foods—containing the different vitamins and minerals that their bodies require on a daily basis.

Fish, beef, and chicken are loaded with protein, vitamins, minerals, no carbohydrates, and widely varying amounts of fat. A 6-ounce serving of fish (halibut) contains 35 grams of protein with 2 grams of fat. A 6-ounce steak (rib eye) contains about the same amount (39 grams) of protein—but an incredible 55 grams of fat as well. A 6-ounce serving of chicken (light and dark meat) contains 46 grams of protein with 25 grams of fat.

Unfortunately, we no longer eat as our ancestors did, or even as our parents did. Meals used to be prepared at home, primarily using fresh foods and without adding much fat, salt, or chemical preservatives.

Today, most of us are too busy to prepare foods from fresh ingredients, so we purchase foods that are partially or fully ready to serve—foods processed with much added fat, sugar, sodium, and chemical additives.

The percentage of meals eaten or prepared away from home (restaurants, take-out) has increased more than 50 percent since 1970. Meals prepared outside the home are much higher in fat and sodium and lower in vitamins and minerals than meals prepared at home—even when compared to meals at home made from highly processed foods.[9] Ironically, as we will see in a moment, being biologically programmed to like the taste of fat—a trait that was responsible for our very survival in prehistoric times—has now become the cause of our worst medical problem.

Economics versus Avarice
and Our Food Supply Problems

Wellness entrepreneurs should keep in mind that as insidious as the manipulation of our food supply may seem in hindsight, none of it was done with insidious intent.

Entrepreneurs and businesspeople added fat to our food to make it taste better, not to create a nation of overweight and obese individuals. Entrepreneurs and businesspeople canned and processed our food to increase its shelf life, not to reduce the amount of vitamins and minerals and decrease wellness. And, as you'll see in a moment, entrepreneurs and businesspeople hydrogenated oils to make foods look better and last longer in the supermarket, not to turn good fats into bad fats and increase heart disease. Unfortunately, compounded by laws of economics that led thousands to imitate their behavior, the effect on our food supply is the same as if this manipulation had been carried out for the worst of purposes.

These actions were taken in response to often misguided or uninformed consumer demand. Chapter 4 examines how the new consumer demand for wellness, by well-guided and informed consumers, is leading entrepreneurs and businesspeople to fix the problems created by their predecessors. Moreover, the same laws of economics that compounded our wellness problems will now be applied to fix them, as virtually every provider in our food supply chain will be forced to embrace the wellness industry or get out of the way for those who do.

> As sad as the problems with our food supply may seem, the creation of these problems has also created the greatest opportunity within the wellness industry—the opportunity to provide consumers with healthy foods and dietary supplements to fix the problems with our modern food supply.

Before we examine these wellness food opportunities, some readers, particularly those focusing on obesity, may want more information on the wellness needs of the 65 percent of the U.S. population that is overweight or obese. Since this is a book on entrepreneurship and not biology, I am including the biological background on obesity in Appendix A at the back of this book. If you are personally or economically focusing on obesity, I suggest you read it now. If not, proceed.

Before Proceeding to the Next Chapter

*Action Plan for Entrepreneurs and
Wellness/Health Professionals*

1. Analyze how individual areas of wellness business opportunity will change our food supply. More specifically, what impact it will have on a consumer's consumption of:

   a. Water

   b. Carbohydrates

   c. Lipids (fats)

   d. Proteins

   e. Vitamins

   f. Minerals

2. Analyze how the obesity epidemic impacts your chosen wellness business opportunity.

3. Analyze the impact of your chosen areas of wellness business opportunity on calories—both the calories your customers consume and the calories they burn.

4. Consider the impact of your chosen area on educating people about what's missing from their food.

   Based on your answers to these questions, think about replacing your chosen individual areas of wellness business opportunity.

CHAPTER 4

Making Your Fortune in Food

Retroactively, in response to consumer demand and potential government regulation, companies in the food industry will begin fixing the problem that they created. But the greatest riches await those entrepreneurs who jump ahead of the consumer demand for wellness—entrepreneurs like Steve Demos and Paul Wenner who each built $100 million businesses by proactively getting their products and distribution in place and waiting for the market to come to them.

The wellness fortunes to be made in food lie in two basic areas:

1. Growing, finding, harvesting, transporting, and preparing healthy foods
2. Teaching consumers how to choose healthy foods and how to limit their overall consumption of food

---

Some of the business opportunities in fixing our food supply are economically distorted because of cultural preferences in choosing the foods we eat and massive government subsidy programs that distort the true cost of producing the foods we eat. Our religious and government institutions have fallen behind the consumer in embracing wellness. Before we examine specific wellness food opportunities, it is important for the entrepreneur to understand how this has occurred and to understand the components of our existing $1 trillion food industry.

As you read this chapter, each time a problem with food is discussed, whether it is based on religion, government, or a specific type of food, you should stop and think how you might be able to turn this problem into a profitable wellness business opportunity.

How Religion and Government Fell Behind on Wellness

The history of human civilization is mostly the history of obtaining food—where humans originally migrated to find it and, later, how they cultivated and preserved it. Growing, finding, harvesting, preserving, transporting, preparing, and eating food dominated our daily existence, and the world economy, until the beginning of the twentieth century.

Then, almost overnight, the green revolution and other technologies shifted our major dietary issues from the problems of starvation and cleanliness to the problems of overeating and malnutrition. This happened so fast that our religious and government institutions have still not had the opportunity to catch up.

Today, in developed nations where food is plentiful, most religious people begin meals with prayers thanking God for providing them with food—as opposed to thanking God for giving them the knowledge of what to eat to be healthy. Gluttony is denounced from Exodus through Jude and is one of the seven deadly sins of early Christianity.[1] The Old Testament predicts that gluttons will become poor (Proverbs 23:21). Yet today gluttony is virtually ignored by most religions. Even those religions that focus heavily on diet, such as Orthodox Judaism and Islam, focus on biologically archaic laws of cleanliness (eating kosher) versus the true dietary needs of most of their congregants (eating healthy food, ingesting sufficient vitamins and minerals, and avoiding obesity).

Even today in the United States, the main mission of the U.S. Department of Agriculture (USDA) is to protect the incomes of farmers, not to protect the food supply of consumers. This may have been good policy in 1776 when George Washington called for the establishment of a National Board of Agriculture—farmers then represented more than 95 percent of the population and farm sales comprised more than 90 percent of the nation's economy. But it is an outdated mission now, when farmers represent less than 2 percent of the U.S. population, farm sales are less than 0.5 percent of our economy, and the majority of our citizens are overweight and malnourished.

In the past century, advancing technology in producing, preserving, and distributing food decreased relative food prices so much that food industry sales now represent less than 9 percent of the U.S. economy, or about $1.3 trillion ($1,300 billion) each year of our $14 trillion gross domestic product. This breaks down roughly as follows:

$1.3 Trillion U.S. Food Industry

Agriculture	$ 55 billion[2]
Food processing and distribution	$ 600 billion
Restaurants	$ 547 billion[3]
Diet supplementation	$ 100 billion[4]
Other	$ 53 billion
Total U.S. food sales	$ 1,300 billion*

*Total excludes the $55 billion in agriculture, as it is either exported or is included as a sub-component of the other categories.

In the previous chapter we saw how this same advancing technology caused the empty-calorie crisis we have to-day—our food contains high amounts of fat and caloric energy but is low (or empty) in essential vitamins, minerals, and proteins. This is about to change as consumers become educated and begin demanding healthier foods of all types.

Agricultural Subsidy Programs

Two major areas of agriculture should rapidly change in response to consumer demand for wellness: (1) which foods (healthier) farmers produce and (2) how farmers produce these foods (e.g., organic farming and genetic engineering).

I say *should* because which foods farmers choose to produce and how they produce them are often determined today by obsolete government subsidy programs, written almost a century ago, rather than by consumer choice and sound economic decisions. Although entrepreneurial opportunities for farmers in the wellness industry still exist, there are fewer opportunities than there would be if farmers were more free from government interference to serve consumer demand.

Even if you are not interested in becoming a wellness farmer, it is important to understand these government subsidy programs for the following reasons:

1. You are paying for them as a taxpayer.
2. Subsidized produce will compete with your wellness food products.

3. **They keep farmers producing unhealthy foods, which increases the demand for more wellness products and services.**

Agriculture today represents a very small part of our food industry and a minuscule part of our nearly $14 trillion economy, yet farmers and their economic issues occupy a great part of the national stage. This is because too much federal power is now concentrated in several low-population agricultural states. The combined population of any 20 mostly agricultural states like North Dakota (637,000) and Wyoming (509,000) is less than the population of any one industrial state like Texas (22,860,000) or California (36,132,000), yet these agricultural states have 20 times the political power of Texas or California in the U.S. Senate[5]—power that is unfortunately controlled and abused by rich farmers and powerful special interests like the American Dairy Association (ADA).

Beginning in the 1920s, when most voters were farmers, the federal government sought to stabilize farm prices to protect individual farmers from falling prices. Over the years, dozens of different government programs evolved into the system we have today, where farmers (or their children, who do not want to farm anyway) are paid corporate welfare *not* to grow certain crops—$25 billion in 2005.

In one county in Texas, federal subsidies make up more than one-third of all farm income, and the top 10 percent of subsidy recipients were paid an average $396,131 from 1996 to 1999—with several farmers receiving more than $2 million each over this period.[6] These subsidy programs are cloaked in names like the "Freedom to Farm Act," suggesting that they benefit consumers and family farms, but most of the money ends up in the hands of a very few rich individuals and corporations who can afford to employ lawyers and lobbyists who are experts in processing government subsidy applications. Unlike virtually every other entitlement or welfare program, federal farm subsidies have no requirements regarding income, assets, or debts.

Even worse than just paying out $25 billion in corporate welfare, these subsidies incentivize the production of certain outdated foods that, for wellness reasons, should no longer be produced.

The Dairy Deception

The worst of these foods, receiving $7 billion in government subsidies, are dairy products. But dairy products cost U.S. consumers many times more than just the $7 billion federal subsidy given dairy producers as corporate welfare.

Milk and milk by-products are leading contributors to the $2 trillion sickness industry—milk causes allergies, gas, constipation, obesity, cancer, heart disease, infectious diseases, and osteoporosis.

Yes, milk causes osteoporosis, despite the massive deceptive advertising campaign by the ADA stating that milk prevents osteoporosis.

Several studies have concluded that drinking milk is more likely to *cause* than to prevent osteoporosis, which is the result of calcium leaching out of the bones and is not directly associated with calcium intake, because the amount and type of protein (casein) in milk results in a great loss of calcium in the bones. For those who believe that taking calcium as an adult will help them have strong bones, calcium contained naturally in vegetables is much healthier, easier to absorb, and more abundant. A cup of the latest Tropicana calcium-enriched orange juice contains more calcium than fortified milk—350 milligrams versus 302 milligrams in a cup of milk. Moreover, whatever benefit calcium intake may have in avoiding osteoporosis probably stops in adulthood when bone mass stops increasing—despite the fact that ADA milk advertising promoting calcium intake to avoid osteoporosis is targeted toward adults and older Americans.

But of far more concern than contributing to osteoporosis, milk contains hormones and carries infectious diseases. A typical cow in nature can produce up to 10 pounds of milk per day, whereas today's tortured modern dairy cows produce up to 100 pounds of milk per day. This is because cows today are given massive amounts of specialized hormones like bovine growth hormone (BGH) to increase milk production—making their udders so large they often drag on the ground. This results in frequent infections and the need for constant antibiotics—the USDA allows drinking milk to contain from 1 to 1.5 million white blood cells (that's *pus* to a nonbiologist) per milliliter. These growth hormones, antibiotics, and pus remain in the milk after processing, which causes dire medical consequences for people, especially children, who consume dairy products.

Any U.S. brassiere manufacturer will tell you that sales have been good the past few decades since the introduction of BGH in milk, because BGH and other hormones have increased the size of the average teenage human female breast and have decreased the age of menarche.* But what the brassiere manufacturer may not be able to tell you is that these same hormones are also a major cause of the increase in breast cancer in adults—as they cause malignant tumors in the human breast to grow as though they were tortured cows' udders filled with BGH. Despite the fact that numerous consumer groups have called for milk containing BGH and other hormones to be banned or at least labeled as such, the FDA continues to bow to the ADA lobbyists and refuses to ban such hormones or to require milk to be so labeled.

Milk production is also terrible for the environment and for the cows themselves. A dairy cow may produce 100 pounds per day of milk, but it also produces 120 pounds per day of waste—equivalent to the waste produced by 24 people, but with no toilets, sewers, or treatment plants. Each cow consumes 81 pounds of grains and vegetables, plus 45 gallons of water—per day. Although natural cows may live 20 to 25 years, cows in dairy production typically live only 4 to 5 years—burning out from the hormones and constant artificial pregnancies that turn them from living creatures into grotesque milking machines.

The worst thing about dairy products is not the disease they cause, the torture for the animals involved, or the terrible impact on the environment—the worst thing about dairy products is that they are the major cause of more than 65 percent of our population being overweight and obese.

Although drinking milk and eating cheese may *possibly* give a young girl the breasts of Britney Spears (one of many celebrities proudly sporting a milk mustache), drinking lots of milk and eating cheese will *definitely* give a young girl the thighs and hips of the late Mama Cass.**

*The age of menarche has been dropping rapidly over the past few decades in the United States, occurring as early as age 10 in many girls. In civilizations that don't use bovine growth hormones, menarche typically occurs around age 15 (Yoffe, Emily, "Got Osteoporosis? Maybe All That Milk You've Been Drinking Is to Blame," *Slate Magazine,* www.slate.com, 2 August 1999).

**"Mama" Cass Elliot (1941–1974), of The Mamas and The Papas, was one of the greatest singers and warmest people in history. Unfortunately, as was sometimes noted affectionately in the group's songs, she was terribly obese and died tragically of a heart attack at age 33 after performing at the London Palladium.

The average American eats over four pounds of food per day, and nearly 40 percent of that food is milk and dairy products. Milk contains no fiber and is filled with saturated fat and cholesterol. A glass of milk gets 49 percent of its calories from fat, and cheeses get more than 65 percent of their calories from fat. Milk really should be called "liquid meat"—one 12-ounce glass contains as much saturated fat as eight strips of bacon. When it comes to obesity and being overweight, milk is even worse than beer—a 12 ounce glass of milk contains 300 calories and 16 grams of fat, whereas a 12-ounce glass of beer contains 144 calories and no fat. Just four tablespoons of half-and-half added to a cup of coffee contain 15 grams of saturated fat— about 80 percent of the saturated fat you should consume in an entire day. To counter the undisputed truth of these facts, the dairy industry came up with the deception of "2 percent" and "low-fat" milk. In reality, 2 percent milk contains 24 to 33 percent calories of fat and is only slightly less fattening than whole milk (which contains 3 percent fat by weight). Milk producers even had the audacity to label cottage cheese, which contains 20 percent calories of fat, as "low fat"— which prompted the FDA to recently order dairy producers to stop promoting milk products as low- or nonfat foods.

How did we get to where we are today—where most Americans drink milk and eat milk by-products every day? Historically, milk was valued by our pioneer ancestors because it could be processed at home into high-energy foods like butter and cheese that could last through the winter.

Because milk was perceived to be so valuable, innovative entrepreneurs figured out ways to produce milk at an amazingly low price, then used their profits to build a self-perpetuating marketing and political organization now known as the ADA.

The ADA lobbied the federal government to subsidize overproduction, then forced milk into the diets of children through mandatory school lunch programs. I say *forced* because, though it is widely known that 95 percent of Asians are lactose intolerant, I suspect that most adult humans of every race are similarly intolerant. Caucasians, who comprise most of the milk market, have sadly learned to accept the accompanying allergic reactions, heartburn, upset stomach, diarrhea, gas, and diabetes as facts of everyday life—and to treat only the symptoms of these diseases, taking addictive over-the-counter remedies on a continual basis.

As consumers become educated about the detrimental effects of drinking cow milk, they will develop a voracious appetite for a wellness substitute. This will occur not only for milk, but for the thousands of unhealthy food products that currently dominate our modern food supply. And, as we see in a moment, the greatest rewards will be for the entrepreneurs who get there first.

The Soy Solution: A New Opportunity Born from Wellness

Fortunately, there is a high-energy low-fat substitute for milk that lasts longer, is incredibly healthy, prevents disease, is great for the environment, and costs less: soy milk and other foods made from soybeans. Unfortunately, few people in the United States and other Western countries know about it. This is ironic considering that, although containing less than 5 percent of the world's population, the United States produces about 50 percent of the world's soybeans. Of the 3 million bushels of soybeans grown in the United States each year, 98 percent is for animal feed or industrial uses and only 2 percent for direct human consumption—with the overwhelming majority of this 2 percent sold to Japan and other countries where consumers already enjoy a soy-rich diet.

Converting more farms from producing soybeans for animal feed to soybeans for human consumption is one of the largest wellness opportunities for agriculturally based entrepreneurs.

Soybeans first came to North America in the early 1800s, not as food, but as ballast aboard clipper ships. In 1904, George Washington Carver, the famous African American chemist, discovered their high-protein value for animal feed and also discovered that farmers could produce higher-quality cotton and other plants by rotating them with soybeans every one to three years. Henry Ford used soybeans to make the plastic parts for many Ford cars—using 60 pounds of soybeans in every Ford by 1935.*

*In 2853 B.C., Emperor Sheng-Nung of China named five sacred plants: soybeans, rice, wheat, barley, and millet (North Carolina Soybean Producers Association, www.ncsoy.org).

But soy's greatest benefits, which could make soy the largest staple in a wellness diet, have only recently been discovered. For human beings, soy is the best low-fat source of proteins, carbohydrates, fibers, vitamins, and minerals we know about today. Moreover, soy has great medicinal qualities that can prevent many of the diseases caused by dairy products, from osteoporosis to heart disease and cancer.

Soy is high in calcium and, unlike milk, does not contain the casein proteins that result in calcium loss in the bones. Soy has even been shown to reverse osteoporosis, as the isoflavones found in soybeans can increase bone mineral content and bone density.* An *isoflavone* is a colorless organic compound (ketone) occurring in a plant in sufficient amounts to affect the endocrine system of animals. Another soy isoflavone, genistein, stops cancer cells from growing when added to live cancer cells in laboratory test tubes. Other soy isoflavones reduce the frequency and intensity of hot flashes in menopausal women, similar to estrogen-replacement therapy. And the protein in soy has such a preventive effect on heart disease that in October 1999 the FDA announced that soy producers may claim that "consuming 25 grams of soy protein a day may help consumers lower their (bad) cholesterol and reduce their risk of heart disease." The American Heart Association endorsed the same claim one year later.

Soybeans contain more protein by weight than beef, fish, or chicken, with no cholesterol and little saturated fat. Moreover, for those individuals wanting to limit or eliminate their consumption of animal proteins, soy protein is the only "complete" vegetable protein. As noted earlier, human beings require 20 basic amino acids from proteins, 11 of which can be produced by our bodies. The remaining nine we must get from the foods we eat. Soy protein provides all nine missing amino acids, making it as complete as the protein in milk or meat products—but without the hormones, the saturated fat, the calories, and the devastating effect on our environment.

Soybeans and soy beverages have been cultivated and produced in China for 5,000 years and enjoyed throughout Asia for centuries. In the West, the term *milk* has been used since the twelfth century to define "a fluid secreted by the mammary glands of females for the nourishment of their young, or the contents of an unripe kernel of grain."[7] But all this didn't stop the cow milk producers from having the au-

---

*A study at the University of Illinois at Urbana concluded that consuming soybean isoflavones can increase bone mineral content and bone density. As little as 40 grams of soy protein, consumed each day for six months, led to positive results in a test group of postmenopausal women. Forty grams of soy protein can be found in two ounces of soy protein isolate (www .unitedsoybeanboard.com).

dacity in February 2000 to file a trade complaint with the FDA requesting that soymilk producers be prohibited from using the term *milk* in their advertisements—claiming "that 'milk' has a standard of identity dictating that it must come from dairy cows."[8] If the FDA insisted on the truth about cow milk and milk advertising, it should rule that cow milk be labeled "cow pus" and carry warnings on each carton similar to the warnings now required on individual packs of cigarettes (e.g., "The Surgeon General has determined that the human consumption of cow milk causes allergies, constipation, gas, bacterial infections, osteoporosis, obesity, heart disease, and cancer").

Many upscale Americans who dine in expensive sushi restaurants already love soybeans but don't know it. The green "snap beans" often served as complimentary appetizers in upscale sushi restaurants, called *edamame,* are nothing more than pure boiled (or steamed) soybeans. Edamame (pronounced ed-ah-MAH-may) is technically the name of a specialty soybean harvested just before the beans reach maturity. While most sushi diners think of them only as something to nibble on while waiting for their fish, edamame is incredibly healthy and actually contains more proteins and nutrients than the fish itself—an amazing 22 grams of protein per cup. Although the farming of edamame is currently a very minor part of U.S. soybean agriculture, it is extremely profitable, and its cultivation is expected to grow exponentially as it becomes more widely known.

From a scientific standpoint, soy foods should already be widely touted as the wellness wonder products of our time. Unfortunately, science has very little to do with the Western diet. When it comes to food, we are ruled by convention, taste, and convenience.

Many people are unwilling to try new foods, seeking out the familiar and expected glass of milk in the morning or the cheeseburger for lunch. Those of us eager to try new foods are often ruled by the immediate sensory gratification of taste rather than the longer-term benefit of how we will feel afterward. Even if soy products were familiar to us and tasted good, they would have to be as conveniently available as McDonald's Big Macs or Coca-Cola to make a real impact on the average diet.

A few wellness revolutionaries are poised to achieve exactly this result in all three areas—convention, taste, and

convenience. Some of these revolutionaries are already entrenched in the largest part of our food industry, the $500 billion food processing business. Fortunately for the wellness entrepreneur just getting started, these successful entrepreneurs are barely scratching the surface of what is possible in developing wellness substitutes for many of our unhealthy foods.

The Soy Wonder: Building a "Right Livelihood"

In 1970, when Steve Demos graduated from Bowling Green University in Ohio, he knew everything he *didn't* want to do to make a living. However, like many of his generation, he also had no idea of what he did want to do—so he ended up dropping out for the next four years and traveling throughout India. There, he became a vegetarian and formulated his desire to construct a "right livelihood" where the Golden Rule could be applied to business. In his own words, this meant that

"Everyone who touches the stream of revenue must be doing good for society."

When he returned to the United States, Demos settled in Boulder, Colorado, and decided that the business of making healthy vegetarian foods, especially from soy products, had all the attributes to which he could apply his "right livelihood" philosophy.

Like many entrepreneurs, Demos tried various approaches before he hit on the one that would make him famous.

He started a natural nut butter company called Naturally Nuts. He ran a retail vegetarian delicatessen called The Cow of China. And he started White Wave Tofu, which today has become the largest soy foods and soymilk company in the world.

White Wave Tofu (now White Wave, Inc.) made its first sale of tofu on September 27, 1977, at 11:30 A.M. Tofu, also known as *bean curd,* is a soft, bland, custardlike food made from crushed soybeans. The tofu was made in Steve's apartment kitchen using $500 he borrowed from a neighbor to start the company. White Wave ran along for the next 20 years making various soy-based products, achieving sales of about $6 million in 1996. During those years, many products were tried and eventually dropped—like Polar Bean (soy) ice cream and ToFruzen—products that Steve didn't realize until years later were viable but were then simply too far ahead of their time.

In 1996, after a successful "getting rich slowly" philosophy that had sustained White Wave for almost two decades, Steve realized that packaged soy foods like tofu and tempeh were probably never going to make the impact on society he had dreamed of when he started his company.

Soy seemed to be a very narrow niche market limited to those vegetarians who knew about it. The company had tried veggie burgers, tofu hot dogs, ice creams, and countless other ideas in attempting to entice the American consumer to embrace soy. Over those years, Steve realized that the product he was searching for would be one that required no customer education—it had to be a "nonthinking" product containing "freshness, familiarity, and convenience." Steve came up with SILK soymilk later that year as the culmination of all of these insights.

SILK, a very fresh soymilk product made entirely from organically grown soybeans, is sold in freshness-dated, refrigerated cartons that look like quarts or half gallons of ordinary milk. It comes in plain, vanilla, chocolate, chai, and mocha flavors—and a companion SILK creamer product comes in Plain and French Vanilla. For the consumer, it is "fresh, familiar, and convenient," especially since it is now available in 91 percent of U.S. supermarkets.

In 1997, soon after launching SILK, White Wave sales rose 37 percent, from $6 to $8.2 million. Led by SILK, sales rose another 24 percent, to $10.2 million in 1998, and yet another 39 percent, to $14.2 million in 1999. Then the FDA and others began touting the benefits of soy products and sales more than doubled, to $29.6 million in 2000, and then almost tripled in 2001, to $80.5 million. Sales were $180 million in 2002, $240 million in 2003, and $362 million in 2004.[9]

When I first phoned the main number for White Wave to set up an interview back in 2001, Steve's voice greeted me on the company's voice mail: "Welcome to White Wave. This is Steve Demos, company president. The following menu will assist you." Since I had read about Steve before calling him for the interview and had seen tapes of his appearances on CNN and elsewhere, I was not surprised to hear him humbly attribute the enormous success of SILK to "the market was ripe, there was nobody present, and we had all the elements."

> **I was surprised to find this former society dropout highly versed in the vernacular of modern business—so much so that I could have been talking to any Fortune 500 CEO or professor at Wharton or NYU business school. When I complimented him on this he explained, "If you are really and passionately committed to what you want to accomplish, you adjust to the language spoken."**

But Steve has done far more than simply learning the language of business in the twenty-first century. He practices it at the highest levels—levels not usually found in a food company or with a startup entrepreneur.

> **According to Steve, "Most entrepreneurs are prepared for failure but not for success. Thus, when they succeed, they end up handing their business over to a competitor."**

In 1998, Steve realized that he had a tiger by the tail and began to prepare for success. First, White Wave identified several strategic targets as investors—targets that could provide capital and operational support if SILK sales continued their meteoric rise. Then, after identifying the proper targets in its industry, White Wave hired an investment banker to execute the transaction and sold a minority interest in the company for $15 million to the second largest dairy in the United States, Dean Foods, Inc. But White Wave never used the operational resources of their new dairy partner.

Instead, Steve retooled the SILK manufacturing process into a virtual process modeled on the best aspects of both the dairy industry and the much more profitable soft drink industry. White Wave began making high quality soymilk extract at three 20,000-square-foot, company-owned facilities that are strategically located in New Jersey, Colorado, and Utah. This highly valuable extract is then shipped in milk-type trucks to five major dairies that make and package the SILK—dairies carefully chosen to ensure that White Wave is an important part of their overall volume and a profitable customer. These dairies not only guarantee SILK virtually unlimited manufacturing capacity, they already have the trucks and sales organizations to keep

SILK in the dairy case at the local supermarkets. As Steve explained in our first interview, White Wave has a totally scalable model—"We draw a 500-mile radius around extraction, find facilities, and then expand."

Although most people see SILK as an alternative to cow milk, Steve doesn't see the dairies as his competition. "We're not an alternative to milk," said Steve, "we're an option. I don't want to be dairy's nemesis—I want to be so superior that there is no comparison. I'm after Coca-Cola as much as I'm after milk." In this regard, White Wave makes an 11-ounce plastic bottle of SILK soymilk packaged like a soft drink but with a 120-day nonrefrigerated shelf life. The average person in the United States consumes 24.2 gallons per year of cow milk, and that same average person also consumes 54.6 gallons per year of soft drinks.

In 2003, Steve made a deal with Starbucks to create an exclusive version of SILK to complement their espresso and chai drinks.

In 2002, soon after I wrote about Steve Demos in the first edition of this book, his company was sold to Dean Foods, Inc. in a highly publicized $295 million transaction. At that time White Wave had about 150 employees, of whom 100 had worked for the company for 2 years or more. In an unprecedented move for a packaged foods business, Steve and his managers refused to sell unless every employee who had been with the company for 2 years or more received something from the sale. The lawyers were astounded by Steve's request—it took them three months to work out the legal mechanics, which could have jeopardized the sale of the company. In the end, $15 million of the sale price was handed out to about 100 people, many of whom didn't speak English. One, a truck driver named Pete, received almost $400,000. There was no legal obligation to do this, and Steve lights up when he speaks about handing them the checks and sometimes having to explain through a translator why they were getting this money.

Reflecting back on the sale, Steve said: "This event was a cause and effect circumstance (proving) that if you choose to do something the right way you end up at a certain point. The ultimate message is that there is a path, and that path is Right Livelihood, to create wealth without guilt or negativity."[10]

After the sale, most people expected the culture at Dean's Foods to decimate White Wave. Instead, the opposite occurred. Steve made new deals with his management team to stay on for at least $1 million each, and together they earned an additional $35 million in sales proceeds by exceeding the new owner's expectations. Steve was promoted to manage not just White Wave, but he became president of the Refrigerated Products Division of Dean's Foods, with sales of $1.2 billion, including Horizon Organic Milk. Steve's favorite speaking topic from 2002–2004 was "Who Bought Into Who?"

The story of "Who Bought Into Who?" appeared on the front page of *The Wall Street Journal* on February 1, 2005.[11] Steve was a national celebrity and, although he was only running a $1.2 billion division of a $10 billion company, he was more popular than the chairman and the board of directors. In a surprising move, just one month after the glowing story in *The Wall Street Journal,* the board fired him.

Steve has agreements with White Wave and Dean Foods that prevent him from speaking freely or going into competition until Spring 2007. He just recently completed an 11-month trek in Asia and the Himalayas, and we are expecting more great things from this Soy Wonder when his noncompete agreements expire, just about the time this book is expected to be published.

The Vegetarian Burger Wonder: A Wellness Cautionary Tale

Steve Demos's concern about handing over your wellness business to a competitor after achieving success is well founded. Entrepreneurs must be prepared for success.

The story of Paul Wenner, the famous vegetarian chef, author, and founder of Gardenburger, Inc., contains an important lesson for wellness entrepreneurs. At the time of this writing, Wenner and his company appear to have lost out financially to competition after pioneering the market for vegetarian burgers. Nevertheless, Paul Wenner is a true wellness revolutionary who has made, and continues to make, a positive contribution to the lives of millions of people.

Paul Wenner didn't start out wanting to be a wellness revolutionary or even a great success. He thought that he had finally realized his lifelong dream in 1981 when he opened his gourmet vegetarian restaurant, The Gardenhouse Restaurant, in Gresham, Oregon. As he explains in his book, "Like all restaurateurs, I was soon faced with what to do with the leftovers. My solution was something I called the 'Gardenloaf Sandwich' made of leftover vegetables and rice pilaf.[12] Later I got the idea of slicing up the loaf into what looked like patties—and suddenly the Gardenburger was born." Soon, one out of every two lunches sold in his restaurant was a Gardenburger.[13]

Then, in 1984, a recession hit Oregon and his restaurant folded. Paul thought it was the end of the world, although, as he reflects now, it was "the best thing that could have happened." Customers started calling to ask where they could still get Gardenburgers, and one day Paul's sister set up a meeting with the CEO of her company to see about financing a business to supply them. The CEO tried the Gardenburger, offered Paul $60,000 to start the business, and asked: "When will this company make money?" Paul had absolutely no idea, so he replied, "In 13 months," based on the notion that if it couldn't make money after a full year he wouldn't be able to stick it out anyway.

As Gardenburger grew, Paul learned to turn every negative experience into a positive one. When 9 out of 10 restaurant owners told him, "We don't get any vegetarians in here," his response was, "Maybe that's because there's nothing vegetarian on your menu."

The company went public in 1992, and Paul Wenner turned over day-to-day management to food industry professionals in 1995, retaining for himself a seat on the board and the title of chief creative officer. By 1998, Gardenburger, Inc.[14] had sold hundreds of millions of Gardenburgers and the company's products were distributed in tens of thousands of supermarkets and natural food stores worldwide.

Unfortunately, as fast as Gardenburger grew, it wasn't fast enough to satisfy the demand for what Wenner had started. In 1993 another restaurateur, in Fort Lauderdale, Florida, decided he, too, could create a good-tasting vegetarian burger and started Boca Foods— which by 1998 was making vegetarian substitutes for ground beef, chicken, sausages, and other popular meat products. Another competitor, Worthington Foods, also entered the "meatless meat" market with a more complete line of soy-based products called Morningstar.

Although Gardenburger achieved sales of $100.1 million in 1998, this represented then only about one-fifth of the market it had created for meatless vegetarian substitutes.

The food industry professionals running Gardenburger were convinced that all they needed was more awareness and trial of their product before someone else acquired their future customers. In 1998, Gardenburger spent $1.5 million for an advertising spot on the last *Seinfield* episode. Although the ad was seen by a record 104 million viewers, critics claimed that the bulk of the benefit went to Gardenburger's competitors, who also reported increases in store sales the next day. To sustain its $100.1 million in sales in 1998, Gardenburger spent an incredibly high $15 million on advertising that year and was planning to continue such spending by raising more equity capital. The company sold $32.5 million in preferred stock in 1999—but that year its sales fell 12 percent to $88.8 million. Sales fell an additional 21 percent to $71 million in 2000, and the company recorded a loss of $32.7 million, or $3.67 per share.

To make matters even worse, in 1999, Kellogg, Inc. ($9 billion sales) purchased competitor Worthington Foods for $307 million, and in 2000, cigarette maker Philip Morris purchased Boca Foods. Wall Street lost confidence that Gardenburger could ever recover against such strong competition, and its stock price crashed from $18 to less than 50 cents a share—causing Gardenburger to be delisted from the Nasdaq.[15] The company subsequently filed for bankruptcy and successfully emerged from bankruptcy on March 30, 2006 as a privately-held corporation called Wholesome & Hearty Foods Company. According to its latest annual report, the company is now refocused on "returning to its roots as a maker of great tasting vegetarian foods that provide positive nutritional benefits."[16]

Paul Wenner is now running a vegetarian restaurant in Hawaii. He wrote a book *Garden Cuisine,* part autobiography, part how to start a business, part how to achieve a healthy body, part how to prevent cruelty to animals, and part how to protect our environment.

Wenner's personal loss today seems almost insignificant considering the billions of vegetarian burgers now sold and the positive impact Wenner has had on the lives of millions of people.

What Restaurant Entrepreneurs Need to Know

Restaurants like Wenner's have introduced more than just vegetarian burgers to society.

The restaurant industry is one of the most dynamic entre-preneurial components of the American economy—con-tinually introducing new products and innovative concepts over the past four decades. How this industry grew over the past 40 years illustrates what is possible for the wellness industry over the next decade.

In 1961, few Americans ate their meals out of the home, and total U.S. restaurant sales were less than $20 billion. Today, about half of Americans eat meals out of the home each day, and total restaurant sales are about $547 billion. If, back in 1961, someone were to have predicted this 27-fold increase in sales, you probably wouldn't have believed it, for the following reasons.

First (you might have thought in 1961), only the very wealthy could afford to eat half of their meals out of the home. Yet advancing technology lowered production costs so much that today it is often less expensive to eat out than to dine at home.

Second (you might have thought in 1961), there weren't enough restaurants in America to seat that many people at mealtimes. Yet over the next 45 years, tens of thousands of shopping centers were built to house the 925,000 U.S. dining establishments that now exist.

Third (you might have thought in 1961), people would be bored eating out so much, because, back then, only three basic types of cuisine were available (diner, cafeteria, and French). Yet hundreds of varieties of restaurants came to exist, many from places like Thailand, that weren't even independently named countries in 1961.

Fourth (you might have thought in 1961), restaurants are labor intensive and there simply aren't enough people in the United States to work in all those dining establishments. Yet advancing technology allowed manufacturers to lay off tens of millions of workers while still being able to serve their customers, and 12.5 million of these workers ended up in the restaurant industry by 2006. The restaurant industry today is the largest U.S. private sector employer.

Fifth, and finally, even if you were able to foresee these incredible changes in lower costs, increased number of dining establishments, unlimited varieties of cuisine, and available labor, you might have thought in 1961 that people just didn't have the time to eat out so often. In fact, a whole new category of restaurants emerged in the 1960s, defined not by their price, location, or country of origin, but by the speed of their service: fast-food restaurants.

> **Restaurant choice now is dominated by price, location, type of cuisine, and speed of service, but a new type of restaurant choice is emerging that will generate fortunes for the Ray Krocs and Dave Thomases of tomorrow who proactively jump in now and wait for the customer to come to them.**

If you haven't guessed it already, it is exactly what Paul Wenner did in 1981 when he decided to open a restaurant focused on healthy food—although he was then too far ahead of his time to have it work out the way he originally thought it would.

> **The reason the time is ripe to open specialty restaurants focused on healthy cuisine has to do with the nature of who is spending the most profitable part of the $547 billion consumed at U.S. restaurants today.**

The average American family spends 45.6 percent of their food budget on meals prepared outside of the home, but households with incomes of $50,000 or more spend *70 percent* of their food budget on meals prepared outside of the home. Those households with incomes above $100,000 spend even more than 70 percent of their food budget at restaurants. Although baby boomers comprise only 28 percent of the U.S. population, boomers account for more than 50 percent of households with incomes over $50,000 and 60 percent of the households with incomes over $100,000.[17] On a per-person basis, boomers today spend more than twice as much dining out as did the generation of their parents.[18]

As explained in Chapter 2, the single item that characterizes most boomer spending to date is the desire for products that remind them of their youth. In restaurants, they have not had much to choose from in this regard, other than a few establishments with themes or menus reminiscent of earlier times. But think for a moment what would happen if boomers could choose restaurants that served healthy cuisine that could actually make them younger or could slow down the effects of aging in the future—cuisine like SILK soymilk or Gardenburger meatless patties, or just ordinary cuisine prepared without the addition of heavy creams or saturated fats.

Boomers would flock to such restaurants, as evidenced by the fact that such health-food restaurants already exist in almost every city, and most regular upscale establishments have added one or two healthy or vegetarian entrées to their menu.

Instead of being considered fringe-type food or something grudgingly added to restaurants' menus, by 2012 healthy cuisine will be almost universal. Whereas today people choose restaurants mostly based on taste, price, and convenience, millions will soon choose restaurants based on the healthiness of the cuisine or how they will feel afterward.

Today, on hearing this prediction, you might think that consumers would never flock to healthy cuisine because it costs too much to prepare—yet history proves that advancing technology drives prices lower and lower in response to consumer demand, especially in the food service industry.

Second, you might think that there aren't enough locations left to open hundreds of thousands of healthy restaurants—yet most of the existing 925,000 U.S. restaurants will be forced to retool their menus or lose their leases to new owners who will. There will be widespread consumer rejection of restaurants perceived to serve unhealthy food. Additionally, today's upscale restaurant patrons limit going out when they are watching their weight—these profitable patrons will eat out even more often if they are given more healthy places to choose from.

Third, you might think that people will get bored eating only healthy food again and again—yet all types of restaurants, from French to Italian to Thai, will be embracing a healthy menu, and the term *health food* will soon become as meaningless in describing the type of food at an establishment as the word *restaurant* is today.

Fourth, you might think that healthy food simply doesn't taste good, yet once you get the toxins, high levels of sodium, and dangerous chemicals from processed foods out of your system, you won't believe what you have been missing. There is nothing more delicious than food in its natural state—from bananas to fresh grains to raw vegetables—but our taste buds have been chemically altered by processed food companies for so long that most of us have been unable to appreciate them.

And finally, even if you now accept my predictions on lower prices, locations, types of cuisine, and great taste, you might think that this type of change in the restaurant industry won't occur because people's dining habits are so well entrenched—yet something even more fundamental than all of these changes is about to happen to the dining habits of society, beginning in the United States.

Consumers everywhere will soon understand that there is a monumental connection between the food they consume today and the way their bodies will feel tonight, let alone tomorrow.

The "professionally beautiful," as explained in Chapter 1, already understand part of this relationship as they navigate through the menus at exclusive restaurants. As you look around, from your nightly newscast to the advertising and packaging that affect and shape our thoughts, you can see that everyone will soon embrace the age-old wisdom of Hippocrates: "Let food be your medicine and medicine be your food."

Before Proceeding to the Next Chapter

Action Plan for Entrepreneurs and Wellness/Health Professionals

1. Analyze how the coming changes in agriculture will impact your current area of potential wellness businesses.

2. How will your current area of potential wellness business rise or fall with a potential consumer flight away from dairy products?

3. How is your current area of potential wellness businesses positioned for the major changes coming in the American diet?

4. Steve Demos (SILK soymilk) spent 21 unsuccessful years trying to change American dietary habits (by getting people to eat tofu). He then succeeded in 1997 when he made a product (soymilk) that required no change in the dietary habits of consumers. Analyze the major changes in dietary habits that need to be overcome for your current area of potential wellness business to succeed. How would you plan to accomplish these necessary changes?

5. Steve Demos made his worst enemy (the dairies) his best ally—by making a healthy substitute milk product for the dairies to distribute. Analyze how you might be able to similarly induce an existing food company or industry to distribute your product(s). How is your area of wellness business interest positioned to take on strategic partners to grow?

6. Paul Wenner's Gardenburger, Inc. eventually failed by not being able to supply its customers before competition took hold. How is your area positioned to succeed without being eaten alive by the competition?

7. In a similar vein, what products will be displaced by your area of potential wellness business, and what action are their manufacturers or industries likely to take for or against you?

8. Analyze the impact of ubiquitous healthy food on your area for development or investment—particularly if your area of wellness business interest is in the restaurant business.

Based on your answers to these questions, think about replacing your individual area of wellness business opportunity.

CHAPTER 5

Making Your Fortune in Medicine

Let thy food be thy medicine and thy medicine be thy food.
—HIPPOCRATES (460–377 B.C.)

Most of the fortunes in medical wellness will be made by people outside of the sickness industry. In this chapter, we will examine a salesperson who invented multivitamins, two unusual MDs who have branched out of traditional medicine, an extraordinary female athlete who has built a $100 million fitness club business, a chiropractor who is developing the "McDonald's" of wellness franchises, and a college professor who is changing the face of a profession.

Many consumers mistakenly still think that their medical wellness should come from their traditional sickness-care providers—doctors, hospitals, and pharmaceutical companies. This is why it is important for every wellness entrepreneur to be able to explain the history of wellness medicine and the current state of scientific knowledge when it comes to keeping our bodies healthy, fit, and youthful.

The Search for What's Inside the Black Box

Throughout most of our history, the human body has been a black box. A black box is a device, like a computer or a car, that does something, but whose inner workings are mysterious—either because its inner workings cannot be seen or because they are incomprehensible.[1]

> **The history of medicine is the search for what's inside the black box called the human body and how it functions.**

In the Stone Age, most of humankind accepted debilitating illness as something that was caused by a higher being for no apparent rhyme or reason—people were not responsible for medicine and thus could not affect it or change it. Those few cultures that did practice medicine believed that cures lay in expelling the disease-causing demon from the body—so-called medicine men developed elaborate rituals and techniques, like trepanning (boring a hole in the skull), as treatments.[2]

Later in antiquity, humankind developed the belief that sickness was punishment from a supernatural being and that the cure for sickness lay in prayer and repentance for the action (or inaction) that had angered whichever god had caused the disease. The thought that you, or someone you loved, were being punished for your actions added even more trauma to the most painful of human experiences.

Hippocrates:
The First Wellness Practitioner

One of the earliest people to refute both of these beliefs was the Greek physician, Hippocrates (460–377 B.C.), the founder of modern medicine.[3] Hippocrates is best known today for the Hippocratic Oath still recited by medical school graduates. Unfortunately, medicine today has evolved far from the most important beliefs of its most famous practitioner.

Hippocrates regarded the body as a "whole" being rather than just the sum of operating parts—whereas today modern medicine often treats each organ or illness in isolation. Hippocrates studied each patient in his or her own environment, from their occupation to their diet. In doing so, Hippocrates came to the conclusion that health was the natural state, that disease was abnormal, and that the role of the physician was to assist nature to regain its natural (i.e., healthy) state. But most important,

> **Hippocrates was the first physician focused on *preventing* disease as well as treating disease. In all areas of medicine, he taught that the right types of nourishment and exercise were the keys to both avoiding sickness and regaining health. This is the key difference between wellness and sickness medicine: avoidance and prevention.**

When we consider what we know today about human evolution, from Charles Darwin's *Theory of Natural Selection* to Michael Behe's *Theory of Intelligent Design,* Hippocrates' teachings about diet and exercise make even more sense.* Our bodies evolved on this planet to exist in their natural state (i.e., *good health*) based on a natural diet and a natural amount of exercise. For more than 99 percent of human evolution and existence, a natural diet consisted of eating the wide variety of carbohydrates, fats, proteins, vitamins, and minerals that were abundantly available by grazing a mostly vegetarian supply of food. A natural amount of exercise consisted of physically laboring throughout each day for food and shelter.

It is easy to see how far we are today from this natural ideal in terms of our health. Our Western diet is far from that of our biological ancestors—it contains much more fat and is low in essential vitamins and minerals. Similarly, few of us get the amount of exercise all day long that our biological ancestors got naturally in their daily search for food and shelter.

Our Limited Vision

In the parable *The Blind Men and the Elephant* by John Godfrey Saxe (1816–1887), six blind men encounter an elephant for the first time: The first, touching its side, exclaims, "The Elephant is very like a wall." The second, touching its tusk, exclaims, "The Elephant is very like a spear." The third, touching its trunk, exclaims, "The Elephant is very like a snake." The fourth, touching its leg, exclaims, "The Elephant is very like a tree." The fifth, touching its ear, exclaims, "The Elephant is very like a fan." And the sixth, touching its tail, exclaims, "The Elephant is very like a rope." Each blind man remains convinced that he alone knows the nature of the elephant.

Throughout history, medicine men and women in every civilization have thought that they could finally explain the human black box and how it functioned. In hindsight,

---

*The *Theory of Natural Selection* and the more recent *Theory of Intelligent Design* both posit that all living creatures evolved from prior-existing organisms due to changes in their DNA. Natural Selection advocates believe these changes came from statistical random mutations that improved an organism's chance of survival (e.g., a leopard growing spots for camouflage). Eventually, the nonmutated organisms became extinct and the mutated organisms survived. Intelligent Design advocates believe that these changes were not random but occurred across the board at the same time by all members of a species due to an already existing code written in the DNA (e.g., all leopards grew spots in 5 million B.C.).

> we can see that they were as foolish as the six blind men,
> because they were similarly blinded by the limited tools
> they had available for observation.

Moreover, each time a new tool allowed scientists to open what they thought was the final black box, scientists saw another, previously unknown black box inside that had to await further tools to be opened.[4]

Early scientists believed that all matter was made of four "elements"—earth, air, fire, and water—since that was all they could see with their eyes. Fledgling biologists believed that all living bodies were regulated by what they could see—the four humors of blood, yellow bile, black bile, and phlegm—and that all disease arose from an excess of one of these humors. Dissection was generally prohibited, and therefore the tools for observation were limited.

> From the time of Hippocrates up to the nineteenth century, medicine didn't focus much on *why* something worked—medicine focused mostly on finding out *what* worked through trial-and-error treatment and observation.

When something worked, it was written down, and thus was medical knowledge accumulated over the centuries and occasionally passed between cultures.

The Scottish physician James Lind is credited with eliminating scurvy in the British navy by prescribing the mandatory consumption of citrus fruits among sailors. Yet Lind had no idea why citrus fruits eliminated scurvy and only came up with his "discovery" after reading that the Dutch navy had done this for hundreds of years. The Dutch probably picked up the practice from some other culture with abundant citrus during their great explorations in the fifteenth through seventeenth centuries.

The invention of the movable type printing press in the fifteenth century spread information to physicians worldwide about treatments that worked in alleviating specific ailments. This knowledge of so many treatments helped medicine establish itself as science (as opposed to religion or magic) by the eighteenth century. Of course, even though by then thousands of medicines or treatments were known to work, doctors were mostly at a total loss to explain *why* they worked.

The breakthroughs of Robert Hooke and others in the seventeenth and eighteenth centuries allowed the development of the inexpensive compound optical microscope. Using this new tool, scientists in the nineteenth century were able to see the previously invisible world of cells, which they then thought were the smallest and "final" building blocks of human matter.

> **The ability to watch cells function, especially in reaction to invading bacteria and medicines, led biologists and physicians to believe that they finally had the tool to discover why medicines worked. Doctors became international heroes as they eliminated major diseases (e.g., smallpox, tuberculosis, typhoid, polio) that had been the scourge of humankind.**
>
> **Emboldened by this success, most Western medical practitioners and researchers also began arrogantly rejecting age-old treatments and cures that had accumulated over the millennia—simply because they could not scientifically explain their function.**

Today we know how wrong they were in assuming that the individual cell was the smallest or final building block of human anatomy. An optical microscope cannot resolve two points that are closer together than approximately one-half of the wavelength of the illuminating light—and an individual bacterial cell, for example, is approximately one-tenth the wavelength of visible light.[5] Although it takes about 10,000 human cells to cover the head of a pin, each cell is composed of *trillions* of molecules that cannot be detected with even the best compound optical microscope. Most important,

> **Virtually everything we know today about the critical biochemical functions performed by proteins, vitamins, minerals, and nutritional supplements takes place on a molecular versus a cellular level.**

Today we also know that it is the individual quality of each cell that matters most when it comes to human longevity, vitality, strength, and everything else we desire from medicine beyond the treatment of disease—in short, wellness.

> Since our cells are constantly being replaced on an hourly to monthly basis, the quality of our cells is a function of the quality of the molecular reactions that constantly occur in manufacturing them.
>
> The quality of these molecular reactions is dependent on the quality of their components—the amino acids (proteins) and minerals that are the building blocks of cellular matter and the vitamins and minerals necessary as catalysts to combine molecules from raw materials.

Scientists generally agree on the daily components necessary to properly regenerate our cellular matter—13 essential vitamins, 14 essential minerals, and 20 basic amino acids (10 of which we must get from external sources). But scientists are far from agreeing on how these components combine in our bodies to form the complex proteins that make up our individual cells. Scientists have identified more than 100,000 different proteins in our bodies, manufactured from the same 20 basic amino acids, and are still identifying thousands more complex proteins faster than they are learning about specific protein deficiencies and how to treat them. We have just discovered that each cell contains its own time clock or biological programming for regenerating itself—DNA—but at this point in time we have a long way to go before we are able to read this programming.

The best we can do today when it comes to preventive or wellness medicine is to seek out the natural type of diet and natural program of exercise originally prescribed by Hippocrates. Today, this means the following:

1. Eating the proper amount (calories) and types of foods (e.g., unsaturated fats, soy, fibers) to maintain optimal health and avoid obesity
2. Avoiding harmful chemicals and hormones in our food—especially those contained in dairy and animal foods
3. Eating foods (including supplements) that yield a daily supply of our requisite vitamins, minerals, and basic amino acids (proteins)
4. Exercising throughout the day to yield the equivalent of a natural amount of exercise

This is much easier said than done in our modern society.

Eating only the amount of calories you need requires a great deal of self-discipline—especially since your body is programmed to eat each meal as if it were going to be your last and to store fat for later consumption. Avoiding harmful hormones and chemicals is virtually impossible, as most of them aren't even disclosed—especially in meat or dairy products. Ensuring a minimum daily supply of vitamins and minerals is difficult because many are missing from our processed foods, and, as we discuss in a moment, many supplements do not currently contain the items stated on their labels. Finally, if you were to try to get the same "natural" exercise as our ancestors, you wouldn't have time during the day to do anything else.

> **Fortunately, a few wellness medical entrepreneurs already exist, but we need thousands more like them, dedicated to making wellness easier than ever before and using technology to solve many of the wellness problems that technology has created.**

Multivitamins and Multilevel Marketing

While working in China as a salesperson for Colgate between 1915 and 1927, Carl F. Rehnborg observed that urban dwellers showed terrible signs of malnutrition, but that this malnutrition was not as widespread among the poorer citizens in rural areas. He began to study the relationship between health and nutrition and realized that there were many plant-based substances critical to the human diet. He thought about making a plant-based supplement for the human diet and, on returning to the United States in 1927, set up a laboratory on California's Balboa Island to study which such supplements were needed.

> **The more Rehnborg studied, the more he could see that the average person needed a single simple solution to the complex problem of dietary supplementation.**

After years of research Rehnborg came up with the then-revolutionary idea of combining every needed mineral and vitamin into a single product. He called his company California Vitamins and produced one of the world's first multivitamin/multimineral food supplements in 1934. The name of the product and the company was changed to Nutrilite in 1939.

Back then, the concept of a single food supplement containing many different vitamins and minerals required a great amount of customer education—especially to a public just learning that vitamins existed. Moreover, since Nutrilite's new multivitamin/multimineral product was a hybrid between a food and a medicine, it wasn't carried by either traditional supermarkets or pharmacies.

> **In order to distribute his product, his wife suggested that Rehnborg set up his own sales force of people—people who were already zealous consumers of Nutrilite themselves. This strategy created a constant need for Nutrilite to recruit and train new salespeople as the company expanded.**

In 1945, Rehnborg and his two main distributors came up with another idea that not only revolutionized the marketing of his nutritional supplements but also created a whole new multibillion dollar distribution industry.[6]

> **Rehnborg's second revolutionary idea was a marketing plan that would allow salespeople both to sell the Nutrilite product and to recruit and train new salespeople— earning one line of income from their product sales and another line of income from the sales of the people they recruited and trained.**

Each individual salesperson, now called a *distributor,* would be treated equally by the company based solely on their sales and the sales of the people they recruited. When the sales of an individual salesperson reached a certain level, they could break away from the person who recruited them and become direct distributors for the company themselves.

In 1949, two young entrepreneurs from Grand Rapids, Michigan, Jay Van Andel and Rich DeVos, purchased a Nutrilite sales kit and quickly rose to the highest sales levels in the company. Ten years later, while keeping their existing Nutrilite sales business, Jay and Rich started a new company to sell household products based on a similar marketing plan. They called their new company Amway, for "American Way." In 1972, Carl F. Rehnborg passed away at age 86, and Amway purchased Nutrilite Products, Inc. Today, Nutrilite is still maintained as a separate corporate entity and, with several billion dollars in annual sales, is one of the largest vitamin/mineral/supplement manufacturers in the world.

Rehnborg successfully used technology to solve a problem with our food supply (lack of vitamins and minerals) that had been created by another technology (food processing). There are thousands of entrepreneurial opportunities today to solve similar problems created by our processed and fast-food industries.

ConsumerLab.com:
Sharing Knowledge Is Big Business

Despite the success of Nutrilite and several other quality manufacturers, the U.S. $70 billion dietary supplement industry has had a tainted reputation. Although hundreds of millions of people use their products every day and often swear by them, millions of people have had similarly negative experiences and call supplement products "expensive urine"—referring to the fact that some of these products just pass through the digestive system without having any effect. Additionally, some people have actually become ill after taking supplements and have called for supplements to be banned from the marketplace. Recent evidence is yielding proof that some of these skeptics and harbingers of disaster may be correct—but not for the reasons they might have suspected.

One-quarter of the dietary supplements (vitamins, minerals, and herbals) sold in the United States today have one or more of the following problems:

1. **The products do not contain what they say they do on the label.**
2. **The products cannot properly release their ingredients due to poor formulation.**
3. **The products contain contaminants or undisclosed dangerous substances, in addition to what appears on their labels.**

The U.S. Food and Drug Administration (FDA) is supposed to monitor and regulate dietary supplements through the Dietary Supplement Health and Education Act (DSHEA) of 1994. Unfortunately, due to woefully inadequate personnel and a limited budget, FDA regulations are rarely enforced when it comes to dietary supplements. This has left the door open for unscrupulous or simply ineffective supplement manufacturers to get away with outright fraud. But it has also opened the door for dedicated medical entrepreneurs, like Dr. Tod Cooperman, to make a significant contribution to wellness while striking out to make their own fortunes in the wellness industry.[7]

Tod Cooperman started his company, ConsumerLab.com, in 1999, and it is already the leading business in the world testing multivitamins, multiminerals, and herbals for consumers.

ConsumerLab.com independently purchases most major brands within each category of supplements and then scientifically tests them to ensure that they contain the ingredients, and only the ingredients, stated on their labels.

ConsumerLab.com provides consumers a wealth of information about each category of supplements, rating the quality of specific products and providing an overview of what is known about the safety and efficacy of the ingredients.

Tod Cooperman didn't start out to become the consumer watchdog for dietary supplements—or even a businessperson or an entrepreneur. He was born in Flushing, New York, and grew up on Long Island. On graduating from public high school he was accepted directly into the prestigious six-year BA/MD program at Boston University School of Medicine. By the time he received his MD at age 24, he found the practice of medicine to be somewhat "cookbookish," and hoped he could find a way to make a greater contribution to society.

While in medical school, he worked one summer at an investment bank in New York, evaluating start-up healthcare companies, where he watched stockbrokers hawk biotechnology stocks with no scientific basis to unsuspecting investors. He worked another summer in the Office of Technology Transfer at the University of Pennsylvania, bringing new medical technology from the laboratory to the marketplace, an experience that landed him his first job after graduation: working for the biotechnology division of medical giant Bristol-Myers. Between 1987 and 1993 he worked with Bristol-Myers and other new medical technology firms until he realized an important point:

> What patients needed most wasn't more new technology, but the ability to make intelligent choices between the dizzying array of competing health plans and new medical technology that was already on the market.

In 1994 Cooperman started CareData Reports, which rated health plans and other HMOs solely on the basis of consumer satisfaction. CareData.com expanded into evaluating pharmacy benefits, dental benefits, and vision care. Cooperman found he liked being an entrepreneur and providing consumers with information that they could act on in managing their health—particularly on a preventive basis. In 1997 he sold CareData.com (which later became part of J.D. Power and Associates) and remained with the company until 1999, when he realized that consumers had an even greater need for information about dietary supplements.

One of his first actions when starting ConsumerLab.com was to hire one of the world's leading experts on dietary supplements, Dr. William Obermeyer, who was then working for the FDA. Obermeyer had already made his mark in nine years at the FDA identifying severe contamination in supplements, and he was ready to bring his expertise to the aid of consumers—helping them make decisions about what to take and what *not* to take. In general, the FDA takes action only in cases where there is an extreme health problem, rarely commenting on manufacturing quality or labeling accuracy of products.

To date, ConsumerLab.com has tested 1600 different products in 50 categories, representing about 95 percent of all supplements sold in the United States. According to Cooperman, "More than one quarter of the products we have tested have failed, and this number has been as high as 60 percent for some categories." They also test popular fortified foods like Tropicana calcium-enriched orange juice, energy bars, and fortified waters.

Products are tested for the following criteria:

1. *Identity and potency.* Does the product meet recognized standards of quality, and does the label accurately reflect what is in the product?
2. *Purity.* Is the product free of contaminants?
3. *Bioavailability.* Can the product release its contents for use by the body?
4. *Ingredient quality.* Does the product (particularly herbal supplements) have the same phytochemicals shown to work in clinical studies?

Examples of products that pass are posted for free on the company's web site www.ConsumerLab.com. Subscribers can get complete listings of every product that passed or failed among those selected for testing. ConsumerLab.com also publishes its reports as a book, *ConsumerLab.com's Guide to Vitamins & Supplements: What's Really in the Bottle?*

ConsumerLab.com launched its subscription program in February 2001 and had 11,000 paid subscribers by August of that year—plus more than 1 million site visits. Today, ConsumerLab.com has nearly 30,000 paid subscribers. But most gratifying to Cooperman are the thousands of e-mails he gets from consumers thanking him for helping them choose the right supplement. Although you may not have tremendous sympathy for a woman choosing a vitamin-enriched antiaging cream that turns out to be plain petroleum jelly, think about the following:

- The father who makes the informed decision to treat his enlarged prostate with saw palmetto only to find out too late that he was taking sugar pills

- The mother who conscientiously gives her four-year-old daughter a daily vitamin that contains more than twice the tolerable level of vitamins for her age

- The father who takes ginseng to boost his energy but chooses a brand that is contaminated with potentially carcinogenic pesticides

- The woman who takes valerian to help her sleep at night but is actually taking a brand that contains no valerian

- The mother whose depression affects her whole family and who turns down Prozac in favor of Saint-John's-wort only to find out years later that she had purchased the wrong brand

To these, and hundreds of thousands of other wellness consumers, the importance of Cooperman's work in the wellness industry cannot be overstated. As Cooperman explained, "You wouldn't buy a car or a stock or bond without knowing how experts rate it. Why would you want to consume a supplement that has not been independently evaluated?"

The wellness industry is growing so fast that the government agencies that normally regulate medicines, food, and commerce cannot keep up. Private, dedicated entrepre-

neurs like Dr. Tod Cooperman, who are stepping in to serve the consumer's need for quality control, may eventually prove more effective for consumers than the traditional government agencies that currently regulate the sickness industry.

Mercola.com—The World's Most Popular Natural Health Web Site

One of the places I often turn for information about wellness and natural health is Mercola.com. With more than 850,000 subscribers and 2.5 million visitors each month, Mercola.com is one of the worlds' most popular health web sites.

"Think of Mercola.com as the meeting place for a real health democracy," says Dr. Mercola. "You'll find a depth of knowledge and information on any health topic, but you'll also get access to the information that thousands of others have voted MOST useful in any given category. It's an invaluable and easy-to-use tool to improve your health."

The story of Mercola.com and its growth to a $100 million web site is, like most stories in the newly emerging wellness industry, the story of a single individual.

Dr. Joseph Mercola was born in 1954 and grew up in inner-city Chicago. At age 13 he read "Aerobics" by Dr. Kenneth Cooper and developed a lifelong passion for exercise that has continued to this day. He graduated college in 1975 and worked for the University of Illinois before attending medical school. At the university, Joseph developed a nationwide system for locating kidney transplant recipients through the Internet. "Once a kidney is harvested," explained Joseph, "you have only 72 hours maximum to implant it in a donor or you have to throw away the kidney." This experience allowed him to see firsthand the positive impact the Internet could have on medicine.

Joseph entered medical school in 1978 and graduated as a D.O. or osteopathic physician in 1982. D.O.s are trained to treat the whole person and to focus on prevention as well as sickness—my wife, who is a UCLA-trained biologist, hired a D.O. as the obstetrician for the birth of our children. D.O.s are complete physicians who, along with MDs, are licensed to prescribe medication and perform surgery in all 50 states. After graduating medical school in 1982, Joseph completed his residency in 1985 and served as the Chairman of Family Medicine for the St. Alexius Medical Center for five years.

During this time, Dr. Mercola wrote prescriptions and practiced traditional medicine until he became aware that this approach was not working for many of his patients. He founded his own clinic just outside Chicago in 1985, The Optimal Wellness Center, based on his belief that people needed to be empowered to take control of their own health. He dug into the research to learn the secrets of natural medicine, and developed a network of alternative medicine physicians to share ideas and patient experiences. And he started a newsletter to share what he was learning with both patients and colleagues. Mercola.com was founded in 1997 originally as just a place to share his newsletters.

Over the next few years, Mercola.com morphed into the world's largest collection of natural health information from all sources, with Dr. Mercola acting as the unpaid editor and gatekeeper to ensure that the information was bona fide. Before he realized it was happening, he had invested $500,000 of his own money, not including years of his life without compensation—and his web site was still 100 percent free to everyone. He realized that he had to do something to create revenue to maintain the web site, but he was determined not to charge his users or to accept advertising from third parties.

Dr. Mercola hit upon the idea of distributing to his readers only those health items that he would recommend as a physician to his patients. By 2002, sales were $1 million and rose to $15 million by 2006. These sales more than supported the main objective of Mercola.com—distributing natural health and wellness information without charge and without advertising—and allowed Dr. Mercola and his family a comfortable million-dollar income.

Mercola.com morphed again in 2006 into a social networking Web 2.0 web site where wellness professionals and consumers can collaborate and share information. One of the most important features on the web site today, in a fast-moving field like wellness, is that readers can vote on their opinion of each article or posting, and share their comments. Thus, you not only get cutting-edge information, you get the opinion of this information from other patients and health professionals.

Mercola.com averages more than 3,000 new subscribers every day, and, with 2.5 million visitors each month, is worth more than $100 million if it were ever sold. Not bad for a web site built by a doctor without any outside investment or external advertising. But Dr. Mercola is the first to tell you that Mercola.com is still in its infancy.

For every million people already visiting Mercola.com, there are tens or hundreds of millions simply unaware of wellness and how much natural medicine can improve their health.

The Wellness Cardiologist: How People Are Transforming Traditional Roles

Dr. Frank Yanowitz tells the following story to his fourth-year medical students.

It was graduation day at Harvard Medical School, and the top student, Michael, was walking along the Charles River with his favorite professor. Suddenly, a drowning man crying for help came floating down the river. Michael jumped into the water, pulled the man above water after he had gone under for the third time, dragged him, unconscious, to the shore, and applied closed-chest cardiac massage and mouth-to-mouth resuscitation—until finally the victim regained consciousness. Michael was elated to have had this opportunity to shine in the eyes of his teacher, and his professor congratulated him on a job well done as the ambulance arrived to take away the victim.

Wet and exhausted, Michael continued walking with his teacher until a second victim crying for help came floating down the river. Again, Michael jumped in to the rescue and brought the victim back to consciousness on the shore. Incredibly, this happened again and again until, when the seventh victim came floating down the river, an exasperated Michael turned to his professor and said: "I know I'm a doctor dedicated to helping people, but I just can't keep this up anymore!"

"Then," replied his professor, "why don't you run ahead upstream and stop whoever is pushing these unfortunate people off the bridge?"

Cardiologist Frank Yanowitz is the medical director and cofounder of The Intermountain Health & Fitness Institute at LDS hospital, a high-technology medical center in Salt Lake City, Utah.

The Fitness Institute is run by some of the best physicians and therapists in the country, but they rarely see a patient with a disease. Instead, the Fitness Institute focuses on the prevention of disease among very healthy individuals—keeping wellness-oriented people from becoming

> customers of the sickness industry. Dr. Yanowitz's personal intrapreneurial[8] story and that of the Fitness Institute provide a glimpse into the future of medical wellness.

Frank Yanowitz was born in 1939 in Malone, New York, a small town at the northern tip of New York State near Montreal. In public high school he developed a love of music and studied classical piano and trumpet. In college at Cornell, he bounced between various engineering disciplines, and became interested in medicine when he took a course in physiological psychology and comparative neurology.

In 1971 he entered the U.S. Air Force School of Aerospace Medicine in San Antonio, Texas, where he had his first encounter with wellness.

> **Unlike the patients of most cardiologists, the patients Yanowitz got to see in San Antonio were extremely well. As jet pilots, they were some of the healthiest and most fit individuals in the nation. They were required to see Yanowitz on a regular basis just to maintain their flying qualifications, and they were required to report even the slightest abnormality in their physical condition.**

Moreover, Yanowitz was given virtually an unlimited budget to investigate the pilots' condition and to work with them to maintain their flying fitness. This gave him a unique preview of the a priori effects of diet and exercise on health.

> **"It was there," he reflects today, "that I began to see the very earliest stages of heart disease—long before I would normally encounter these patients in a typical hospital setting." This experience taught him a lot about the connection between diet, exercise, and disease.**

After serving in the Air Force, Yanowitz accepted a position as a cardiologist at LDS Hospital in Salt Lake City and as an instructor at the University of Utah School of Medicine. The first thing he noticed when he came to Utah was the need for a specialized cardiac rehabilitation program to work with patients following heart surgery, but there was little support back then for such a program. The prevailing view was that a patient who had had heart surgery was "fixed" and that you shouldn't waste time and money on someone who was already fixed. Undeterred, Yanowitz and a physical therapist named Marlin Shields started a cardiac rehabilitation program, but they got very few patients. Although they received tremendous gratitude from the few patients they had, who were happy to be regaining their health and learning how to diet and exercise, "We got very few referrals from the medical community, who felt no need to send patients after they had been 'fixed.'"

In the late 1970s, Yanowitz began working with three colleagues: a student working on his PhD dissertation in exercise physiology (Ted Adams), an orthopedic surgeon (Tom Rosenberg), and physical therapist Marlin Shields. The four of them formed the Fitness Institute in 1980 to focus on prevention and wellness, screening individuals at high risk for heart disease, cardiac rehabilitation, and sports medicine. But by the end of its first year, the Fitness Institute was almost entirely focused on prevention and wellness.

> When they first opened, the expected referrals from other physicians never occurred, and their business lost money for its first 10 years. This forced them to learn how to market directly to their customers, and today they put fitness tips on the radio and meet directly with major employers and executives in the area.

I first became aware of their work when I was a 47-year-old patient completing my annual physical. After telling me I was in perfect health, my internist (Dr. Mary Parsons) asked me if there was anything I wished I could change about my body. Completely in jest, I said, "Sure, when I bike up to Jupiter Peak [10,300 vertical feet] I collapse on the dirt, as I have trouble breathing after riding for 10 miles uphill!" Dr. Parsons then referred me to the Fitness Institute for a VO2 Max test before recommending that I begin a strenuous bike training program. A VO2 Max calculates the maximum amount of oxygen that can be removed from circulating blood and used by working tissues during a specified period.

> When I arrived at the Fitness Institute I thought I was walking into a very modern, high-technology fitness club—until I looked closer and saw that each of the workout machines had a dizzying array of meters and probes attached to them.

As Dr. Yanowitz explained to me, "People don't come here to work out but to be evaluated." The institute offers a complete line of internal medical care, but it does not manage any chronic problems, catering mostly to a market for periodic checkups and to people dissatisfied with their HMOs or primary care physicians. Here's what a typical six-hour first visit to the Fitness Institute (which costs about $1,500) includes:[9]

- An analysis of all body systems, including cancer screening

- Blood and urine tests to assess your risk for heart disease, diabetes, infection, and anemia

- A maximal treadmill stress test by a cardiologist to screen for heart disease and to assess your fitness level

- Written evaluations to assess medical history, personal stress factors, and nutritional adequacy

- Hydrostatic (underwater) weighing to determine your percent of body fat and ideal body weight (based on BMI)

- Pulmonary function tests to screen for obstructive lung disease

- Orthopedic evaluation by a physical therapist to assess your strength, flexibility, and risk for orthopedic problems

- One-on-one wellness counseling to review results and recommend necessary changes in diet, exercise, and stress management

- Screening test for colon and breast (women only) cancer

- A take-home copy of *Maintaining the Miracle: An Owner's Manual for the Human Body,*[10] a comprehensive personal wellness encyclopedia published by the Fitness Institute

Not surprisingly, Frank Yanowitz has had his own wellness transformation. In 1978, at age 37, while teaching some high school students how to use a sphygmomanometer, one of the students took his blood pressure, whereupon Yanowitz was shocked to see an unexpectedly high reading. He had the student repeat the test again and again, in front of the entire class, to confirm the results. That night he realized the irony of his developing an interest in wellness when he himself was overweight, sedentary, out of shape, and now had dangerously high blood pressure. He began a regular program of watching his diet, taking medication to lower his blood pressure, and exercise. Within a year he was running 40 to 50 miles a week and doing 10K runs and half marathons.

Today, at age 67, although never athletic as a child or in college, Frank Yanowitz has completed four marathons, runs 10 to 15 miles each week, mountain-bikes, road-bikes, hikes, skis, and snowshoes.

His curriculum vitae includes 80 publications and 18 major research projects. He has written a full-length book titled *Coronary Heart Disease Prevention.* He was the first chairperson of the Utah Governor's Council on Physical Fitness. He has personally affected the lives of tens of thousands of patients. But Yanowitz lights up the most when he talks about the groups of medical students assigned for one-month tours of duty at the Fitness Institute—the cardiologists of tomorrow—who will hopefully go forth from his tutelage dedicated to *preventing* heart disease rather than just treating its symptoms.[11]

Physical Exercise: A Wellness Entrepreneurial Opportunity

The words *physician* and *physical,* as in physical exercise, come from the same Greek word, *physis,* which loosely translates as "nature." This connection is more than just etymological. Many people today mistakenly think of physical exercise as something primarily for aesthetic rather than medical wellness benefits. This is far from the truth—a lack of regular physical exercise is attributed as the cause of approximately 12 percent of the 2.1 million deaths in the United States each year, about 250,000 people.[12]

Thousands of studies have shown direct relationships between a lack of physical activity and coronary heart disease, hypertension, cancer, diabetes, anxiety, and depression.

Yet amazingly, only 15 percent of U.S. adults engage in regular vigorous physical activity, and 60 percent report getting effectively no exercise at all from a regular or sustained leisure time activity.[13]

It is difficult today to get what Hippocrates might have prescribed as a "natural" amount of exercise.

Many of us have sedentary occupations, with little time for exercise outside of work. Most of us live in urban environments with inclement weather. Moreover, when it comes to exercise, our bodies require both generic aerobic exercise (running, biking) and specific exercises (weight training, flexibility) to keep us healthy and functional.

Fortunately, just as there are wellness entrepreneurs using technology to change our diets and to ensure we get the minimal daily building blocks of our cellular material, wellness entrepreneurs are also beginning to use technology to change how and where we get our exercise.

One who stands out in particular is fitness entrepreneur Jill Stevens Kinney—the woman *Club Insider News* called "America's #1 Female Club Entrepreneur."[14] Her story, and the rapid rise of her company, Club One, Inc., illustrates some of the potential for the $24 billion fitness industry in the coming $1 trillion wellness economy.

America's #1 Female Club Entrepreneur

Jill Stevens Kinney has always been very healthy. She grew up in a family agribusiness in Fresno, California, eating lots of fresh fruits and vegetables. She started jogging regularly with her father at age 6. And she had a successful career as an athlete (as a downhill ski racer) before graduating from the University of California at Berkeley in 1979.

After graduation, Kinney met Dr. Jack Bagshaw, a successful cardiologist in wealthy Marin County, who was fed up with treating the symptoms of heart disease. Bagshaw wanted to open a holistic health center that would teach people how to avoid getting heart disease in the first place. He hired Kinney to be his business manager, and together they opened a facility called Physis, catering to senior executives in the San Francisco Bay area. Physis charged $3,000 for a three-month program consisting of an initial assessment, three personalized 90-minute training sessions each week, educational workshops on topics from healthy cooking to stress management, and a final assessment of progress at completion.

Kinney was optimistic, but even she was truly amazed at the results. "People didn't just get more fit," she lights up as she reminisces, "marriages got better, careers improved, and in some cases whole lives were turned around—emotionally as well as physically."

"By the end of the three-month program I was positively hooked on what balanced exercise and a holistic professional approach to fitness can do for people!" Kinney feels very fortunate to have started out first in a wellness center, not a health club:

"The health club industry was launched by people out to make a buck versus people out to make a difference."

After the initial success of Physis and while still in her twenties, Kinney was hired by a national sports and fitness club chain, where she rose to become the chief operating officer, with a staff of 800 people. In 1985, after getting calls from several real estate developers wanting to have sports and fitness facilities as part of their projects, she was hired to open one of the most prestigious clubs in the nation: the Sports Club LA in Los Angeles. The great success of this project—her staff presold the 5,000 memberships needed to break even before the club even opened—led to a series of similar entrepreneurial assignments throughout the United States. Kinney became *the* person to hire if you wanted to open the most prestigious sports and fitness club in your city.

During this time, Kinney, who was also chairperson of the market research committee for the International Health, Racquet & Sportsclub Association (IHRSA) from 1984 to 1989, began to notice a shift in the marketplace. Her prime clientele, the baby boomers, were moving past their twenties and becoming more concerned with wellness and aging issues than with sports and social activities. Most of the megasize sports and fitness clubs opened in the 1980s were inconveniently located for aging baby boomers, who now, with families and more intensive jobs, had less time for exercise. Kinney's research showed that these boomers now wanted a convenient location near home or work (as in choosing a dry cleaner) more than they wanted sports activities, social activities, and megasize physical facilities. But at the time, 98 percent of the local conveniently located fitness clubs were single-unit, inexpensive mom-and-pop facilities with few amenities—not the kind of places that would appeal to baby boomers used to high-quality clubs like Sports Club LA. In 1989, Kinney began to work with businessman John Kinney on a business plan to serve this market for high-quality fitness facilities at convenient locations.

In 1990, she and John Kinney wrote the business plan for Club One and also got married that same year. On June 17, 1991, they opened their first Club One facility at Citicorp Center in San Francisco, followed by a second facility later that year at Embarcadero Center.

Originally, the Kinneys thought they might keep opening similar 12,000-square-foot facilities and become the "Starbucks of fitness clubs," but John Kinney quickly saw a greater financial opportunity in consolidation—purchasing existing single-unit clubs in good locations and updating their facilities. This strategy not only saved money in most cases, it attracted instant members while eliminating a local competitor.

In addition to focusing on convenient locations, one of Club One's unique approaches was to attract the best fitness professionals (trainers, nutritionists, yoga teachers, massage therapists, etc.) as dedicated professional employees rather than as independent contractors without benefits, continuing education, and defined career paths. Over her years in the fitness business Jill Kinney had seen some of the best of these professionals leave the industry when faced with the task of continually marketing themselves or trying to balance their need for continued professional education against their need for current income. Just as some of the best doctors and other professionals function better in salaried, nonentrepreneurial environments, Jill Kinney felt that her customers and some fitness professionals themselves would benefit from a similar professional-employee approach. She says, "When you make the commitment to empower them to grow their career, everyone benefits."

Their plan worked. Club One quickly went from start-up to sales of $60 million per year and 71 locations—one of the fastest growing businesses in the fitness club industry. The Kinneys are most proud of their fitness professionals, all of whom work as salaried professional employees, with Club One charging customers standard hourly rates for their services, depending on their education, experience, and expertise.

Despite executing a well-thought-out business plan, most of the Club One success came from a surprise phone call Jill Kinney received in 1995. Autodesk, Inc., one of the leading software companies in the world and a prestigious employer in the Bay Area, called to ask if Club One would be willing to design, open, and manage a proprietary onsite fitness club solely for Autodesk employees. After determining that Autodesk was motivated by a real concern for the wellness of its employees and not just adding a perk to attract new

Fitness careers of the future include the following certified professionals:

Fitness trainer

Personal trainer

Specialty trainer/sports conditioning

Clinical exercise specialist

Chiropractor

Physical therapist

Nutritionist

Massage therapist

Seniors trainer

Youth trainer

Personal coach

Group exercise instructor

Yoga instructor

Pilates instructor

Performance training coach

hires, Club One took on the contract. A year later the company opened similar onsite corporate fitness facilities for The Gap and Electronic Arts. By 2000, the Kinneys had 50 such corporate facilities under management, with 500,000 corporate members—onsite corporate employees with free access to a private fitness club managed by Club One. The "convenience" objective of Club One had always been a five-minute desk-to-club experience. Having such a private facility located at the workplace more than met this objective.

> **Jill Kinney sees the corporate centers managed by Club One as the greatest challenge and training ground for her organization because her customers in these centers closely parallel the typical U.S. employee—not someone who walks into a private fitness facility ready to join with their own funds.**

These corporate members need much more education and motivation. According to Jill Kinney, this "gives us the opportunity to serve people who really need us—people who are overweight, people with clinical issues and addictions, people with eating disorders—and we can use exercise as the medium to start helping them make the right changes in their life." Club One has recently expanded its contract management program to a new location in Redwood City, California, where several corporations share the same private facility adjacent to their offices.

The corporate customers of Club One are motivated by a sincere desire to help their employees achieve wellness. But irrespective of their altruistic motivations, a key advantage of such a program is that it enjoys a 2-to-1 financial advantage over employees purchasing Club One membership for themselves. The company receives a deduction from its state and federal income taxes for the cost of the Club One facility, and the employee does not have to pay state and federal income taxes on the monthly value of the membership.

Club One also has had great success managing the fitness centers for six large Jewish Community Centers (JCCs), including one new 220,000-square-foot JCC in San Francisco that was custom-designed around their fitness facility. At these sites, the uniforms worn by fitness consultants, from personal trainers to nutritionists, may say "JCC," but they share the same certification, continued training, and professionalism as Club One professionals at all of their private and public locations. Jill is especially proud of the success of these nonprofits, since they bring professional fitness to a larger audience, and have become significant revenue generators for their nonprofit sponsors.

In the past few years, Jill and her husband John have moved away from the day-to-day operations of Club One and started a new entrepreneurial business—developing the real estate for new Club One facilities. Jill personally does the site selection, acquisition, and real estate development work—and when completed, Club One gets a turnkey facility with a management contract similar to a hotel management contract for a third-party owner. This is not without risk—like with any real estate deal, the tenant or manager could slip. But if this should occur, Jill and John are among the most able fitness club operators in the world to step in and fix whatever has gone wrong.

Some of the world's greatest fortunes have been made by real estate professionals who simply supplied buildings and locations to specialty retailers, fast-food companies,

Blockbuster video stores, or whatever new concept was in vogue. As illustrated by the Kinney's latest venture, the next wave of real estate fortunes is already being made by perspicacious developers who understand the wellness industry.

Creating Wellness, Inc.

Dr. Patrick Gentempo has always been into wellness. While he was growing up, his family ran a health food store, "Here's Health," in Ramsey, New Jersey. His parents were ahead of their time and it was a great struggle just to keep the doors open. Although they never made any real money, their investment paid off handsomely for their son Patrick, who grew up to be a multimillionaire wellness revolutionary that has brought wellness to hundreds of thousands of people.

"I can remember taking vitamins and eating Tiger's Milk bars when my friends in school were all drinking soda and eating Baby Ruth bars," Patrick recalls. "I liked being different and it was important for me to perform on a high level so I could demonstrate by example the results of my non-mainstream choices." Patrick performed—he was a five-time New Jersey State and two-time national AAU karate champion, and also wrestled his senior year of high school.

Everything changed for Patrick one day when he injured himself during wrestling practice.

"I remember bridging up on my neck and feeling something give," Patrick reflects. "I had immediate pain in my neck that radiated down both arms. My muscles were in spasm and something was swollen. My family medical doctor explained what happened: 'You have cervicalgia, myospasm, and inflammation.' I asked, what's that? He said neck pain, muscle spasm, and swelling, and explained that 'for the pain we will give you a pain killer, for the muscle spasm we will give you a muscle relaxant, and for the swelling we will give you an anti-inflammatory.'"

The drugs made Patrick feel sick and did not alleviate the pain. After two weeks of pain and missing school, his mother brought him to a chiropractor. After his adjustment, he felt 90 percent better and became fascinated about the practice of chiropractic—gathering and reading everything he could about chiropractic. He decided to become a chiropractor.

Chiropractors focus on the nervous system, that master system of the body that controls healing, regulation, and general wellness. Chiropractic adjustments help remove subluxation; interference in the nervous system that is caused by lifestyle stress. This nerve interference reduces a person's ability to express health and well-being.

Patrick graduated chiropractic school in 1983 and entered practice. He also developed educational programs for chiropractors with another chiropractor, Dr. Christopher Kent. They both quickly realized that Dr. Gentempo's practice, and the profession of chiropractic itself, needed better diagnostic tools and standardized training materials for its professionals.

Patrick and his partner founded the Chiropractic Leadership Alliance (CLA), which today provides the chiropractic profession with advanced technology, educational programs, and business development strategies.

I first became acquainted with CLA when I visited my local chiropractor, Dr. E. J. Raven, in Park City, Utah. Instead of just checking out my spine with his hands, before I was examined by Dr. Raven his assistant performed a series of high-tech scans of my spine and nervous system with CLA's Insight technology. These scans produced a colored map of the temperature around my spine as well as a pattern of electrical activity produced by the muscles surrounding my spine. When I then consulted with Dr. Raven, he used the colored scans to tell me about my clinical status and also used them as a guide to completing the exam. Moreover, as my care progressed, he reperformed the scans on a regular basis to track my results.

Patrick and his partner grew CLA into a multimillion-dollar company with thousands of chiropractor customers. In addition to maintaining his own practice, he achieved personal wealth and success far beyond his wildest dreams. But something was missing. Everywhere he traveled he saw the same thing again and again. Millions of people were discovering wellness, chiropractic care, and how to take better care of their bodies. But many millions more were getting more unhealthy every day because they lacked the information they so desperately needed about nutrition, exercise, and psychological well-being.

His observation struck home in 2000. His Aunt Joanne, a 48-year old schoolteacher and mom with two young children, dropped dead of a heart attack in front of her daughter while visiting a local nail salon. Patrick's entire family was devastated, but no one felt more to blame than Patrick. Aunt Joanne was obese, and everything Patrick had done until then to help millions of chiropractic patients had been in vain when it came to helping this member of his own family.

Shortly after this tragedy, Patrick began to focus on what he could do to bring wellness not just to chiropractic patients, but to the tens of millions of Americans who didn't even know that wellness existed. His solution was the Creating Wellness Alliance, which he founded in 2002.

Dr. Gentempo knew that baby-boomers, who drive half of our economy, were looking for longer and better lives through wellness. He also knew that there were multitudes of deconditioned soccer moms who wanted to reclaim their health and fit bodies. And there were millions of business executives who had lost their health while building their careers. He wanted to create a model that allowed wellness to be affordable to the masses, not just the wealthy. He recalls, "The big question was, how do I massively customize a meaningful wellness program that is affordable to the masses?"

He knew that he had to have a program that worked. "When somebody tries and fails, it is worse for them than not trying at all. It lowers their self-image and they give up." In order to do this right he would have to (1) define wellness, (2) measure wellness, and then (3) customize a wellness program for the individual that covered all three dimensions of lifestyle stress that cause one to lose one's wellness. These three dimensions are *physical,* what you do to your body; *biochemical,* what you put into your body; and *psychological,* which relates to the mind/body connection. In his words, "be fit, eat right, think well."

This is exactly what he and his team at Creating Wellness built. They developed an operational definition of wellness based on the three dimensions of lifestyle stress. They developed technology and software, the Creating Wellness Assessment Station, which measures an individual in all three dimensions and calculates their Wellness Quotient. And finally, they developed a system to produce a customized wellness program that covers all three dimensions, which is assembled and shipped to the client.

Every week while on the Creating Wellness program, the client gets a weekly wellness coaching visit to hold them accountable and provide education and motivation. Since a core value of Creating Wellness is measurable results, every five weeks a new Wellness Quotient is performed on the client to track progress. The minimum program is 15 weeks, because Dr. Gentempo feels it takes that long to make real changes that become habits that stick. As he states, "If someone is not committed to 15 weeks, they are not committed to changing their life and this program is not for them. There are too many wellness failures out there and I won't be a part of it."

To really make it turnkey, the Creating Wellness System includes all necessary products in each dimension. This includes exercise DVDs with the necessary equipment to perform them at home, daily supplements, a meal planner that directs the client on what to eat and the timing of the meals, customized audio programming to give psychological support, and weekly coaching. The suggested retail price for the Creating Wellness System, including all the products and services, starts at $800, which can be paid with $200 down and $40 a week for 15 weeks.

The biggest surprise for Dr. Gentempo and Creating Wellness has not been the number of individual customers, but the number of employers signing up to bring wellness into their workplace.

At this time, there are over 200 Creating Wellness Centers across North America. Dr. Gentempo projects Creating Wellness to have over 1,800 centers by 2010. He explains: "Millions of Americans have lost their lives to the fast food industry, the beverage industry and other industries who market life-depriving products to them in overwhelming ways. Our goal is to have them reclaim their life from these industries so they can live longer and better. When we have as many Creating Wellness Centers as there are stores in a major fast food chain, then we will have done our jobs."

From a child who was born to a mother that was told not to have any more children after spinal surgery, to a wellness revolutionary, Dr. Gentempo is a passionate wellness entrepreneur who drives a business with a purpose. As he explains, "Creating Wellness is a purpose-driven business. We earn a profit by creating worldwide wellness. It is crystal clear to me how capitalism is completely compatible with a social conscience."

Revolutionizing a Profession from the Inside

Dr. Fabrizio Mancini did not set out to be a wellness revolutionary. Nor did he set out to compete against traditional medicine. He planned to be a traditional MD, but at the age of 33 he had already emerged as one of the world leaders in wellness and alternative medicine. Today, at age 41, he is still just getting started.

I became aware of Dr. Fabrizio Mancini ("Fab") after the first edition of *The Wellness Revolution* was published in 2002. My original book contained very little on chiropractic care because, like most Americans, I had never visited a chiropractor. During the publicity tour for the book several chiropractors expressed to me their dismay that I had not included more about their profession in my book.

One of these chiropractors was Dr. Fabrizio Mancini, who at age 33 had become president of Parker College of Chiropractic, making him one of the youngest college presidents in the United States. Parker College of Chiropractic, in Dallas, TX, is a fully accredited institution offering both undergraduate degrees and Doctors of Chiropractic.

When Dr. Mancini contacted me I was first expecting another upset chiropractor, and was pleasantly surprised. Fab slowly walked me through the history and principles of chiropractic care, where the profession was today, and how he and other national chiropractic leaders were retooling the profession into becoming the wellness providers of the future. Although he and I had not yet met in person, I could sense the deep compassion this man had for his patients, and his dedication to bringing wellness care to millions of people from all walks of life.

I was also aware that chiropractic care had recently been elevated by the IRS to the same status as traditional medicine, and was thus one of the few segments of the wellness industry that enjoyed the same tax and accounting advantages of sickness care.

Chiropractic care is based on the principle that health is the natural state and the human body has the ability to heal itself, but sometimes parts of the nervous system (vertebrae) become sublaxated (interfered with) and cannot properly communicate with each other. Chiropractic care seeks to eliminate vertebral interference to allow the body to return to its natural state—optimum health.

While most people think of a chiropractor as someone to see when they are ill or have had an accident, the best use for chiropractic care is to keep the nervous system functioning at an optimal level before organs begin to malfunction and symptoms appear—preventing patients from becoming ill in the first place.

Although I was skeptical when Fab first explained this to me, I listened because I was, frankly, overwhelmed at the presence the man projected, even over the telephone. I later found out that this is what Fab really does best—identifying and educating authors, celebrities,

and other people of influence who are simply ignorant of chiropractic care.

Dr. Mancini eventually convinced me to see one of his graduates
in my town, Dr. E. J. Raven. After I began a series of chiropractic
wellness visits, my wife, who is a scientifically minded, UCLA-trained
biologist, was very pleased with my results—so pleased that she
started taking herself and our four children to Dr. Raven for a weekly
adjustment. We credit our wellness care with eliminating the regular
colds that come from living in a ski town with four small children, but
there are simply no words to describe how much better than healthy
we feel since adding quality chiropractic wellness care to our lives.

Dr. Fabrizio Mancini was born in Colombia and moved to the
United States with his family, speaking only Spanish, at age 12. In
1987, while a premed student, he was surprised when his orthopedic
surgeon referred him to a chiropractor after a car accident. He
switched from premed and enrolled at Parker College of Chiropractic. It was here he first realized the powerful connection between chiropractic and wellness and began his odyssey to bring health and
wellness to the masses.

After graduation he developed a very lucrative practice, but was
also recognized for his leadership potential, and was asked to become
president of Parker College in 1999. As president, he has greatly expanded the enrollment, curriculum, and quality of the incoming students. To attract the best and most dedicated students, in addition to
offering the Doctor of Chiropractic degree, Parker now offers BS degrees in anatomy and in health and wellness.

As president of Parker College, and president of Parker Seminars
(which runs the world's largest annual educational conventions of
chiropractors), Fab has emerged as an international leader for the
profession—educating chiropractic students, already-practicing
chiropractors, and potential chiropractic patients. As he explains:

**"Consumers must be counseled and educated relative to
their spines, the need for proper exercise, diet, as well as
the adverse effects of pollutants, obesity, smoking, stress
and negative thoughts. Unfortunately, much of the general public does not realize that today's chiropractor is
well educated (more than seven years of university studies) and recognizes that the body was designed to be
healthy, and not sick."**

Dr. Fabrizio Mancini,
president of Parker College of Chiropractic

A frequent guest on popular television shows, Fab has received awards from the state of Texas, the White House, and from chiropractic organizations and colleges worldwide. To expand the knowledge of chiropractic, he created the book *Chicken Soup for the Chiropractic Soul,* which became an instant bestseller.

Fab is most proud of what he is doing to bring the benefits of wellness and chiropractic to the less fortunate, both in the United States and abroad. Hispanics, as some of the newest immigrants to the United States, are often at the lower end of the socioeconomic ladder and have thus been less influenced by the wellness revolution. To reach this group, Dr. Mancini, who speaks fluent Spanish and Italian, has developed programming for CNN Español and its 38 million viewers.

Parker's Clinic Abroad program makes it possible for American students to study and live in Mexico. The students treat patients at the university's public clinic, and students also study Spanish and Mexican culture in order to better prepare them to serve the U.S. Hispanic population when they return home.

Mexico has a population of 100 million people and only 100 chiropractors. Dr. Mancini assisted the Secretary of Education to establish the first and only chiropractic school in Latin America. The first group of students has already graduated and are practicing in the Mexican hospital system. Mexican chiropractic faculty study and are trained at Parker College in the United States.

Before Proceeding to the Next Chapter

Action Plan for Entrepreneurs and Wellness/Health Professionals

1. Analyze how a return of medicine to a whole-body approach (Hippocrates) would impact your chosen area of wellness business opportunity.

2. Dr. Yanowitz and his MD colleagues (The Fitness Institute) run a completely wellness-focused business within the traditional medical arena. Analyze how a shift in medicine toward prevention would impact your chosen area of wellness business opportunity.

3. Carl Rehnborg (Nutrilite) had to set up his own sales force of distributors because his product was neither a medicine nor a food that could be carried by pharmacies or grocery stores. Analyze the individual products of your chosen area of wellness business opportunity from the standpoint of how they will be distributed, and by whom.

4. Rehnborg hit upon network marketing as the most cost-effective way to continually educate new distributors. How could network marketing impact your chosen area of wellness business opportunity?

5. Analyze the products of your chosen area of wellness business opportunity from the standpoint of manufacturing quality. If more businesses similar to ConsumerLab.com emerge, will this help or hurt you?

6. Jill Kinney (Club One) has been able to build what was formerly a local mom-and-pop business into a $100 million national chain for the reasons listed here. Analyze how your individual area of wellness business opportunity could be similarly impacted by these reasons.

   a. Riding a quality-demand shift from sports fitness to convenience

   b. Riding a quality-demand shift from sports fitness to wellness

   c. Standardization of product quality

   d. Marketing directly to employers

   e. Tax advantages of having employers versus consumers pay for products or services

7. Dr. Patrick Gentempo (Creating Wellness) is organizing existing wellness practitioners (e.g., chiropractors) into a brand-name scalable business. Is this model possible for your area of wellness business opportunity? It is easier to get people already doing something to slightly modify their course than to get someone to move in an entirely new direction.

   Based on your answers to these questions, think about replacing your chosen area of wellness business opportunity.

CHAPTER 6

What You Must Know about Health Insurance

One of the greatest opportunities for wellness entrepreneurs lies in redirecting part of our $2 trillion sickness industry into products and services that prevent disease versus just treating the symptoms of disease.

Our $2 trillion sickness industry, which is paid for mostly through health insurance, occupies almost one-sixth of the U.S. economy—about $6,667 per year per citizen, or $27,000 for a family of four. The opportunity exists for you to help educate almost every U.S. family how to save $5,000 or more on their health insurance and healthcare (sickness) expenses—money they can invest today in their wellness or save tax-free for their future wellness or retirement.

Every U.S. wellness entrepreneur must understand the American health insurance industry that finances U.S. sickness, and ultimately decides what type of health products and services most American consumers receive.

Understanding U.S. health insurance is about more than just helping your customers save money on sickness that they can invest in their wellness. The current employer-based U.S. health insurance system is collapsing, causing the financial ruin of millions of Americans each year. You can help your customers avoid financial catastrophe by helping them get permanent, renewable, lifetime (until Medicare) health insurance coverage for less than half the total cost of their current employer-sponsored plan.

As you will see in this and the next chapter, a new consumer-based health insurance solution is already in place, although most people don't yet know about it. The early adopters of this new system are receiving immediate cash savings and lifetime financial protection.

Financial rewards await the wellness entrepreneurs who help more consumers understand and implement the new health insurance solution.

The Crisis in Health Insurance for the U.S. Economy

Health insurance expenses now threaten the U.S. economy more than all other economic threats combined, including paying for the war in Iraq, repairing the damage of terrorist activities, and the retirement needs of aging baby boomers. This is because rising health insurance costs threaten the very viability of our businesses, which generate the gross domestic product that we use to pay for everything else.

In 2005, for the Fortune 500 as a group, the cost of providing sickness industry health benefits for employees exceeded profits. Moreover, the cost of employer-sponsored health benefits are increasing at 15 percent per year or more—few companies expect their profits to increase at even half this rate over the long term.

Stop and think about this for a moment. While you may enjoy a relationship with a company because of the products or jobs it provides you, the company itself only exists because of its actual or perceived ability by investors to make a profit. Without profit, investors will simply close the company and redeploy their assets elsewhere—either overseas or in another less employee-intensive operation.

On a macroeconomic scale, if left unchecked, the U.S. sickness industry's expenses will exceed GDP itself in 18 years and cause the collapse of the entire U.S. economy long before then.[1]

Fortunately, the solution for both U.S. employers and for the U.S. economy is in sight.

U.S. employers are now allowed to switch from expensive, wasteful, "other people's money" Defined Benefit plans to cost-effective, efficient, "your money" Defined Contribution plans.

With a Defined Contribution plan, the employer simply gives each employee a fixed monthly tax-free allowance to buy their own health insurance and pay medical expenses—allowing the consumer to choose their desired level of sickness coverage, the amount they can invest in their wellness, and the amount they wish to save tax-free for future medical expenses and retirement.

The greatest immediate financial return from the wellness revolution will be reduced sickness industry costs. This is being already realized today by innovative employers who have implemented workplace wellness programs, like those described in the previous chapter by Club One or Creating Wellness. These employers understand that the only long-term alternative to escalating sickness industry costs is wellness, starting with weight-reduction, nutrition, exercise, and smoking cessation programs.

The Crisis in Health Insurance for U.S. Individuals

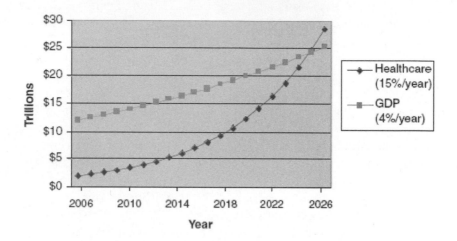

The Dirty Secret about Employer-Sponsored Health Care

Have you ever been in a work situation where a person got promoted in lieu of someone more deserving of the promotion? Or have you ever made a promotion recommendation only to have it overruled by the owner of the company where you worked? Here's what could have been going on behind the scene.

Assume a typical situation where a 100-employee U.S. company provides medical benefits at an annual group premium cost of $500,000 per annum ($5,000 per employee or family). Now assume that one of the employees, or one of their children, develops a chronic disease like diabetes or becomes permanently disabled in an automobile accident—a condition that allows the employee to continue working but ends up costing $75,000 in recurring annual medical expenses for drugs and treatment. Initially, the employer's insurance company bears this $75,000 expense, but next year it will raise the employer's $500,000 annual premium to $575,000 or more to cover this now-anticipated additional expense (as well to try and recoup its prior loss).[2] The employer, although free to shop around for a different insurance provider, is unlikely to find a better deal, since the main criterion used to underwrite and price a group policy is the prior year's medical expenses of that group.

The employer and the employee are both trapped.

The employer needs to get rid of the employee to lower its total group medical insurance premium, but under federal law cannot fire someone for medical reasons if that person is still "doing their job." Fortunately for the employer, but unfortunately for the employee, a person with a chronic medical condition or a very sick child is unlikely to be able to continue doing their job.

In the event that the employee is still capable of doing his or her job, often by putting in extra hours, the employee cannot quit. Many new employers will not hire a liability, and the employee's preexisting medical condition will probably prevent him or her from obtaining affordable health insurance without an employer-sponsored plan.

In 1985 I testified before the U.S. Congress as follows:

Show me a person who owns their own 100-employee business, and I'll show you an employer who knows the first name of each child of an employee who has diabetes—even though they are not supposed to know. A small employer with a $35,000-a-year employee should not be burdened with the $75,000-a-year medical cost for a child of that employee who has diabetes—or have to face the terrible choice between staying in business versus taking care of the sick child of an employee.

This is the dirty secret of employer-provided healthcare. Most business owners know the name of each employee who has a family member with such a preexisting condition. While compassion suggests that the owner try to ignore this fact in making decisions regarding promotion and termination, competition and the need for economic survival often dictate otherwise.

The U.S. Health Insurance System Is the #1 Cause of Personal Bankruptcy

Since the 1980s, each year between 1 and 2 million American families file for personal bankruptcy. Until recently, the causes of these bankruptcies were unknown, and most people assumed credit card spending, divorce, and loss of employment to be among the major reasons. In February 2005 Harvard University released the results of its study, "Illness and Injury as Contributors to Bankruptcy."[3]

The study interviewed 1,771 Americans in bankruptcy courts and determined that about half were "medically bankrupt"—driven to bankruptcy by medical bills not covered by health insurance. Equally surprising, the study concluded:

- Three-fourths of the medically bankrupt had (employer-sponsored) health insurance at the beginning of their illness.

- The majority of the medically bankrupt owned their own homes and had attended college.

- Many of the medically bankrupt who had health insurance were simply unable to pay the thousands of dollars in annual deductibles, coinsurance, and other out-of-pocket expenses not covered by their health insurance.

If you are a healthy family, you may be more likely to incur a healthcare expense from an accident (e.g., playing sports, cooking, falling) versus having an illness. New accidental medical coverage for as little as $10 to $40/month can cover your out-of-pocket medical expenses not covered by health insurance, up to $10,000 per accident (see www.zanebenefits.com).

This study was completed in early 2005, when all Americans still had the option to file for bankruptcy protection from medical expenses. A new bankruptcy law was signed into law on April 20, 2005, that prevents millions of Americans from being able to discharge their debts and start over, including those whose bankruptcy was caused solely by an unexpected medical expense.

The health insurance most Americans receive from their employers shouldn't be called "insurance." It's not insurance because you lose it when you are no longer able

**to come to work, either because you are ill or you are
needed at home to take care of a family member with an
illness.[4]**

Once you lose your employer-sponsored health insurance, your
nightmare has just begun. Not only are you going to have to worry
about how to pay for healthcare, you are also going to have to worry
about how to get good healthcare. Many medical providers refuse to
schedule an appointment for people without health insurance, and
those who do agree to see you will typically charge from 150 to 500
percent of what they would have charged you or your insurance carrier if you had health insurance and were thus a member of their
provider network.

The Crisis in U.S. Health Insurance for Wellness–Treating Symptoms versus Preventing Illness

The biggest problem with our current medical care insurance system,
where more than 90 percent of expenses are paid by someone *other
than* the patient and the doctor deciding on the treatment, is that it is
focused on paying for treating the symptoms of illness rather than on
curing or preventing illness.

This is partly because it is much more profitable for medical companies to produce products that create customers for life—products
that treat symptoms of disease rather than products focused on cures
or prevention.

**Suppose you were a member of the board of directors of a
pharmaceutical or medical company—appointed to your
position by a pension fund for the purpose of increasing
the value of their investment. Would you direct your company to spend millions of dollars in R&D to make a one-
time-use product costing $50 a pill that could cure or
prevent a disease, or would you direct your company to
spend millions of dollars in R&D to make a product costing only $3 a pill that consumers would take every day for
the rest of their lives, 365 days a year.**

It's easy to see why the overwhelming majority of new medical
technology today is focused on treating the symptoms of disease

rather than on cures or prevention, and why 90 percent of the pharmaceuticals sold today are maintenance drugs consumers take daily for the rest of their lives.

> **But the major reason that U.S. medicine is not focused on curing or preventing illness is because the insurance companies, and ultimately the employers, do not have a financial stake in the long-term health of their employees.**

Employees used to stay with one company for 25 years or more. Today, the average employee changes jobs more than 10 times over his or her 45-year working life. Most of the major illnesses on which you can spend $1 today to save $100 tomorrow (like heart disease from obesity or cancer from poor nutrition) will not show up until an employee is long gone or retired, at which time the $100 cost is picked up by another employer or by taxpayers through Medicare.

As medical costs have escalated, employers have, in effect, told their medical insurance companies to pay for only those expenses related to keeping or getting the insured back to work—and this does *not* include paying for the prevention of a disease that will not manifest itself during the expected tenure of the employee with the company.

> **Weight reduction, nutritional advice, vitamins, minerals, smoking cessation, and hundreds of other wellness-related or preventive-type treatments are currently excluded from most corporate- and government-sponsored medical plans.**

This causes even greater escalation in medical costs. Many physicians I interviewed believe that the majority of nongeriatric medical expenses are caused by poor diet and smoking, both of which they are effectively limited from treating in the current PPO or HMO[5] environment.

> **It is critical that you, and your wellness customers, take control of your own health insurance and do not depend on your employer to provide health benefits for your family. I will show you how in the next chapter.**

How the United States Got into the Current Health Insurance Crisis

How Employers Became the Providers of Most U.S. Medical Care

Today about 150 million Americans, 50 percent of the population, receive their health benefits through an employer-sponsored health benefits plan. The rest of Americans receive their health benefits through government-paid care such as Medicare (15 percent) or Medicaid (15 percent), and 5 percent purchase their own individual or family policy. Fifteen percent of the U.S. population is uninsured.

Despite the popularity of employer-sponsored health benefits, one of the last entities anyone should want to have involved in their family's medical care is their employer. That is because today people spend less than 25 percent of their time at work, about 40 hours out of a 168-hour week, and typically change jobs up to 10 times over their lives. One hundred years ago this was not the case. People worked from dawn to dusk, six days a week, and often for the same employer their entire life. But even then, company-provided medical care was limited to having a company doctor on-site at large places of employment, and then only to treat injuries that arose at the workplace.

Prior to WWII, most Americans paid for their own medical care themselves, either directly to their chosen provider or through Blue Cross nonprofit health insurance entities created by hospitals offering guaranteed service in return for a fixed fee.

When consumers paid their medical providers directly, they also chose each medical provider wisely and made intelligent decisions about the potential benefits, effectiveness, and cost of each prescribed treatment.

During WWII, government leaders and economists were greatly concerned with potential postwar inflation. They had seen firsthand what happened in Germany after WWI, and blamed Hitler's rise to power on Germany's postwar inflation and economic ruin. The U.S. Congress and President Roosevelt instituted wage and price controls during WWII that they were determined to maintain after the war.

In order to politically grant a concession to labor during WWII without appearing to violate wage and price controls, Congress exempted employer-paid health benefits from wage controls and income taxation—in effect allowing off-the-books raises for employees in the form of nontaxable health benefits. This created a "black market" for employer-paid health benefits—equivalent to paying employees off the books cash for their healthcare expenses that they legally didn't have to report to the IRS.

This off-the-books compensation in the form of health benefits created an enormous tax advantage for employer-sponsored health benefits over health insurance or healthcare purchased by employees with their own after-tax dollars. By the mid-1960s, employer-sponsored health benefits were almost universal.

This huge government subsidy, which still exists today, results in the following:

- It allows employers to deduct from their taxable income 100 percent of the cost of employer-sponsored health benefits.
- It allows employees to receive unlimited employer-sponsored health benefits without having to pay wage or income taxes on these benefits.

Originally, employers thought providing health insurance was a great way to compensate employees, with federal and state governments paying about half the bill through a hidden tax subsidy.

With third-party employers and government footing the consumer's medical bill, the medical industry was given free rein to develop thousands of new treatments. Some of these were powerful, but others were not economical or merely preyed upon the hopes of desperately ill people and their families.

The pharmaceutical industry drove up costs by inventing solutions to problems that weren't previously defined as medical issues: prescription drugs to allow people to eat bad foods, Viagra to treat impotence caused by old age, and so forth. By classifying these solutions as "prescription drugs" rather than over-the-counter medicines, the pharmaceutical industry was able to sell them to consumers with a 50 percent tax subsidy through their employer-sponsored health insurance plans. The American taxpayer was thus forced to provide billions of dollars in unintended tax subsidies to the pharmaceutical industry to develop these lifestyle drugs, driving up costs for everyone.

As a result of this and other problems, U.S. healthcare costs, funded mostly through tax-free employer-sponsored health benefits, rose from $27 billion in 1960 to more than $2,000 billion. Today the cost of employer-sponsored health benefits exceeds profits for most large companies, and threatens the viability of many of our best employers. In 2004–2005, despite a rising Dow over the same time period, GM's stock value dropped 50 percent after the company announced a $60 billion retiree healthcare obligation.

Looking back, by making employer-sponsored health benefits tax deductible, Congress created more problems than just escalating medical costs:

- The U.S. healthcare marketplace has been discouraged from developing innovative healthcare solutions for consumers at affordable prices because it has focused only on solutions that could be sold to employer health benefits and insurance company executives. This is in contrast to the dramatic innovation in every other part of the U.S. economy such as automobiles, restaurants, personal computers, telecommunications, and so forth, which are focused on solutions sold directly to consumers.

- The U.S. insurance industry, until recently, was preempted from developing affordable health insurance policies that could be sold direct to all consumers—just as it did with automobile insurance, homeowner's insurance, and life insurance.

- Employers and insurance companies have become the nation's healthcare gatekeepers, deciding, in advance, what type of medical care employees should receive—which by definition often means yesterday's treatments versus today's treatments. This also has, until now, prevented entrepreneurial medical providers and alternative medical providers from developing better treatments, since they cannot easily get paid for them.

- As the average length of employment fell from 25 years to only 1 to 4 years, employers and their insurance carriers shifted to paying for short-term fixes versus long-term cures—treating the symptoms of disease instead of curing disease.

As you will soon see, this has recently changed, thanks to new federal legislation and regulations that have leveled the playing field between employer-sponsored health insurance and individual/family health insurance policies that you purchase yourself.

How Most U.S. Consumers Waste
Thousands of Dollars Each Year on Their
Health Insurance

Most people have comprehensive insurance on their automobiles. Yet they don't file a claim with their car insurance company when they buy gasoline, have their car cleaned, replace the tires or brakes, or change the oil. Even if they have an accident they are typically 100 percent responsible for any costs below the deductible on their policy.

Most people have homeowners insurance on their homes. Yet they don't file a claim with their property insurance company when they buy heating fuel, have their house painted, or install a new roof. And here, too, they typically have a deductible where the insured pays entirely any claim below $500 or $1,000 per event.

Any financial advisor will tell you that it is foolish to buy insurance covering an expense that you can afford to pay on your own. The cost of the paperwork involved on each transaction, plus the costs incurred by the insurance company in issuing and enforcing the policy, would cause the premiums to far exceed, over time, any potential benefits. Many consumers have discovered that they can save hundreds or thousands of dollars a year by raising the deductible on their automobile and homeowner policies.*

In homeowners, automobile, life, and all other types of insurance except one, insurance is used to cover only those catastrophic expenses that the insured party cannot comfortably afford to pay on their own. In these cases, most of the money paid for insurance serves a valuable function for the insured and his or her family.

In health insurance, most of the money healthy consumers pay for premiums does not serve a valuable function for the insured or their family.

Most people have a health insurance policy with coverage for incidental maintenance expenses that healthcare consumers don't really

---

*Raising the deductible on an automobile policy from, say, $500 to $1,000 often reduces the annual premium by $500 or more—the insured typically pockets the $500 per annum and only loses out if he or she has more than one major accident per year on a regular basis. The only ones who lose in such a situation are the insurance agents—who are paid a percentage of the total premium and sometimes paid lesser percentages on less-profitable products like high-deductible insurance.

need covered. In addition to being economically foolish, this cover-age supports a byzantine distribution system and payment mechanism that wastes hundreds of billions each year.[6]

Consider how inefficient it would be if you had to file a claim with your automobile insurance company every time you bought gasoline or changed your oil—or if you could only buy gas or have your car maintained at a particular service station where your insurance company had negotiated a discounted rate for such services.

Consider how difficult it would be if you had to get approval from your homeowner's insurance company to pay utility bills, or change your carpets, or paint your house—and if you could only purchase such items from a store selected by your insurance company, and only purchase certain types of carpet or paint colors that your insurance company had preapproved.

Consider how much lower the prices are, and how better the selection is, at the mass-merchants and category-busters, ranging from Home Depot to PetSmart to Staples—and consider how none of these retailers would exist if the consumer were not free to shop competitively in each of these areas.

A significant part of the money consumers and employers pay for health insurance goes toward prepaid medical care that most consumers never use. Healthy consumers would be much better served purchasing just insurance in the event of a medical catastrophe and paying out-of-pocket themselves for doctor visits, prescriptions, and affordable, incidental medical items (if they could get these items at the real usual and customary price).

When you stop and think about it, it doesn't take long to see how inefficient we are in distributing medical products and services, and what great opportunities are probably being missed. But our medical services distribution system actually looks efficient when compared to our medical services insurance and payment system.

The Three Major Components of Health Insurance

As just explained, health insurance is different from all other types of insurance. When you buy life insurance, automobile insurance, or homeowner's property and casualty insurance, you do not expect to have a claim in the near future. You purchase these types of insurance for financial protection against the occurrence of an unlikely event that you wish to avoid—like a death, an auto theft, or a fire. If such an event occurs, you generally receive money that you are free to spend any way you wish.

In contrast, with health insurance, you expect to have some claims in the near future and you almost never receive money when you have one. Instead, your insurance carrier directly pays the medical providers that have taken care of you—typically paying them either a flat monthly fee or a small fraction of what they would charge you directly if you didn't have health insurance.

This is because what we call "health insurance" in the United States consists of three separate but related components, only one of which is actually insurance. These three components are:

1. *Medical discount networks*—Access to a network of physicians, hospitals, and other medical providers, who provide services at greatly discounted rates.

2. *Prepaid medical care*—Basic medical care from these providers, prepaid and usually forfeited whether you utilize them or not.

3. *Financial protection*—Insurance against the medical expenses of an accident or illness.

(1) Medical Discount Networks

Health insurance began in the United States during the Great Depression, when local hospitals began adopting the Blue Cross plans—providing groups of individuals with hospital care in return for a fixed monthly fee. Insurance for hospital stays is truly insurance, since no one expects to spend time in the hospital during the coming year.

Around the same time, employers and groups of individuals began contracting with doctors to provide care for a discounted or fixed monthly fee—these were called Blue Shield plans. Over the subsequent decades, thousands of these plans were merged and consolidated into the 70 independent Blue Cross Blue Shield health insurance companies that exist today. These companies, collectively known as "the Blues," maintain their own networks of independent doctors and hospitals to provide benefits at discounted prices to their policyholders.

Hundreds of other health insurance companies and independent noninsurance companies also developed their own networks—contracting with medical providers in their local areas to provide service to their policyholders or members for either a flat monthly fee or a discounted rate.

> These medical provider networks originally provided a good service to both sides—getting medical providers new patients and getting patients reasonable discounts off the price of medical services.
>
> A similar opportunity exists today for financially oriented wellness entrepreneurs to organize wellness networks in their communities.

As new medical providers entered the marketplace, from ordinary physicians to specialized blood testing laboratories, the only way for them to get patients was to offer great discounts to the largest purchasers of healthcare—the medical provider networks. As medical providers lowered their prices to these large purchasing networks, the same medical providers raised their prices to patients *outside* the network—sometimes just to show the networks that they were giving them increasing discounts off the prices they charged some other (poor) patient.

Soon almost every patient became a member of a medical provider network and there were very few people left to charge the higher out-of-network price—except very poor people who were uninsured and probably couldn't pay anyway. Today, most medical providers, from local pediatricians to big-city hospitals, charge the few patients who don't belong to their health insurance medical provider network far higher prices (sometimes five to ten times higher) than they charge to those in their network for the exact same service.

This is one of the most tragic parts of U.S. health insurance today. Patients who don't have health insurance, and are thus outside of the discounted network, are typically charged multiples of the usual and customary rates paid by insurance carriers for patients with health insurance. Even worse, when these patients don't pay these exorbitant rates, their bill is sold to a collection agency and they are forced into bankruptcy—and under the new bankruptcy law they are still forced to pay the exorbitant five to ten times amount after bankruptcy rather than pay the usual and customary amount that was all the medical provider really wanted to receive in the first place.

In my book *The New Health Insurance Solution* (Wiley, 2007), on pages 50–52, I examine medical expenses incurred by my family and my partner's family over the past five years. What our medical providers profitably provided us for $3,466.53, they charged $16,311.53 for identical services to families who were outside of their medical provider network—typically poorer families without health insurance.

(2) Prepaid Medical Care

Most people, especially those with young children, expect to utilize some basic medical services in the coming year, if for nothing more than an annual checkup or OBGYN exam. A significant part of the premium paid for health insurance is typically for prepaid medical services at the offices of the providers in the medical provider network.

This is the area where healthy people waste the most money on their health insurance, either because they utilize a very low amount of medical services, or because they utilize wellness-oriented medical providers that are typically outside of their health insurance carrier's medical provider network.

For example, you or your customer might be paying $5,000 a year for a health insurance policy with a $20 medical doctor co-pay— valid only at sickness-oriented doctors in the insurance carrier's medical provider network. If you are not visiting medical doctors that often, or if your primary care physician is a chiropractor or osteopath outside the network, you could save up to $3,000 on your annual premium by switching to a high-deductible policy. Such a policy requires that you pay your medical providers directly for each visit, although you typically receive the lower in-network price that the insurance carrier would pay to your provider if you had a lower-deductible or co-pay policy.

Switching to a high-deductible policy was not possible only a few years ago. Many states used to have regulations requiring minimum annual deductibles, or 100 percent coverage (i.e., no deductible) for certain items like maternity or specific treatments. While these regulations always seemed good at the time to a state legislature overreacting to the issue of the day, they ended up driving up the cost of health insurance for everyone and pricing millions of consumers and employers entirely out of the health insurance marketplace. Today, less than 60 percent of U.S. jobs include health benefits, and two million fewer jobs offer coverage every year.

Fortunately, as you'll learn in the next chapter, the recent federal initiative for Health Savings Accounts (HSAs) has increased the popularity of high-deductible health insurance policies, and caused most states to amend their regulations to allow high-deductible coverage.

The new availability of high-deductible health insurance is one of the biggest blessings for the wellness industry. High-deductible health insurance policies save wellness-

oriented consumers thousands each year on sickness industry health insurance, savings they can now channel
into their wellness.

(3) Financial Protection

Financial protection (insurance) against the medical expenses of an
accident or illness is the main component of health insurance that
everyone needs. Until 2005, good financial protection was difficult to
obtain, because the only way to get affordable tax-deductible health
benefits for most people was through employer-sponsored health
benefits—health benefits that terminate when you quit, are fired, or
are no longer able to come to work.[7]

Fortunately, new federal laws and regulations have leveled the
playing field between employer-sponsored health benefits and individual or family policies that wellness-oriented and self-employed individuals can obtain for themselves. Such policies offer permanent,
lifetime (until Medicare) financial protection and typically cost
healthy people one third to one half the price of employer-sponsored
policies with similar benefits. Here's why.

- Employer-sponsored group health insurance policies are required to accept all employee applicants, at the same price, without regard to age, weight, smoking status, or health history.
  When an employee has a $100,000 medical expense, that ex-
  pense is passed through to the employer and/or to the other employees in the group. Even if you are healthy, live a wellness
  lifestyle, and stay with the same employer your entire life, your
  financial protection and benefits are subject to the medical experience of the entire employee group.

- In contrast, 46 states now allow individual insurance carriers to
  medically underwrite each applicant and their family members—and then either reject each individual applicant, accept
  with exclusions for preexisting conditions, or uprate (charge
  more) for higher risks.

- If you or your wellness customer are among the 80 to 90 percent
  of applicants who currently get accepted for their own individual or family policy, your policy is "guaranteed renewable" and
  your premium cannot generally be increased because of a future
  illness—it can only be increased with your age and general
  medical inflation.

- In 2005, the federal government issued new regulations allowing employers to offer employees tax-free allowances to purchase
  their own individual or family policies. This not only leveled
  the tax playing field between employer-sponsored and individ-
  ual/family plans, it took away the original reason employers
  got involved in providing health benefits for employees more
  than 60 years ago. Thousands of employers are closing their
  employer-sponsored group health plans and switching to new
  Defined Contribution individually purchased health insurance
  policies. You can learn more about this phenomenon at
  www.zanehra.com

In the next chapter, we will examine what you and your wellness-
oriented customers should do to obtain an individual or family health
insurance policy yourself that offers you:

1. *Your choice of medical discount networks*—Access to the best
   medical providers in your area at the lowest rates paid by the
   major insurance carriers, even when you are paying these medical providers yourself as a single patient.

2. *Better prepaid medical care*—Instead of prepaying your insurance carrier for medical products and services you may never
   use or want, you can redirect these funds tax-free into your own
   personal Health Savings Account—keeping what you don't
   spend for future sickness expenses, wellness, or even retirement.

3. *Permanent financial protection*—Health insurance independent of any employer on which the premium cannot be increased, nor the policy cancelled, because you become ill or
   have a high claim.

The New Solution
for Wellness-Oriented Entrepreneurs

Author's note: This section was titled "The *Coming* Solution for
Wellness-Oriented Entrepreneurs" in the 2002 edition of this book,
where I explained why Congress should soon allow universal Health
Savings Accounts (then called "Medical Savings Accounts") for all
Americans. In 2004–2005, Congress did exactly what I predicted,
and I received an honorary doctorate for the role the book played in
educating our elected officials to take action.

Since 1985, I, along with many other economists, have argued in the White House and in Congress about the unfairness of allowing only corporate employees tax-deductible health insurance. These policies have had detrimental effects on our entire healthcare insurance and delivery system. Congress finally listened.

In 2003, self-employed individuals were allowed to deduct from their taxable income 100 percent of the amount they spent on health insurance premiums for themselves, their spouses, and their dependents.

In 2005, all Americans, whether they had employer-sponsored or individual/family health insurance, were allowed to have a Health Savings Account (HSA). An HSA, as you'll learn in the next chapter, is like a super IRA or 401K for health expenses.

In 2006, employers were allowed to offer employees tax-free allowances to purchase their own individual or family policies rather than be forced to participate in the expensive one-size-fits-all company-sponsored group health insurance plan.*

While the effects of these three epochal events have not yet been felt, they will go down in history as the crack in the wall of the corporate sickness insurance monopoly, similar to what the fall of the Berlin Wall in 1989 was to the demise of communism.

No one yet has any idea of how efficient, and even how enjoyable, shopping for wellness (and sickness) services might be if consumers were given the ability to choose freely among competitive, cost-effective providers, but we are about to find out.

Competitive forces are now in place that will soon force all medical providers to allow their customers to choose the wellness and sickness products that they desire, versus the products and services forced on them by cost-cutting corporate employers and lobbyist-controlled government medical plans.

---

*A few states and insurance carriers are (unsuccessfully) fighting this new federal rule, since their healthy insureds, who typically pay $14,000 per family in an employer group plan, are switching to their own individual plans, which typically cost $7,000 or less for the same benefits.

No one knows how innovative and efficient we will become when we get the federal government out of large segments of the healthcare business and apply good old Yankee ingenuity to the distribution side of our healthcare system. But when we look at the growth of so many other industries (food service, transportation, consumer electronics), we begin to get an idea of what might be possible.

Food service outside of the home used to mean either a dull cafeteria or an expensive restaurant. Through innovative technology, the restaurant industry lowered its prices and increased its product offerings so much that the demand for its product increased 1,000 percent. From 1950 to today, Americans went from spending 5 percent to 50 percent of their household food budget on meals prepared outside of the home. Fifty years ago a child's "Can we go out to dinner?" was met with "What do you think we are, millionaires?" Today, such a request is usually met by "What kind of food do you want?" and dining out is an enjoyable and affordable experience for almost everyone.

Similar examples abound for air transportation, vacations, fashionable clothes, consumer electronics, and hundreds of other luxury services and products that people thought could never be made affordable to mass markets.

In the next chapter we examine this opportunity and see that you and your wellness customers can provide yourselves with wellness-oriented health insurance that allows you to freely control how and where you spend—or save—your healthcare dollars.

Before Proceeding to the Next Chapter

Action Plan for Entrepreneurs and
Wellness/Health Professionals

1. Analyze the impact of the current health insurance system on your individual area of wellness business opportunity. How would the collapse of the current health insurance system impact your wellness business?

2. Analyze how continued cost-cutting efforts by medical providers will impact each of your areas of wellness business opportunity.

3. Employers and employees play cat-and-mouse games to get around existing healthcare regulations and restrictions. Analyze how these games help or hinder your area of wellness business opportunity. If everyone were to receive free government-provided sickness care, how would it impact your area? Conversely, what would happen if existing employer-provided sickness coverage were greatly reduced?

4. Analyze how your area of wellness business opportunity is affected by the laws leveling the tax playing field between employer-sponsored and individually purchased health insurance.

5. Analyze how your area of wellness business opportunity will be affected by the shift of consumers to Health Savings Accounts.

6. Analyze how your area of wellness business opportunity could be affected by proposed legislation to make dietary supplements tax deductible.

7. Analyze how your area of wellness business opportunity would be affected if employers began giving each employee a wellness allowance or spending option.

CHAPTER 7

The New Health Insurance Solution: Helping Your Customers Finance Their Wellness

In this chapter, you learn three things:

1. How your healthy wellness customers can get better, safer, and much cheaper health insurance by getting their own individual or family health insurance policy versus participating in a group plan sponsored by their employer.

2. How you can help your customers save $5,000 or more on their health insurance by wisely choosing a higher deductible and only the benefits they really need—money that they can then invest in their wellness through your wellness business.

3. How and why you and your wellness customers should open new Health Savings Accounts (HSAs) to save, tax-free, for your future wellness.

As explained in the previous chapter, most (150 million) Americans receive their health insurance today from an employer-sponsored group health insurance policy. Our current employer-sponsored group health insurance system is the number one cause of personal bankruptcy and is the greatest threat to your financial future. This is because if you or your customer become too ill to work, you would lose your job and lose your health insurance.

The solution, which has already been found by about 15 million wellness-oriented healthy Americans, is an individual or family health insurance policy that you purchase directly from a major insurance company in your state.

What Is an Individual/Family Health Insurance Policy?

An individual or family health insurance policy is a policy purchased from an insurance company or government entity covering a single individual or selected family members.

There are two main differences between employer-sponsored group policies and individual or family policies:

1. Employers and their group-policy insurance carriers are legally required to accept all applicants regardless of their health or lifestyle. In contrast, insurance carriers offering individual policies in 46 states (including Washington, DC) can reject, or charge more for, applicants who are unhealthy, smoke, or are obese—this allows carriers to offer far lower rates to healthy wellness-oriented applicants (except in the five states of NY, NJ, MA, ME, and VT).

2. The premium paid by employers for their group policies is typically increased every year, based on the previous year's healthcare costs of the employee group. In contrast, the premium you pay for an individual or a family policy cannot be raised each year, nor can the policy be canceled based on your health or your prior year's healthcare costs.*

Unlike employer-sponsored health insurance, individual and family health insurance is real insurance because it guarantees protection or safety. As long as you pay the premium, your policy cannot be canceled nor the premiums increased just because you lose your job, change jobs, or have an illness in your family.

So, what's the catch? If individual/family health insurance policies are cheaper than similar-benefit group employer-sponsored plans, if their premium cannot be increased based on future illness, and if you can keep your individual/family policy when you change jobs:

---

*Individual premiums increase with your age and general medical inflation based on the claims on all individual policyholders in your area. Some states, like Utah, allow a relatively small one-time increase based on claims history, although you can usually find a policy in these states that contractually does not allow such an increase.

Why Doesn't Every American Family Have an Individual/Family Health Insurance Policy?

There is no catch, except that only about 80 to 90 percent of Americans who currently apply for an individual or family health insurance policy from a private carrier can medically qualify (based on their past health experience).* Furthermore, until very recently, individual/family policies have gone from being effectively twice as expensive as employer-sponsored group policies to half as expensive. This is because:

1. Healthcare expenses, and particularly catastrophic healthcare expenses, used to be more of a random event for most consumers. In the past, it seemed as if anyone could become tragically ill with heart trouble or Type 2 diabetes with no rhyme or reason—which is why people banded together to protect themselves financially like they did with life, auto, or fire insurance. Today, healthcare expenses are extremely predictable, based on a person's prior health history and the choices they make, starting with being overweight, having poor nutrition, or smoking.

2. In many states, it used to be illegal for insurance carriers to medically underwrite applicants for individual health insurance and charge more or less based on their health expectations for each applicant or each family member. Today, 46 states allow such medical underwriting and allow insurance carriers to price the premiums on policies much lower for healthier applicants.

About 15 percent of people age 18 to 65 consume 85 percent of the medical expenses of this group—which is why insurance carriers, in the 46 states where it is now legal, offer healthy applicants individual or family policies for one third to one half the price of similar-benefit employer-sponsored group plans (which automatically accept all participants regardless of health or lifestyle).

---

3. The income tax regulations allowing employers to reimburse employees tax-free for individual or family policies only just changed, in 2005—prior to this an employee purchasing his or

---

*This figure, while accurate, may be misleading, since only the relatively healthy currently apply for individual or family policies. I estimate that approximately 65 to 75 percent of the total nongeriatric population might qualify if everyone applied for individual or family policies.

hcr own individual or family policy paid effectively up to twice as much, since they had to pay their premium with after-tax dollars versus the pre-tax dollars used to pay for group employer-sponsored plans.

Employers who offer group-sponsored health insurance plans don't tell employees they can purchase individual or family policies for less money than the cost of participating in the company's group plan, particularly if the employer charges the employee a majority of the cost to add a spouse or dependent to the employer plan. If employers did tell employees, more of their healthy employees, who would be accepted by private carriers, would purchase their own policies—leaving the employer without the premium from the healthy employees and stuck paying for the medical expenses of the remaining unhealthy employees and unhealthy dependents.

If you have to pay your employer to allow your healthy spouse and/or dependents to participate in the company health benefits plan, your employer doesn't want you to know you can purchase similar coverage in the private market for half the price.

Another reason is that few people are aware that individuals or families who don't medically qualify for a policy from a private insurance carrier can now receive state-guaranteed coverage from their state—such state-guaranteed coverage is typically the same Blue Cross Blue Shield-type coverage from a private carrier except the state pays the carrier for losses. State-guaranteed coverage costs about two to three times the price per applicant of a private sector policy (which works out to about 50 percent more for a family of four with one unhealthy member). While the states have been federally required to offer such coverage since 2005, many states make it difficult to apply for, or even find out about their programs offering state-guaranteed coverage to their unhealthy citizens.

State-guaranteed health insurance can be the bargain of a lifetime if you are very ill—an annual premium of $3,600 a year can get you $100,000 a year or more in health benefits. Unfortunately, for obvious financial reasons, states don't spend money advertising their state-guaranteed coverage—often, only people who know

someone in state government get to take advantage of it. To learn about State-Guaranteed Coverage in your state visit www.tnhis.com.

How to Help Your Wellness Customer Save $5,000 or More on Their Health Insurance—Money They Can then Invest in Their Wellness through Your Wellness Business

Teach Your Customers about Individual/Family Policies

The first thing you can do to help yourself or your wellness customer save money on their health insurance is to explain what you have just learned about individual and family health insurance policies, and how they cost one third to one half the price of employer-sponsored plans with similar benefits

Many of your customers may tell you that they don't care because they receive "free" health insurance through their job. However, this may soon change for them. About 60 percent of U.S. jobs today include employer-sponsored group health insurance—this figure used to be 80 percent, and each year 2 million fewer U.S. jobs include health benefits. Moreover, employer-sponsored health insurance is the number one indirect cause of bankruptcy in the U.S. today.

But despite these facts, it is unlikely that an employee will forego receiving free health benefits from an employer and purchase an individual or family policy with their own money, unless they soon plan to leave their job and go into business for themselves.

However, while most U.S. employers today still pay for most of the health benefits cost for their employee, almost all private employers today charge 50 percent or more of the cost to add the employee's spouse and/or children to the company plan. If your customer's spouse and/or children are healthy, you could show them how to save 50 percent or more and get permanent coverage for their dependents by buying their dependents their own individual or family coverage.

If your prospective wellness customer or their family members are unhealthy, smoke, or are overweight, show them how much more they are paying for health insur-

ance to demonstrate the benefits of making an investment
in their wellness. Once they lose weight and/or become
healthier they may qualify for better, cheaper, and safer
individual or family policies.

For more on how to purchase an individual or family health insurance policy, including pricing from most carriers in all states,
please see *The New Health Insurance Solution* (Wiley, 2007) or visit
www.tnhis.com.

Explain the Benefits of High-Deductible Health Insurance

Most of your customers, whether they receive their health insurance
through an employer or from their own individual or family policy,
can save money by increasing the annual deductible on their health
insurance. This not only saves them money, it reduces the amount of
prepaid medical care they are wasting on sickness-oriented doctors
and gives them more money today to invest in their wellness.

If you contacted a health insurance company or employer and told
them that from now on you would like to pay directly the first $2,500
per year of your medical expenses, they would probably lower your
annual premium by about $3,000. This puts you ahead by $500 per
annum even if you had a medical catastrophe every year.

As illogical as it may sound, most health insurers would
lower your annual premium by roughly 120 percent of
the increase in your annual deductible, approximately
$3,000 savings in annual premium for a $2,500 increase
in your deductible—putting you ahead by at least $500 a
year, even if you become very ill. Here's why.

When you incur a $50 expense at a doctor or other medical service
provider, your insurance company incurs an expense of $75 or
more—$50 to pay the doctor and at least $25 for the paperwork and
overhead required by the transaction. This is one of the reasons insurers have been pushing their insured to enroll in health maintenance
organizations (HMOs), which pay the provider a flat annual amount
per patient (capitation) rather than paying for each service rendered.

On average, health insurance companies and employers providing
employer-sponsored plans spend about 20 percent on overhead, but
this average number masks the true picture of what is happening. To

approve and pay a single $10,000 hospital bill might cost an insurance company only $500 (5 percent) in transaction costs—dealing with the hospital and cutting them a check. But to approve and pay a $50 medical bill from a single provider might cost the insurance company $25 (50 percent) or more in transaction costs—sometimes even more than the actual cost of the medical service itself.

The first $2,500 of a family's annual medical expenses are typically spent in $50 to $125 increments in 20 to 30 different transactions—which costs the insurance company the $2,500 plus an additional $500 to $1,500 in transaction processing costs.

No wonder an insurance company or employer might lower your annual premium by $3,000 if you would agree to increase your annual deductible by $2,500. Most, in fact, already have, by incorporating such a 120 percent or greater reduction of premium into their published rates.

The main benefit of increasing the annual deductible on your employer-sponsored or individual health policy is not the money you can save—the main benefit is that it puts you in control of where you spend your first health-care dollars and allows you to choose wellness medical providers versus just the sickness doctors typically allowed by most insurers or company-sponsored plans.

Some consumers who are concerned about not having enough cash to pay the annual deductible choose an uneconomic lower deductible health insurance policy. Agents sometimes recommend such products because the agents make a higher insurance commission on the higher premium.

If you are wellness-oriented, live a wellness lifestyle, and are healthy enough to qualify for an individual or family policy, you may have a greater health expense risk from having an accident (e.g., playing soccer, falling on ice) than from having a disease or illness. If this is your concern, you can purchase inexpensive accident medical coverage.

Visit www.ZaneAMC.com to learn about Accident Medical Coverage that pays your deductible and other medical

expenses not covered by your health insurance. You can
get your family up to $10,000 in coverage for as little as
$10 to $40/month.

Help Your Customers Save 10 to 75 Percent on Their Prescription Drugs

Approximately 131 million people in the United States, about 66 percent of all adults, use prescription drugs. Once your customer or you
switch to a high-deductible health insurance plan, you have a big incentive to be smart about the way you buy prescription drugs.

As explained in more detail in *The New Health Insurance Solution*
(Chapter 9), you can save 10 to 75 percent on prescription drugs as
follows:

1. Get a drug discount card.
2. Choose the right drug plan from your health insurer.
3. Shop overseas pharmacies.
4. Substitute generic drugs.
5. Use a different drug that has similar effects.

> **However, for wellness-oriented customers there is an
> even better way that can save them 100 percent of the cost
> on prescription drugs—stop taking them entirely by
> working with a medical or wellness professional to either
> change your diet or find safer natural substitutes. See Ap-
> pendix B to learn how to do this.**

> **Today about 95 percent of the prescription drugs sold are
> *maintenance drugs*—drugs that treat only the symptoms
> of a disease and that you are expected to take for the rest
> of your life.**

From an economic/business perspective, at least, it's easy to
understand why this is so, and you need to understand this if you are
taking any prescription drugs on a regular basis. I'll put the answer
in the form of a question: If you were the CEO of a major pharmaceutical firm, would you spend your R&D dollars to make a pill that
a consumer would only take once (e.g., a vaccine) or for only a short
period of time (e.g., an antibiotic), or would you spend your R&D

dollars on creating products that consumers would take every day, or two or three times a day, for the rest of their lives?

For the past three decades, the majority of private R&D dollars in the pharmaceutical industry have been spent on products that treat merely the symptoms of disease rather than cure or prevent disease—thus creating customers for life.

As explained in greater detail in Appendix B in this book, today the world's top-selling prescription drugs, Lipitor, Zocor, Nexium, Prevacid, and Zoloft, have the following things in common for most people taking them:

- They do not prevent a disease.
- They treat only the symptoms of a disease.
- They are designed to be taken for the rest of your life.
- They are not narcotic or controlled substances and thus should not be prescription (versus over-the-counter) medicines.
- They would have less chance of being sold directly to consumers as real products without first coopting trusted physicians as sales agents.
- They are dangerous to your long-term health, because by treating only the symptoms of a deadly disease, they prevent you from modifying your behavior to cure the disease.

If you or any of your customers are taking these or other prescription drugs on a regular basis, please read Appendix B to better understand:

1. The economics behind these products;
2. How to consider changing your diet, exercise, or other lifestyle factor; and
3. How to locate a doctor to work with you to stop taking these drugs.

Health Savings Accounts

Health Savings Accounts (HSAs) represent the biggest change in U.S. health and retirement care since Social Security and Medicare.

They allow you to save hundreds of thousands of dollars, tax-free, for your future medical expenses or retirement—while financially reforming the entire U.S. healthcare system.

Three million Americans have already opened an HSA since they became legal in 2004. But HSAs are really just getting started because they are only now becoming available from major employers and most financial institutions. This is similar to what happened with IRAs and 401(k)s more than 30 years ago—back then, some people thought it was ludicrous to allow consumers to manage their own retirement savings. Today 48 million U.S. households have an IRA and 45 million have a 401(k).

When people say they have a "Health Savings Account," they typically mean that they have a high-deductible "HSA-qualified" health insurance policy from an employer or that they obtained themselves, combined with an IRA-type savings account called an "HSA." An HSA consists of:

1. A high-deductible HSA-Qualified health insurance policy that qualifies you to open an HSA bank account. The maximum annual deductible on your HSA-Qualified health insurance policy is $10,500 per family ($5,250 per single) in 2006 (these figures increase annually with inflation).

2. A savings or brokerage account that functions similar to an IRA, except that both you *and* your employer may make tax-free contributions, up to the maximum amount of your annual deductible but no greater than $5,450 per family ($2,700 per single) in 2006.

Why You Should Always Fully Fund Your HSA before Your IRA or 401(k)

With a traditional IRA or 401(k), you receive a deduction from your taxable income for 100 percent of the contributions you make each year, but after age 65 you must pay state and federal taxes at high ordinary income tax rates on all distributions—even on capital gains in these accounts.*

*Traditional IRAs and 401(k)s have proven to be tax traps for millions of Americans because most of the money in IRAs or 401(k)s at retirement is from capital appreciation—which is then taxed at higher ordinary income tax rates instead of lower capital gains rates. Also, many seniors are not in lower tax brackets after retirement. Seniors dislike taking money out of their retirement accounts and paying ordinary income taxes so much that Congress now requires Required Minimum Distributions (RMDs) beginning at age 70 1/2, based on life expectancy, for 100 percent taxable distribution. At death, unused IRA/401(k) balances are taxed at ordinary federal and state income rates, with the remainder subject to estate taxation.

In contrast, with a Health Savings Account (HSA), you receive all the same benefits you do with a traditional IRA or 401(k), except you *never* have to pay income taxes on distributions used for qualified medical expenses—and you can take these distributions without penalty anytime before or after age 65.

HSA funds can also be withdrawn for any purpose other than qualified medical expenses—in which case they are treated as if they were withdrawn from your IRA or 401(k)—there is no penalty if you are over 65, though you do pay income tax.

HSAs have essentially the same benefits of traditional IRAs and 401(k)s—plus distributions from HSAs are allowed tax-free at any time for qualified medical expenses.

HSAs have triple tax advantages:

1. Contributions are tax deductible going in.
2. Appreciation is tax-free.
3. Withdrawals are tax-free (when used for qualifying medical expenses).

Why HSAs Are So Important

There are many advantages to having a Health Savings Account (HSA), including:

- HSAs make healthcare more affordable for tens of millions of Americans—in 2006 the average individual/family HSA-qualified policy cost less than half the price of a traditional lower-deductible policy. HSA-qualified high-deductible coverage from employers is typically also half the price.

- HSAs allow your customers to save thousands each year on their sickness insurance—savings they can invest in their wellness or save for their future.

- HSAs reward consumers for making financially smart but medically sound choices—like choosing generic drugs over chemically identical name brand ones, or better yet, not taking prescription drugs entirely and using less-invasive natural remedies.

- HSAs provide your customers with the financial and health coverage buffer they need between jobs—withdrawals from HSAs

to pay health insurance premiums are tax-free at any age if unemployed.

- HSAs significantly reduce the 20 percent ($400 billion) of the
  $2.0 trillion U.S. healthcare budget that goes to paperwork.

- HSAs help Medicare by ensuring that baby boomers have the
  necessary funds to supplement Medicare during their retirement.

- HSAs return entrepreneurial innovation to U.S. healthcare,
  since tens of millions of Americans with HSAs will be allowed to
  select the medical provider of their choice, and medical providers can offer new products and services direct to consumers
  without getting them approved by health insurance carriers or
  employers.

- HSAs promote proactive preventive care and wellness care
  instead of offering reactive sickness medicine provided by third
  parties who cannot make optimum long-term choices.

Why HSAs Are Especially Good for Wellness

Having a high annual deductible does not mean that your HSA-
qualified health plan cannot provide full coverage for certain items.
Congress was concerned that people with high-deductible coverage
might be reluctant to spend their own money on wellness, preventive
care, or annual checkups. HSA-qualified health policies are allowed
to provide unlimited first-dollar coverage for benefits outside of the
minimum annual deductible amount, with or without co-pays.

Items Allowed Outside of Minimum High Deductible for HSAs

Periodic health evaluations (e.g., annual physicals)

Screening services (e.g., mammograms)

Routine prenatal and well-child care

Child and adult immunizations

Tobacco cessation programs

Obesity and weight loss programs (doctor supervised)

Preventive care

Preventive care does not include treatment of an existing condition, but does include drugs and medications designed to prevent a
disease that has not yet manifested itself or to prevent reoccurrence

of a disease—such as cholesterol-lowering medication for people with high cholesterol.

Every day thousands more employers are offering HSA options to their employees. This is a great time for these employers to implement a workplace wellness program, since the company can pay for these benefits without violating the rules on their HSA high deductible coverage.

HSA insurance coverage is also allowed to have first-dollar health insurance coverage for specific diseases, accidents, disability, vision care, long-term care, and drug discount cards—without violating the HSA-qualified minimum high-deductible requirement.

Accident Medical Coveage programs are available that pay maximum benefits of up to $10,000 per accident for about $10 to $40 per month. These programs are excellent supplements to high-deductible HSA coverage, since they can protect your HSA balance.

Helping Your Customers Finance Their Wellness

Every wellness professional needs to know about health insurance, and needs to know how to educate their customers how to get better, cheaper health insurance. The money your customers save on their health insurance can be redirected into investments in their wellness.

Specifically, you can teach your healthy wellness-oriented customers:

1. How to get better health insurance for much less money by purchasing their own individual or family policy;
2. How they can save money by reducing their prepaid medical expenses (i.e., raising their deductible) and invest the savings in their wellness; and
3. Why every U.S. citizen should have a Health Savings Account.

If you have customers with employees, show them how to institute a workplace wellness program at virtually no net cost to their company using a Health Reimbursement

> Arrangement (HRA). An HRA can make every one of their employees your wellness customer.
> Visit www.ZaneHRA.com to learn more.

To help you explain these concepts to your customers, Zane Benefits LLC has a new no-cost Affiliate program that allows wellness professionals to receive, for free, a 400-page personalized web site to educate their customers about health insurance.

Thousands of wellness professionals and entrepreneurs have signed up for this program, with spectacular results for both their businesses and for their customers. Moreover, if your customers start purchasing health insurance through this free web site, you can sign up for an Associate program that pays you a referral fee each time your customer purchases better health insurance for his or her business or family.

Visit www.zanebenefits.com to learn more about how these Affiliate and Associate programs can affect your wellness business.

Before Proceeding to the Next Chapter

Action Plan for Entrepreneurs and Wellness/Health Professionals

1. Analyze how educating your customers about their health insurance fits into your wellness business.

2. As consumers shift to individual/family policies, their annual premium is determined by their health. Develop a formula to show your customers how much they will save on their health insurance premium alone by being healthy, and then show how your wellness business can help them get there.

3. Virtually every healthy consumer can save money today by raising the annual deductible on their health insurance. Show your customers how to do this and simultaneously invest the savings in their wellness—by purchasing products or services from your wellness business.

4. Prescription drugs are a significant cost for more than 100 million U.S. consumers. See Appendix B for how to work with a doctor to get your customers off prescription drugs, and invest their savings in their wellness through your wellness products or services.

5. Every U.S. consumer should have a Health Savings Account. Educate yourself more about HSAs, and use this knowledge to introduce yourself to potential new customers and earn their trust.

CHAPTER 8

Making Your Fortune Distributing Wellness

The fastest-growing area of wellness distribution is Direct Selling, which is so important today that it is discussed in its own chapter, following this one.

Throughout history, there have been fortunes made and fortunes lost in manufacturing or controlling some particular commodity. However, consistent success has come only from distributing the ever-expanding production of cutting-edge technology.

This is especially true today, because distribution costs now represent approximately 70 percent of the retail price for most products and services, and distribution costs represent approximately 80 percent of the retail price for most wellness products.

However, before we examine some of the opportunities in wellness distribution, it is important for wellness entrepreneurs to first understand the biological concept of *unlimited wealth,* which has created most of these opportunities.

Unlimited Wealth: The Biological Principle behind Modern Economics

Here's an exercise I use to teach the concept of unlimited wealth to my students. I have the members of the class pretend they are shipwrecked on a desert island with no provisions. In order to survive, they must organize a society and divide the work according to specific chores—gathering food, building shelters, collecting firewood, and so on.

At first, the students want to democratically rotate various chores in their new island society. However, as we role-play the various chores, they soon learn that it is much better for each person to specialize.

The person who goes out to find apples on Monday not only returns with apples, she knows exactly where to get the apples on Tuesday. By Wednesday, she not only knows where to find the apples, she has made tools like a sack or a wheelbarrow to carry them all back to the camp in one trip. By Thursday, she has made a tool to pick the ripe apples from the higher branches before they fall to the ground. By Friday, she is able to accomplish a former day's work in less than an hour, so she starts learning how to make apple cider and apple preserves.

Eventually, all of the chores necessary for survival (obtaining food, shelter, fuel, etc.) are performed in a fraction of the time and by a fraction of the people originally required to complete them. This frees some members of the society to explore new pursuits—producing new products, more tools, and even providing entertainment.

As the society grows, so much quantity and variety of goods are being produced that a new need arises—distributing all these goods and services. Before long, some people are engaged full-time in distribution, which mostly entails educating everyone about what the others are doing and what is available. These distributors, or merchants, end up being the wealthiest members of the island society because they add the most value—especially when the island society encounters another island society and the merchants begin trading more produce and more tools.

In this lesson, my students learn the two main principles of unlimited wealth underlying our modern economy.

First, over time, individuals can produce an unlimited amount of a single good or service (i.e., *unlimited wealth*) by making use of the advancing technology that automatically results from specialization.

Second, the total overall wealth of a society is thus limited only by distribution: the number of individuals available to consume and trade their specialized produce and tools.[1]

The economic power of the United States is based, in part, on distribution laws that initially made it the world's largest open marketplace for goods and services. The U.S. Constitution generally allowed each state to rule itself, with one very powerful exception: no state was allowed to make any law or rule that infringed on the rights of its citizens to freely trade with the citizens of any other state.

Similarly, the economic power of the developed nations today—Western Europe, North America, Japan, and the other Asian tigers (Taiwan, South Korea, Singapore, etc.)—is based on effectively free trade between their 1 billion or so citizens.

This trading block of 1 billion citizens—Western Europe, North America, Japan, and the other Asian tigers—comprises the international wellness marketplace of the immediate future.

From a political standpoint, the challenge for the less developed nations is how to allow their 5.5 billion people to join the free traders while fighting the political instability at home that often results from rapid economic change.

How Distribution Opportunities Surpassed Manufacturing Opportunities

In the 1967 movie *The Graduate,* actor Dustin Hoffman was offered a confident, one-word solution to the quest for economic success: "Plastics." Back then, due to a short-term shortage of raw materials that peaked in the 1970s, economic success for many did lie in finding less expensive ways to make things.

Today, however, thanks to plastics and so many other better ways of making things, economic success for most people no longer lies in manufacturing. Today the greatest opportunities lie in the distribution sector of our economy.

Back in 1967, a manufactured product that sold for $300, for example, such as a camera or a fashionable dress, typically had a manufacturing cost of approximately $150 and a distribution cost of approximately $150. Manufacturing costs accounted for approximately 50 percent of retail prices, so it was possible to make a great deal of money by lowering the costs of production. Back then, even a 10 or 20 percent reduction in manufacturing costs could lower your retail price by $15 or $30.

> In the 1960s and 1970s, entrepreneurial fortunes were made by those who found ways to lower manufacturing costs significantly (e.g., from $150 to $30 or less), often by using plastics or relocating production facilities overseas.

Today, 40 years later, the same product of similar quality typically retails for approximately $100 (although people sometimes don't realize this because they have shifted to purchasing higher-quality products). This two-thirds price reduction for similar-quality items has occurred primarily because technology has lowered production costs from $150 down to approximately $30 or less.

> Distribution costs on that same product have also fallen, from $150 to approximately $70, to where they now account for approximately 70 percent of the price of a typical $100 retail product.

Typical Retail Product Cost Breakdown

	1967		2007	
Manufacturing costs	$150	50%	$ 30	30%
Distribution costs	$150	50%	$ 70	70%
Total retail price	$300	100%	$100	100%

Relative distribution costs have not fallen as much as relative manufacturing costs because we have not yet applied to distribution many of the innovative methods that we have applied to manufacturing.[2]

Today, manufacturing costs represent only about $30 of a typical $100 retail price, so a 10 or 20 percent reduction in manufacturing costs might represent only a $3 to $6 retail price reduction on a $100 item.

But distribution costs represent about $70 of a typical $100 retail price, so a 10 or 20 percent reduction in distribution costs might represent a $7 to $14 retail price reduction on a $100 item. A 50 percent or greater reduction in distribution costs—sometimes feasible by eliminating a single link in the distribution chain between the factory and the consumer—might represent a $35 or even greater retail price reduction on a $100 item.

Due primarily to this increased percentage of distribution cost in retail prices, many of the production facilities that moved overseas in previous years have moved back to the United States. The majority of the foreign cars sold in the United States are now made in the United States. The largest auto plant in the world is the Honda Accord plant in Marysville, Ohio, which exports much of its production to Japan; the hottest new line of Mercedes SUVs is made in Alabama, and the most popular BMWs are made in South Carolina.

The increasing percentage of distribution cost is why, over the past three decades, the majority of great personal fortunes have been made by people who found better ways of distributing things rather than better ways of making things.

In 1992, Sam Walton, of Wal-Mart, who first became an entrepreneur at age 44, became the richest man in the world. Sam never manufactured anything during his life; during his rule, Wal-Mart simply distributed name-brand merchandise made by other companies. In the 1980s, Ross Perot, of Electronic Data Systems, became a billionaire by discovering better ways of distributing other companies' hardware and software. In the 1970s, Fred Smith, of Federal Express, became a billionaire by building an entire airline for distributing products rather than transporting people. The list goes on and on.

More recent examples can be found in the megafortunes of Internet billionaires like Jeff Bezos of Amazon.com, who was chosen as *Time* magazine's Person of the Year in 1999. These cyberspace entrepreneurs found ways to use a new tool (the Internet) to distribute things more efficiently.

How Distribution Has Changed in the Twenty-First Century

When we look more closely, especially at the fortunes that have been made most recently, we see that the nature of the distribution opportunity has changed.

Distribution is really two processes:

1. **Educating consumers about products and services that will improve their lives.**
2. **Physically distributing products and services to consumers.**

Sam Walton, Fred Smith, and most of the distribution billionaires of the twentieth century made their fortunes by finding better and cheaper ways to physically distribute products to consumers *that consumers already knew they wanted.*

On the other hand, Jeff Bezos and other distribution billionaires of the twenty-first century are making their distribution fortunes mostly by educating consumers about new products and services—typically products and services *that consumers don't even know are available.*

It is important for wellness entrepreneurs and investors to understand that this flip-flop in the nature of the distribution opportunity has occurred at least once before.

Prior to the nineteenth century, the work of distribution (of finished goods) mostly entailed educating consumers about products and services that would improve their lives. The peddler and the Main Street merchant alike prided themselves on the knowledge of what they sold, and explaining their products to customers took up the bulk of their time.

In the nineteenth century, these peddlers and merchants evolved into the department stores that characterized most of twentieth-century distribution, from Marshall Field in Chicago (1865) to Filene's in Boston (1881). Technological advances (e.g., centralization of credit, real estate, and buying functions) allowed department stores to quickly replace the peddlers and individual Main Street merchants from whom they themselves had sprung.

These department stores did a lot more than just use technology to lower the cost of selling merchandise. They prided themselves on the customer service of small retailers. This fueled the never ending cycle of consumer demand that defied conventional economic logic. Instead of going to the department store to purchase something you wanted, you went to the department store to find out about something you didn't know existed but that you couldn't live without once you learned about it (e.g., electric lamps, dishwashers, icemakers, self-cleaning ovens).

Looking back on those days before the advent of television and mass media, the department store best served the two distinct functions of distribution today. The department store first *educated* its customers about new products that would improve their lives. Then, once it had taught customers what was available and assisted them in choosing the right product for their needs, it *physically distributed* the product from the factory to the consumer.

From this point forward we use the following terms: *intellectual distribution* and *physical distribution.*

Intellectual Distribution
versus Physical Distribution

Intellectual distribution is the process of educating customers about products and services, typically items that they either don't know exist or don't know are now affordable.

Physical distribution is the process of helping customers physically obtain products and services that they already know they want.

The wellness entrepreneur, like every other business today, must perform these two distribution functions in serving his or her customers.

From 1950 to 2000 the traditional department stores declined, partly because advancing technology, such as universal credit cards and shopping malls, made most of their original innovations (like charge accounts) obsolete.

But department stores declined mostly because they failed to keep their physical distribution service at the same level as their intellectual distribution service.

As the consumer retail dollar shifted from traditional durables (major appliances, furniture) to more consumables (cleaners, paper towels, batteries), consumers desired to quickly obtain these items— items that they already knew they wanted—in as short a time as possible and on a regular basis. The physical layout of the typical multistory department store was ill suited to this task, and department stores were slow to retool their layout. Many of us can remember running into a department store to buy a roll of film, only to have to wait while the same clerk who operated the cash register took 20 minutes to explain a new camera to a potential customer.

This led entrepreneurs like Sam Walton to open mass-merchandise stores dedicated almost entirely to physical versus intellectual distribution. These stores sold the customer exactly, and only, what they knew they wanted before they entered the store—in the shortest time possible and at the lowest possible price. The mass merchandisers decimated traditional department stores.[3]

The mass merchandisers also benefited from the development of radio and television. Mass media allowed manufacturers of wide-appeal products to bypass the traditional department stores in communicating directly with their customers. Today most manufacturers handshake with their customers through the mass media, and the surviving retailers for most products are the lowest-cost, most efficient, physical distributors of merchandise—like Wal-Mart, Kmart, and Target stores. Customer loyalty has shifted from individual retailers (Sears, Macy's, J. W. Robinson's) to individual manufacturers (Sony, Levi's, Procter & Gamble).

When this trend began 30 years ago, a commonly heard shopping complaint was that the customers knew more than the clerks about what they were selling. Today, most retail store shoppers just assume that *they* are more educated about their purchases than the people who sell them.

This story about how the mighty department stores declined contains an important lesson for wellness entrepreneurs:

You must maintain your physical distribution service at the same level as your intellectual distribution service, and vice versa, constantly riding the flip-flop that occurs in the nature of the distribution opportunity.

Applying the Lessons of Business History

Business history, such as this story of the department stores and mass merchants, contains many important lessons for the wellness entrepreneur. However, when you study these stories and then seek to apply them to the distribution of wellness products and services, you must do so with one very important caveat:

Changes that used to take place in 50 to 100 years or more now take place in 5 to 10 years or less.

Starting in 1981, it took only seven years for the 70-year-old carburetor industry to be displaced by electronic fuel injection. Starting in 1985, it took only five years for the 50-year-old phonograph record to be displaced by the compact disc, which is now being displaced by MP3 files. Starting in 1995, it took only three years for the 30-year-old fax machine to be largely displaced by e-mail.

In studying the past, you must condense time when considering solutions applicable to your wellness business of the future—as changes that now take place in five years may soon take place in five months, or even less.

The Category Busters: A Supersized Wellness Opportunity

Recently, a new retailing trend has emerged—*category busting,* which preserves the physical distribution benefits of the mass merchandisers while exceeding the intellectual distribution services of traditional department stores.

These category busters, which include stores like Home Depot, PetSmart, CompUSA, Toys "R" Us, and Babies "R" Us, are effectively mass merchants in just one category—carrying the largest array of merchandise in their category at the lowest prices. This makes consumers willing to travel greater distances to reach them and thus allows the category busters to continue to open even larger stores with greater selection at lower prices.

Since they are focused on only one type of merchandise, they attract employees who are interested in the product category itself. Plus, most category busters hold onsite classes for employees and for customers interested in learning more about their products. Category busters often know more than manufacturers about their products and how consumers use them.

This knowledge, coupled with the extremely favorable buying and marketing power of the category busters, has led to a new phenomenon in retailing: custom-packaged, brand-name merchandise that is retail-priced below the average single-unit manufacturing cost. In effect, retail goods that are priced below wholesale.

Here's one example of how this arrangement works. In 1992, a particular company sold a tool air compressor for $300 wholesale (200,000 units per annum) that retailed for $600 at high-end hardware and tool shops. The company manufactured this item for $200 per unit—$50 in variable labor and material costs and $150 in five-year-amortized design, tool, and die costs. To make a five-year production run of 1 million units, the company had to spend $150 million up front ($150 per unit) on the plant, research, tool dies, engineering design, and so forth.

In 1993, Home Depot hypothesized that at a much lower retail price than $600, say $200 retail, it could sell 500,000 units of this product. Home Depot offered to purchase 500,000 units—for $100 each. At first the company resisted, stating that it cost them twice this price just to make them. After reflection, however, the company realized that the offer would technically be profitable on a marginal basis, and, if they didn't accept the offer, Home Depot would go to a competitor who could build a higher-volume plant and put them out of business. They accepted, and Home Depot actually ended up selling 800,000 units. Subsequently, the manufacturer used the higher volume to retool and lower their fixed costs to less than $50 per unit—far below the initial $150 per unit.

The ultimate beneficiary of this story was the consumer, who was and still is able to purchase a formerly $600 product for $200—50 percent below the original wholesale price of $300.[4]

Similar innovations (e.g., purchasing during slow periods or downtimes of manufacturers) are allowing both category busters and innovative mass merchants to continually sell top-quality goods below actual wholesale.

For example, certain stores, like Costco, don't carry any specific items on a continual basis. Costco gives open orders to name-brand manufacturers that are typically filled when their manufacturing plants have idle time. Since the manufacturer has to pay for labor and overhead anyway during these time periods, it accepts these orders at far less than normal wholesale cost. Moreover, Costco suppliers are typically required to take back (including freight) any items not sold in a short time period, so Costco is assured that it gets only the most fashionable, top-quality merchandise.

Category busters currently represent the state of the art in retailing technology, combining the best customer education and physical distribution services with the ability to continually sell first-quality merchandise at below-wholesale prices. Yet at this time no significant category buster has emerged in the wellness industry.

This is one of the greatest opportunities in wellness: creating a one-stop supersized shop, or perhaps a mall, for many wellness products and services that combines the best intellectual and physical distribution services.

Moreover, as we now examine, the category-buster opportunity can be especially lucrative for the wellness entrepreneur because of the unique nature of many wellness products.

The New Era of
Zero Marginal Product Cost

Category busters can profitably sell top-quality goods below whole-sale because of a profound change taking place on the economic landscape:

We are entering the era of effectively *zero* marginal production and physical distribution costs.

This statement has enormous implications for suppliers and retailers in every industry, but especially in wellness, because of the low or zero marginal cost of most wellness products and services (e.g., vitamins, supplements, and fitness club memberships).

The per-unit price of raw materials and automated labor has fallen so low that the amortized per-unit research and development (R&D) cost and the amortized per-unit marketing cost are almost all that matters for many types of goods.

The pipeline from raw materials to finished products travels through four stages:

1. Research and development (R&D)
2. Physical manufacturing or production
3. Intellectual distribution
4. Physical distribution

Traditionally, the largest component costs in products and services were in variable per-unit physical manufacturing costs (item 2) and physical distribution costs (item 4). Expensive raw materials and hand labor made up the bulk of manufacturing expenses and went up or down almost directly with each unit (or 1,000 units) produced. Similarly, the physical distribution costs of storing, transferring, and delivering the finished product made up the bulk of distribution expenses, and also went up or down almost directly with each unit (or 1,000 units) distributed.

But today, most of the expense in making products and services is in research and development costs (item 1) and intellectual distribution costs (item 3). This applies to almost 100 percent to new products and services like software, entertainment, communications, and especially wellness—products whose costs are composed almost entirely of R&D and marketing expenses. It even applies to traditional physical products and services like cameras, clothes, and other consumer items.

Thus, the nature of the opportunity in manufacturing and in distribution is changing—especially for products with low marginal manufacturing or physical distribution cost, like wellness products and services.

The opportunity in manufacturing is now in the design or invention of the product rather than in finding a way to simply lower the per-unit cost of physical production. And the opportunity in distribution is now in intellectual distribution versus physical distribution.

Mass merchants are the first retailers to feel this change. Millions of consumers are discovering how much more efficient it is to purchase their household consumables online or via some type of automatic, direct, factory-to-home replenishment system. In addition to lower prices resulting from bulk buying and from direct shipment from the manufacturer, the cost of physical delivery from UPS or FedEx is often lower than the time and mileage cost for consumers to lug these items home from retail stores.

And these initial savings are just the beginning. As millions more consumers embrace direct delivery of household consumables, manufacturers will eventually ship the bulk of their products directly to homes rather than stocking items at intermediate waypoints like mass merchants. Increased volume will drive prices down even further.

Anticipating this trend, we built our family residence with an enclosed glass-door front porch, so delivery people can leave items when no one is home—it has a refrigerator, heater, a hanging rod for dry cleaning, and an electronic camera that takes a picture when someone is present. Such electronic butler areas, perhaps with magnetic card access, should eventually become standard household fixtures.

At the beginning of the twentieth century, railroads dominated the national physical distribution of manufactured goods and raw materials. The railroads diminished in importance because of an us-versus-them mentality (i.e., railroads versus the transportation industry)—and thus they failed to capitalize on customer relationships and make the transition from railcars to trucks. Several mass merchants are determined not to make this same mistake.

Wal-Mart, Costco, and other merchants that specialize in physical distribution are rapidly building cyberstores like Walmart.com and Costco.com, hoping to beat the technological clock that threatens to put them out of business. But they are fighting an uphill battle, because they are collectively still focused on a shrinking component of overall cost: physical distribution. For now and for the foreseeable future, the greatest retailing opportunities will be in intellectual distribution.

Within intellectual distribution, the greatest entrepreneurial opportunities exist with wellness products and services—because consumers don't know many of these products exist and because many wellness products and services have low or effectively zero marginal-unit product cost.

The Importance of Combining High Touch with High Tech

New products and services have always required one-on-one customer education that only a trained user of the product can provide—"high touch" combined with "high tech." Some of these items were VCRs in the 1970s, discounted long-distance service and telephone answering machines in the 1980s, and, of course, better vitamins and nutritional foods in the 1990s.

Every year for the past few decades, more and more of the consumer dollar has been spent on such new products and services. Yet even with the recent growth of the category busters, there are still far too few places for the consumer to learn that such products exist, let alone how to use them.

This required combination of high touch and high tech in new products accounts for much of the growth of person-to-person direct selling companies—particularly in areas of new technology, and especially in wellness.

In the 1980s, Amway distributors launched consumer discount long-distance telephone service through an arrangement with MCI, as well as home-based electronic voice messaging through Amway's proprietary Amvox service.

In the 1990s, the most successful vitamin and nutritional supplement products were launched through direct marketing companies. Many of the most popular categories of supplement products, like ephedra (weight loss), pycnogenol (antioxidant), and echinacea (colds and flu), were available only through direct selling companies before they became off-the-shelf store products.

Led by wellness products and new technology, sales of direct selling companies in the United States alone recently rose 70 percent, from approximately $17 billion in 1995 to $29 billion in 2004. This is almost twice the sales growth rate of traditional retail stores during a similar period.

> **Despite this 70 percent increase, direct selling companies have a long growth curve ahead of them before they reach the saturation now being experienced by their competition.**

Annual U.S. direct selling sales of approximately $30 billion today amount to less than 1 percent of the more than $4.5 trillion ($4,500 billion) in sales at traditional U.S. retail stores. The sales of just one mass merchant, Wal-Mart, exceeded $300 billion in 2005.

Despite the growth of both direct selling companies and category busters, each year the backlog of unused but more efficacious consumer products continues to grow. For every household that starts using a better consumer product, from the latest digital camera to educational software to healthier foods and nutritional supplements, there seem to be dozens more new products and services that consumers haven't yet learned exist.

> **Thus, teaching consumers about such products and services—intellectual distribution—is the greatest entrepreneurial opportunity now and for the foreseeable future.**

Some direct selling companies themselves don't fully understand their own business. They still refer to end users of their product as *customers* to whom they sell versus *clients* whom they educate.

> **Direct selling distributors need to understand the differences between selling and education, and between physical and intellectual distribution, in order to fully exploit the high-touch advantage they have over traditional retailers.**

The Impact of the Internet
and Dot-Com Companies

Every businessperson today must consider the impact of the Internet—how his or her business will use the Internet and how Internet-based companies will compete with his or her business.

Wellness entrepreneurs, in particular, must understand the history of the Internet and its function in distribution—to incorporate the Internet into their business plans and to be able to answer questions about the Internet from their investors and business associates.

The Internet of today was started in the 1960s by Pentagon weapons researchers who sought to develop a system of communication that could survive the most catastrophic nuclear holocaust. This system was designed to connect disparate locations in a manner such that there was no one central processing location. Thus the surviving systems could continue indefinitely, regardless of how many others were destroyed.*

It is this distinct feature, treating every sender and every receiver as a unique client/server or mainframe unto itself, that has allowed the Internet to evolve into the incredible democratizer it is today—changing the focus of world and economic power from the organization to the individual.

The first node on the Internet was installed in 1969 at the University of California at Los Angeles, connecting computers on a network at UCLA with another computer at Stanford Research Institute. Two more nodes were soon added at the University of California at Santa Barbara and the University of Utah. This original Pentagon-funded net, called ARPANET, quickly grew to connect thousands of scien-

*It is fascinating to note, almost theologically, what happened when the Pentagon hired three different groups to begin working on the concept of the Internet in the early 1960s—at MIT, at Rand, and in the United Kingdom (at the National Physical Laboratory). When they all came together in Washington to agree on a standard in 1968, they had all come to the same conclusions regarding packets and independent client/servers, even though they had all proceeded under strict security guidelines and without knowing of each other's work.

tists and universities around the globe. A new standard for communication, called TCP/IP for short, was implemented in 1983.

Although originally funded by various government agencies to connect only defense-related scientists, in 1985 a decision was made to give access to all qualified users on-campus access, regardless of their academic discipline. This led to a nine-year program to privatize the backbone communication lines of the Internet—the backbone being the high-speed communication lines that connected one university's network to another's. By the time this privatization was accomplished, the Internet had grown to over 50,000 networks on all seven continents and outer space—even so, the Internet as we know it today had not yet begun.

In 1995 the historic decision was made to allow individual users to obtain their own Internet accounts, accounts independent of their university affiliation or the organization to which they belonged.

We noted earlier that distribution costs as a relative percent of retail prices rose over the past three decades, from about 50 percent at the end of the 1960s to about 70 percent today, and that thus the greatest fortunes during this period were made by pioneers who found better ways of distributing things versus better ways of making things. These distribution pioneers succeeded by using electronic real-time communication to connect retailers and producers with their suppliers. For example, Wal-Mart, whose computer database is now second only to that of the Pentagon,* was able to greatly reduce distribution costs while actually improving customer service—delivering just what their customers wanted, when and where they wanted it.

At the beginning of the 1990s this just-in-time technology was generally limited to large companies that could afford to establish proprietary communication links between themselves and the mainframe computers of their suppliers. This real-time high-speed communication ignited the fire of economic expansion that characterized the decade of the 1990s. The historic decision that was made in 1995, allowing individual users to obtain their own Internet accounts, had the effect of pouring gasoline on this fire.

Overnight, the economic and lifestyle benefits of instant realtime communication became available to everyone—leveling the playing field from the smallest entrepreneur to the largest Fortune 500 company. Companies that had already built their own proprietary communication systems now found themselves having to start over, since

---

*Although he is rarely remembered that way, the late Sam Walton was really the first information age CEO. After starting his company in 1962 at the age of 44, Walton attended an IBM school in computers in 1966 with the goal of hiring the smartest person in the class.

consumers (their ultimate customers), as well as thousands of smaller suppliers, were all going to be on the Internet themselves.

The results of this decision are just beginning to be felt on Main Street, from the act of waiting for a bus to the task of shopping for food. Bus stop shelters will be electronically connected so that drivers pull off the road only when passengers are waiting. Shoppers with electronically connected pantry closets will find their basket of re-plenishables (paper towels, milk, eggs) already pulled, loaded, and waiting for them when they arrive at the supermarket—or groceries may be automatically delivered to their homes.

But the results of this decision have already been felt on Wall Street, where the smart money has already anticipated what is about to oc-cur on Main Street.

Today the majority of the companies with the largest market capi-talizations (i.e., net worth) on any Top 100 Wall Street list are the high-technology "toolmakers." Toolmaker companies don't produce a single product that can feed, house, clothe, transport, heal, teach, inform, or do anything else that a consumer might ultimately want.

Instead, toolmakers make products that help *other* companies produce these ultimate consumer products even better—so much better that the toolmaker companies have become worth more than their customers (because of their value-added ability).* Some of the highest-valued companies in the U.S. stock market today (Cisco, Microsoft, Intel, Oracle, Google and Vodaphone) are companies that effectively didn't exist 20 years ago but whose combined net worth today exceeds $1 trillion.

This is the most misunderstood part of Internet dot-com compa-nies today: These and thousands of other technology-based compa-nies are toolmakers. They do not produce end-use products desired by consumers—instead, they help *other* companies that *do* produce and distribute end-use products to lower their costs and better serve their customers.

Eventually, the companies that produce and distribute end-use products or services and who have the relationship with the ultimate consumer will have the final say. Since 2001, Wal-Mart has been the largest company in the United States, in both sales and number of employees,[5] because, as John Maynard Keynes once said, "Con-sumption is the sole end of all economic activity."

Many entrepreneurs and investors have made the unfortunate mis-take of seeing the Internet as a business unto itself. The Internet is a

---

*To put it another way, the majority of the economic value or cost in finished goods today is in the tools used to make them rather than in the traditional labor and raw material costs.

powerful tool that can be used to leverage the opportunities in another business.

The success or failure of any Internet-based business, and particularly Internet-based wellness businesses, will depend mostly on the products and customers of the business itself.

Before Proceeding to the Next Chapter

Action Plan for Entrepreneurs and Wellness/Health Professionals

---

1. Changes that used to take place over centuries now take place over decades, and changes that now take place over years will soon take place over months. Analyze how this accelerating pace of change will impact each of your wellness business opportunities.

2. How do you plan to educate potential customers for your wellness business opportunity? Analyze the cost of doing so. Do you receive revenue for performing such education, or is such education a cost of doing business? If it is a cost of doing business, are the costs of such education affordable for your business?

3. *Intellectual distribution* is the process of educating customers about products and services that they either don't know exist or don't know are now affordable. *Physical distribution* is the process of helping customers physically obtain products and services that they already know they want. Analyze the type of distribution opportunity for your wellness business opportunity. Keep in mind that the greatest distribution opportunities for entrepreneurs are now in intellectual versus physical distribution.

4. Assume that category busters like Home Depot or PetSmart emerged in the wellness industry. Analyze how this would impact your wellness business opportunity. Could you survive such competition? Could you become a provider to wellness category busters?

5. What is the marginal cost of each product for your wellness business opportunity? Will it approach zero? Why or why not? Could another supplier provide the same products or services at a much lower cost? If so, how can you become this type of supplier first?

6. What role would the Internet play with respect to your wellness business opportunity? Analyze how you could utilize this powerful tool for each area. Is there another type of business or individual who could better use the Internet in supplying your customers? If so, what can you do to become this type of individual or business?

Based on your answers to these questions, think about replacing your wellness business opportunity. Look back at your notes, and the Action Plan at the end of the previous seven chapters, and reconsider all of the potential business areas you have thought about.

CHAPTER 9

Direct Selling—
How to Get Started

Th>here are many ways to create fortunes in the wellness revolution. One of my favorites, particularly for new entrepreneurs starting out, is Direct Selling, also called Network Marketing and sometimes referred to as Multilevel Marketing (MLM), based on its compensation formula.

Direct selling is very different today than it was in the past. Today:

- Quality direct selling companies and their distributors only make money when they either sell product or when the new distributors they sign up make money from actual product sales— not by convincing people to sign up for a business opportunity.

- Most quality direct selling companies today are members of the DSA (Direct Selling Association), an organization that holds member companies accountable to a very strict code of conduct that includes things like returns of unused merchandise and no false representations of potential earnings.

What I like most about direct selling is:

- Anyone can choose to become successful without having to get through the traditional hiring process or risk a large cash investment, and

- The personal growth and training provided by most direct selling opportunities.

In the 33 years since I graduated college, I've been a government official in the White House, a vice president with Citicorp, the founder and CEO of several companies, and a professor at New York University. Looking back today on all of these experiences, the place where I have seen the greatest positive impact made on the largest number of individuals has been in the direct selling industry.

Personally, I've never been directly involved with a direct sales company, or endorsed any individual company's product or business opportunity. Although I am sometimes referred to as an expert on the direct selling industry, I didn't even know what direct selling, multi-level marketing (MLM), or network marketing was when I was first invited to speak at an Amway convention in March 1991.

How the Direct Selling Industry Found Me in 1991

Ever since I first became an economist, I've been fascinated by distribution and its changing role in our economy. In February 1991, as part of the book tour for *Unlimited Wealth,* I presented my theories about distribution on the *Larry King Live!* television show. After this appearance, the first person who called me to discuss the show was Sam Walton, the founder of Wal-Mart and at that time the richest man in the world. The second person who called was Don Held, an Amway "diamond" who invited me to speak at an Amway convention in St. Louis the following month.

I remember frantically trying to understand what Amway or network marketing was all about before giving this speech. My host told me not to worry about his business, but to just concentrate on speaking about my business—economics and distribution.

When I received the itinerary for the event, I was surprised that my speech was scheduled for Saturday evening at 9:00 P.M. and that the attire was formal wear—who hires an economist to speak on a weekend, let alone on a Black Tie Saturday Night? I thought I must be at the wrong place when I came to the ballroom at 8:00 P.M. to check out the venue—the lights were low and 3,500 people were dancing to singer Crystal Gayle, who was onstage. Then, at 9:00, they turned up the lights and ran a video introduction for my speech. Everyone became silent and returned to their seats, took out pen and paper, and began taking detailed notes. After my two-hour speech, I ended up talking about economics in a hotel suite with sixty of their leaders until 6:00 A.M. the following morning. Over the next decade, the sponsoring organization distributed 10 million tapes of my speech.

Since this first encounter with the direct sales industry in March 1991, I have given approximately 200 speeches for 20 different DSA (Direct Selling Association) companies around the world—a typical venue ranges from 5,000 to 50,000 attendees. I've studied the industry and written articles about the role of direct selling in the economy, some of which are posted at www.paulzanepilzer.com. My wife and I have developed friendships over the years with many of the leaders we've met from the direct selling industry—we know hundreds of people who have made multimillion dollar fortunes as direct selling distributors. But what we like best about the industry is the life-changing impact it can have when a person first joins a direct sales organization—even if he or she doesn't make his or her fortune in direct selling.

The Elevator Man—One Man's Ex-Direct Selling Experience

In 2002, my wife and I were meeting with our architect over an addition to our ski house. The architect explained that we had three bids for the elevator, but that one of them made no sense—it was from Advanced Lifts, the best quality supplier, but for 40 percent less than the other bids. We agreed to meet with this elevator vendor onsite the following morning.

When I met Matthew Hyde, the owner of Advanced Lifts, I noticed that this 29-year-old looked like a college student but carried himself like a seasoned CEO. After we made a deal for the elevator, I asked him about his background.

"We've already met," exclaimed Matt, "back at an Amway speech in 1991. Your speech helped change my life—that's why I wanted so much to get this contract to build your elevator." Matt went on to tell me how at age 17 he dropped out of high school, got married, and had his first child. At age 19, without a high school diploma, Matt was working for an oil change store, at minimum wage, when he signed up to be an Amway distributor.

As a first-level distributor with a premier company, Matt was exposed to training, exciting people, and a whole new way of thinking without limits—particularly at very large functions where no expense was spared to hire speakers and motivators. This was the first time Matt ever witnessed firsthand what could come from education. As Matt progressed in his direct selling business, he was given the opportunity to chauffeur VIPs and attend group dinners with speakers like Norman Vincent Peale and Zig Ziglar. At age 24, Matt went full-time in his direct selling business, and reached the level of Amway "Pearl" at age 25. That's when he also started working part-time on a small stairway elevator business.

At age 27, Matt realized that although he loved direct selling, he had an even greater opportunity if he could apply the training and limitless thinking he had learned from his Amway business to his elevator business. He left Amway and decided to concentrate on the elevator business full-time. In the next few years, Matt grew his elevator company to $20 million in sales, earning his first million dollars before age 30, and many times more later on. Today, Advanced Lifts is the largest residential elevator company in the western United States, the fifth largest in the world, and Matt has his sights set on becoming a $100 million company. And he's only 34 years old!

"Baby boomers do not want to grow old in a nursing home," Matt said. "They will spend whatever it takes on things like elevators so they can live in their own homes the rest of their lives."

Matt and I sometimes speak about how much he misses direct selling and network marketing. He beams when he talks about his 62 employees and his three children, and how much he is able to teach them based on what he learned during his eight years in direct selling. He admits that he is making a lot more money now, but is not having the enormous impact that he used to have on so many people when he had thousands in his downline. Each time he reminisces, I am expecting him to tell me that he is joining a direct selling company and starting over.

Matt is typical of thousands of people I've met since 1991 who are not currently involved with a direct selling company, but who credit their direct selling experience as the pivotal event that helped them succeed somewhere else. At Matt's first direct selling convention, he heard a speaker tell him that he should read at least two new books every month—one on personal development and one on leadership—for the rest of his life. Matt has been out of direct selling for seven years but still reads two new books every month. In our interview, I asked Matt what were the three things that he learned most from direct selling. He replied:

1. Education—"Until I joined Amway, I hated learning because I didn't know the importance of education and I didn't have a high school diploma—today I have a lot of people working for me with PhDs."
2. Focus.
3. Goal setting.

Matt's story has had an impact on my life. Each time someone applies to work for my company, and their application is dismissed for a lack of education or experience, I think to myself: "Could this be another 19-year-old Matt Hyde?" Unfortunately, in a corporate-based field like health benefits, we don't have the training opportunity available for someone to start at the bottom, or a multilevel financial model that rewards us for training people even if they don't remain with our organization.

In my youth, I took opportunity and training for granted. I graduated from Wharton at a young age and had companies chasing to hire me. During my years at Citibank, I was sent to corporate retreats every few months, where professionals helped me focus on the areas in which I needed to improve. Once I became successful I realized how much of my success was because I was initially given the opportunity to prove myself, and the training to grow as I climbed the ladder. I also noticed how few of my close friends and relatives had gotten the same lucky breaks—some of whom were more talented and/or more deserving than myself.

Then, beginning in 1991, I started meeting many of the Matt Hyde's who hadn't been given their opportunity to go to Wharton or start their career at Citibank, but who had found their initial opportunity and training in the direct selling industry. This is why I am so supportive of the direct selling industry:

1. It allows anyone to succeed without having to first pass through a gatekeeper who decides their future based on their past; and

2. It allows people to make their own decision to succeed, and then to get the training they need from people who only succeed when they succeed.

The Direct Selling Industry Today

Direct selling is actually the oldest form of selling. For most of human history, direct sellers were peddlers; as the primary distributors of tools and technology-based goods, they handled both the intellectual and physical aspects of distributing their wares. This changed with the development of third-party shipping and postal systems, allowing direct sellers to concentrate more on intellectual distribution. In the nineteenth century, many direct sellers put down roots and became the general store and department store merchants of yesterday.

Technological advances over the last few decades have dramatically shifted the significance of direct selling in the new economy.

Here are a few statistics that will give you a sense of what the direct selling industry looks like today.[1]

- Direct selling is a rapidly growing industry, with U.S. sales more than doubling in the last decade. U.S. sales in 2005 were more than $30 billion. Worldwide sales are nearly $100 billion.
- There are currently more than 15 million people involved in direct selling in the United States, and nearly 50 million worldwide.
- Three quarters of the U.S. population (75 percent) have purchased goods or services through direct sales—more than the total number of those who have purchased through TV and Internet shopping combined.
- Nearly half of the U.S. population (45 percent) say they want to buy from direct sellers.
- About 90 percent of all direct sellers operate their businesses part-time.

These figures reveal only the tip of the iceberg. Direct selling is perfectly positioned to take advantage of many opportunities in the emerging wellness industry.

Direct Selling Today = Intellectual Distribution

In the 1960s and early 1970s, when the modern direct selling model was in its infancy, the business very much resembled having a store in your living room. No longer.

Direct selling today is almost wholly *intellectual distribution*. When a direct seller discusses a product or service with a consumer, they rarely hand over the product. They rely on UPS, FedEx, or some other delivery service to ship the product to the consumer. In fact, chances are good that the consumer will go online or call a 1-800 number and order the product or service direct from the company, which in turn credits the sale to the direct seller. Direct sellers are typically out of the loop of physical delivery and serve a wholly educational function.

I saw this first-hand in the early 1990s, when I developed an educational software product line. Here was a product that could make a real difference in a child's life—but telling people about it was far more expensive than producing it. We had a great new consumer product, but no way of telling the consumer it existed, and we were pretty much dead in the water—until we connected with a large network marketing company that took on the distribution of our product.

The companies that are prospering and will continue to prosper in direct selling are those that have adopted a model of having their independent distributors (also sometimes referred to as *representatives, associates,* or *brokers*) focus almost entirely on intellectual distribution, teaching people about new products and services that will improve their lives. Those that really flourish have some sort of unique or proprietary technology, product, or service. And not just unique products or services, but efficacious ones—better than anything else out there.

Traditionally, where direct selling shines is in working with what are called "information-rich" products or services. This means products or services that people don't already know about, that are not widely known or understood, and that therefore need a significant amount of information to go with them. In practical terms, this often means products or services that are of especially high quality or high value: premium products or services.

Successful direct selling companies understand the continuous shift between *Quantity Demand* and *Quality Demand,* discussed in Chapter 2, and understand that only the highest-quality products will survive over the long-term.

The reason direct selling is especially well suited to wellness premium products and services is that they really need to be sold by people who can explain them. Direct selling today is typically done person-to-person by someone who is also a user of the product or service. Unlike the car salesperson, electronics salesperson, or clothing salesperson, the direct seller is an educated, enthusiastic, experienced user of the product or service they sell.

Direct Selling Is an "Active" Medium

I am sometimes asked if the Internet will replace all the people making their living selling products. As powerful as the Internet is, it hasn't replaced the one-to-one, personal function of the modern direct seller any more than did the television infomercials of the 1980s and 1990s, and it never will. The reason for this is one of the great limits of the technology. What's lacking with the Internet is the same thing that's lacking with television: it's a passive medium.

Conventional advertising media are not effective at delivering "intellectually challenging information"—which is a euphemism for "new ideas." This is because most of our information media today are forms of passive media. Television is a very passive medium for learning, so we can't really use it to teach new ideas. It's the same with newspapers. And to a great extent, the same is true of the Internet.

Think about how you watch television: you're sitting back, you're relaxed, on your couch; the last thing you want is to be challenged with new information. In fact, when you *do* see something that challenges you, something that disagrees with what you already know or think is true, what do you do? You change the channel. This is true of most of our media. Any time you encounter something that challenges your view of the world, you change the station, turn to another page, or click the "BACK" button on your Internet browser.

When you go onto Amazon.com, you may not know exactly what book you want, but you know you are looking for a book on a particular topic, or a particular type of book. You only go to learn about a product on the Internet when you want to learn about it—that is, you already know that something like it exists.

Direct selling works because a one-to-one personal conversation is the best way to actively learn and start to consider brand new information about a completely new way of doing something.

The person who can teach or share with me a new way of doing something that's important to me is one of the most valuable people in my life. The investment advisor who shows me tools to help me maximize my wealth; the wellness advisor who introduces me to a product that will stop the ache in my knees; the financial advisor who shows me a type of health insurance that would fit my needs; these are people whose services I value.

I do business with people whose services might cost a bit more than what I might find on the Internet, but because they're always teaching me something or adding some value, they're more than worth it. The more new products that come along, the more I need these people to advise me and educate me.

The Internet will soon take over the information function of teaching people things they already know they want to learn, and it will do that better, faster and in far more detail than ever before possible. But the really vital sales function of teaching people about things they *don't yet know* they want to learn—because they don't yet know they're available—will always be an educational model that will function best person-to-person.

Direct selling is the single most effective medium we have today for teaching people about new products and services that will improve their lives—either products and services they didn't know existed, or ones that they didn't know had now become affordable.

The Value of Residual Income

For most people, the only way to accumulate a significant amount of wealth is through passive income, which is another term for residual income. Residual income is income that continues to flow after the work that created it has been completed—income that is, in other words, *residue* remaining from the original effort.

The way you achieve a residual income flow is to create some sort of property, whether real or intellectual, that continues to yield cash flow to you year after year, long after the initial work is completed.

In real estate, you work hard to put together a good deal; once you have it completed and the property is in the condition you want, you get the income flow from it month after month. This was the original meaning of "royalties," because only the royalty (i.e., kings and queens) were in a position to own large amounts of land and derive residuals from the people dwelling on it.

In 1989, after I had been successful at developing commercial real estate, I decided it was time to explore the world of intellectual property. I began writing books, and also created a publishing company to develop and acquire intellectual properties for publication on the Internet. Now, with a number of strong-selling books in print, every month I receive royalties for work I did more than 10 years ago.

This is a critical distinction, because it makes the difference between economic freedom and servitude. If your income consists exclusively of *compensation* income, then even if you work at a very high rate, such as a highly-qualified lawyer, surgeon, or corporate consultant, you are still tied to your work hours. Every day, you have to start over from scratch and earn all over again. If you stop working, you stop earning.

In contrast, a residual income stream can continue, month after month, and conceivably for a lifetime. Like the American farmers learning how to increase the productivity of their land, when you earn residual income you are greatly increasing the economic productivity of the hours you spend so that they generate yield after yield for years to come.

This is another one of the features I like best about direct selling. Not everyone is going to develop a significant piece of income-generating real estate, and not everyone is going to write a best-selling book. But direct selling provides an opportunity—open to anyone, regardless of background, specialized skills, or accrued capital worth—to create a significant residual income.

In direct selling, the "property" that you develop is the network of direct sellers whose sales volume generates a commission to you, the creator of the network.

Helping Others Succeed

With a direct selling business, your greatest financial opportunity comes from recruiting and training others, who each start their own businesses and consume your company's products or services, generating additional business volume, a small percentage of which is paid to you. They also in turn recruit and train others, who do the same.

If someone were to sell you a franchise kit for a huge fee—and franchises can cost hundreds of thousands of dollars—they would have made their money and you would now have the risk. If you then failed, who would have lost? You.

But in direct selling, if someone recruits you and then you fail, they are the one who loses. They lose all the time they spent recruiting you and training you. And all you've lost is the nominal cost to get started, typically less than $100.

Most direct selling companies subscribe to the DSA code of ethics, which says, "We will not pay you money or give you points for recruiting people; we only pay our people when the people in their organizations actually move product and sell something." Because of this, it is *structurally in the best interests of the people recruiting you* that you become as effective and as well trained as possible.

This is the opposite of the competitive traditional corporate workplace. There is a saying people have in direct selling, that "you only win when you help others win."

Helping other people make smart economic choices, create a business that they can operate from home, spend more time with their families, and build a stream of residual income at the same time—and helping *so many different people* do this—offers its own rewards, far above and beyond the monetary rewards.

How Should You Choose a Direct Selling Company?

Let's say you've decided to start and build a direct selling business in wellness. Among the hundreds of companies out there, how do you choose which one is right for you?

The Product or Service Is the Most Important Factor

Here is the cardinal rule of direct selling: *You should absolutely use and believe in the products or services you sell.*

Because the essence of direct selling is the person-to-person conversation, your own personal belief in the value of the product is essential. Here is a litmus test: Ask yourself, "Would I buy this product or service if I were not part of the sales organization?" If the answer is "No," run from the opportunity.

Are they me-too products with a "business as usual" message, or is this a product or service on the cutting edge of technology? Is there something distinctly new and unique about it? Is it a new and better way of doing something? Does it improve people's lives?

The Company and the Opportunity

Direct sellers are fond of saying that you are in business "for yourself, but not by yourself." While you are in business for yourself as a direct seller, you should choose a company that has a good support structure as well as a good product.

Support structure includes marketing materials, training opportunities, online ordering systems, operations, and, most important, emerging new products and technology.

Choosing the right company as a direct seller is actually more critical than choosing the right employer. If you make a mistake choosing an employer, say because a competitor comes out with a better product, you can always transfer to the competitor and distribute their superior product to your customers. But if you have already built a direct selling business with thousands of consumers in your downline, you cannot simply call them up and transfer en masse to a new direct selling supplier.

You should assess the background, experience, and strength of the corporate principals. What is their track record? How long has this company been in business, and what businesses have they run prior to this one?

How committed are they to providing the best in information, training, and education? One of the greatest strengths of direct selling lies in the extent to which it develops you personally and both broadens and deepens your skills. Are they using the latest, best technology? What does their Internet presence tell you?

Direct selling is a business vehicle especially well suited for global expansion. What is the company's present international exposure, and what are their plans for further international expansion?

You will probably find reams of information about the company on their web site, as well as in their printed and audio-video literature. In addition to company-generated material, before you decide upon a company, talk with others who've had direct experience with this company to verify the information and get as much perspective as you can.

When you choose a direct selling company, you're not simply affiliating with a supplier—you're selecting a partner for your business.

The Direct Selling Association (DSA)

A company you choose should either be a member of the Direct Selling Association (DSA), or preparing themselves for membership if they are a new company. The DSA is the trade organization that represents direct selling corporations.

The company should subscribe to the DSA Code of Ethics, which requires, among other things:

1. Nominal start-up costs

2. Optional purchases for inventory or materials

3. All income is earned based on the actual sale of products and services to the end user; in other words, there are no monies paid for the sheer act of recruiting ("head-hunting" fees)

4. Product buy-back policy, so that the company will allow you to return unsold inventory in saleable condition, purchased within, say, the past 6 to 12 months, usually for 90 percent or more of the price you paid.

For more information on such basic criteria, refer to the web site of the Direct Selling Association (www.dsa.org). The DSA publishes a list of member companies, and all DSA member companies pledge to uphold and abide by the DSA Code of Ethics.

The Final Criterion—
Patience and Expectations

Because there are so many examples of ordinary people achieving extraordinary economic results in direct selling, newcomers to the business sometimes embark on their new career with unrealistic expectations.

One hallmark of a mature, high-quality direct selling company is that the personnel will present the income opportunity as a serious commitment that will yield reasonable results when pursued with commitment for a reasonable length of time. It is not, in other words, a vehicle for getting rich quick. However, it is definitely a potential vehicle for getting rich.

So, how long does it take? Most responsible direct sellers will advise that you should expect to put in consistent effort for two to five years, and in this time be able to create a significant stream of long-term residual income.

Before Proceeding to the Next Chapter

Action Plan for Entrepreneurs and Wellness/Health Professionals

1. Analyze how direct selling fits into the business plan for your wellness business. Could your products or services be distributed through direct selling?

2. What makes your products or services uniquely qualified for direct selling, and if they are not, is there something you could do to make them more attractive to direct selling professionals?

3. If your wellness business is already in direct selling, carefully re-read this chapter asking yourself the key questions raised in "How Should You Choose a Direct Selling Company" about the:

   Product

   Company and its support systems

   Owners or managers.

4. Based on your answers to these questions, think about replacing your chosen individual areas of wellness business opportunity.

CHAPTER 10

Staking Your Claim:
The Next Millionaires

In narrowing down your possibilities for entering this trillion dollar industry, you are probably continually asking yourself: where is the best place for me to stake my claim in this emerging $1 trillion industry that does incredible good?

Should you become a manufacturer of wellness products like Steve Demos (SILK soymilk) or Paul Wenner (Gardenburger)? Should you become a provider of wellness services like Jill Kinney (Club One) or Dr. Frank Yanowitz (The Fitness Institute)? Should you become a specialized wellness consultant distributing the best wellness products to your friends and associates—focusing on intellectual versus physical distribution? Should you become an investor, or even an investment banker, specializing in this emerging dynamic industry? Or should you become a tool provider for others who enter these and other wellness professions, like Dr. Tod Cooperman (ConsumerLab .com)? What about pursuing more than one of these opportunities simultaneously?

On an individual level, I cannot answer these questions for you any more than a surgeon could tell you what type of operation you should have without first doing his or her own individual diagnosis. But I can lay out some general parameters to help you assess your prior experience and answer these questions for yourself.

It is first important to understand that the wellness industry will encompass parts of virtually every sector of our economy—from the food we eat and the medical care we desire to the air we breathe and the bedding we sleep on at night. You need not necessarily be in the wellness industry directly (i.e., food, medicine) to join the wellness gold rush.

Many of the wellness fortunes will be made by bankers, lawyers, accountants, marketing executives, distributors, insurance brokers, and thousands of other professionals who provide tools and services to the wellness industry.

Providing Tools and Services to the Wellness Industry

Since 1876, the term *gold rush* has been a euphemism for staking your claim to "sudden wealth in a new or lucrative field."[1] But many of the fortunes made during the California gold rush weren't made mining gold—they were made by businesspeople providing services to the gold rush industry. The names Henry Wells and George Fargo are synonymous with the California gold rush industry, yet neither of them ever mined an ounce of gold. Both were freight-forwarding agents in western New York before cofounding the American Express Company in 1850 to handle freight west of Buffalo.[2] In 1852 they decided to focus their shipping expertise on the needs of a group of their customers, the California miners, and formed Wells Fargo & Company. Over the years, their connections with stagecoaches, transporting gold, and financing miners led them to become leaders in general banking, travel, and insurance—they (and their successors) introduced the American Express Money Order in 1882, the American Express Travelers Cheque in 1891, and the American Express Travel Department in 1915. American Express actually remained in the freight-forwarding business until 1970.

In extending credit to miners, shipping their produce, and providing banking services, Wells and Fargo ended up knowing more about the gold mining industry than most of their successful gold miner customers.

In a similar vein, certain providers of services to the wellness industry today have already emerged as wellness professionals, even though they do not manufacture or distribute wellness products themselves.

As you begin your wellness business, whether in network marketing or wellness manufacturing, take note of your challenges and ask yourself if you think others pursuing the same path are having similar challenges. If the answer

is yes, make a list of tools you could develop to help yourself and others on their way to success.

You may find out, as did Dr. Bob Hoffman in building The Masters Circle, or as did Peter and Kathie Davis in building IDEA and ACE, that you'll be more successful helping train or manage others to run their business than in actually running the same type of business yourself.

The Masters Circle

The Masters Circle is a premier leadership coaching organization run by Doctors of Chiropractic for Doctors of Chiropractic. It allows each individual chiropractor to function as if he or she had a staff of hundreds—helping them manage their practice, recruit patients, negotiate with suppliers, and most important, analyze and keep abreast of new developments in their profession.

The Masters Circle story is but one example of what will emerge in all areas of the wellness industry as some wellness professionals realize they have a greater calling educating and training other wellness professionals than in just practicing wellness.

Dr. Bob Hoffman remembers his first chiropractic experience, at age 18. He had developed a critical case of mononucleosis, with lemon-size swellings, and his family medical doctor ordered him quarantined for four to six months. As luck would have it, his mother attended a luncheon club speech by a chiropractor and asked the speaker if he could help her son.

Bob was amazed when he sat in the waiting room of the chiropractor. Patients walked in limp and sad, and walked out strong and happy. Bob had never seen a doctor's office like this. Bob was his last patient of the day, so the chiropractor was able to sit down and explain both mononucleosis and chiropractic care.

The X-ray of Bob's spine looked like a roadmap, and when Bob got his first adjustment he "instantly felt a rush, as if my body was just reconnected to the universe." He began to sweat profusely until all his clothes were soaked—which the chiropractor told him was an excellent sign. That night he had his first perfect sleep in months and when he awoke the next day his swellings were down 50 percent.

Bob returned to the chiropractor every two days for two weeks until he was completely healed. The chiropractor sent him back to the medical doctor for bloodwork, which showed normality, and the MD explained that he must have originally misdiagnosed the mononucleosis since he had never a seen a patient recover that quickly.

Three years later, when Bob graduated college, the same chiropractor sponsored Bob for chiropractic school at Columbia Institute of Chiropractic. Bob graduated in 1978 and began his practice on Long Island. In chiropractic school, Bob had been taught that the goal of a successful practice was to have 100 patient visits per week in 10 years—Bob reached this level in four months. By 1981 Bob was up to 700 visits per week and soon had the most successful chiropractic practice in New York state. Professionally, he served on multiple boards and was later elected president of the International Chiropractors Association.

By the early 1990s, Bob had three full-time Doctors of Chiropractic (DCs) working for him, and his practice had made him a millionaire many times over. Looking back over his first 20 years, he says: "I was constantly reinventing my practice over this period, adjusting it to changing times and new technology, without ever losing its purpose or the history and heritage of chiropractic."

During his years in practice, Bob became friends with Dr. Larry Markson. In 1981, after 20 years as a chiropractor, Larry broke his elbow and couldn't practice chiropractic, so he started consulting other chiropractors while he healed. He found that he was so good at consulting that he never returned to practicing, and built a successful chiropractic consulting business known as Markson Management Services (MMS). He was joined by another well-known chiropractor, Dr. Dennis Perman,* and together they grew their consulting business into The Masters Circle.

In 2000, The Masters Circle had 270 DC members paying approximately $7,000 a year each for consulting services—with each chiropractor member receiving service as if he or she personally had this $2 million staff coaching their business. But wellness was taking off, and something was needed to take The Masters Circle, and the businesses of their chiropractor members, to the next level.

The next level occurred when Larry and Dennis made a deal with Bob Hoffman, the most successful chiropractor in the state, to become president and CEO of The Masters Circle. Looking back on the last six years, Bob reflects: "At first, I was reluctant, but now I re-

---

*I first met Dr. Dennis Perman in Hawaii in 1991 when he was the head trainer for speaker/author and personal coach Anthony Robbins.

alize that no matter how many people I was able to help in my practice, it pales in comparison to how many people I am able to help now by helping thousands of chiropractors."

Under Bob's leadership, The Masters Circle has grown almost 400 percent in less than 6 years, to 1,000 DC members each paying an average of $9,000 per year. In our interview, Bob pointed out that the average practice of his members, which was already $300,000 per year, increased 27 percent last year alone.[3] Or put another way, "each chiropractor paying $9,000 a year got a ten times (1,000 percent) return on their investment in The Masters Circle."

Each member of The Masters Circle receives the following benefits.

1. **Five National Seminars**—Each seminar is two to three days long, and teaches the latest techniques, personal development skills, success principles, leadership, business acumen, and current healthcare trends. Seminars are attended by both DC members and their staff.

2. **Year-Round Think Tank**—Eighteen chiropractic consultants available by appointment or at open hours each day for consultation or problem solving.

3. **125 Mini-Seminars**—These virtual seminars, called PODs (for Practical Open Discussions), are telephone conferences attended by up to 20 members at a time. They consist of a 15-minute, single-topic lecture with "cross-podination" afterward. Some members take two to three PODs a year and some take two to three PODs a week.

4. **Eight-page Monthly Newsletter**—Secrets to creating the practice of your dreams.

5. **MasterTalk**—Audio magazine sent every month

6. **Monthly Statistical Analysis**—Computerized statistical analysis of each member's practice each month, analyzing retention, practice trends, strengths, and weaknesses.

7. **MasterMemo**—A monthly editorial and member update from Dr. Larry Markson.

8. **Chiropractic Assistant Newsletter**—A monthly newsletter for Chiropractic Assistants.

9. **Weekly E-column every Monday morning.**

10. **Online Bulletin Board**—A place where members can post anything they wish and contact and share ideas with other members.

In 2000, the average member of The Masters Circle received coaching, training, and education equivalent to his or her each having a staff of 10 people costing $2 million. Today, each member receives the equivalent of having a staff of 100 people costing $9 million.

In 2004, The Masters Circle (TMC) started a new education and training program for CAs (Chiropractic Assistants); last year they graduated their first class of 268 certified CAs in full cap and gown.

Bob Hoffman really lights up when he talks about what's coming next. He, Dennis, and Larry realize that as important as chiropractic care is, it is just one component in the emerging $1 trillion wellness industry. Looking back on what TMC has been able to bring to the chiropractic profession, Bob wants to see similar coaching, training, and professionalism made available to all wellness professionals— TMC already has a few non-DC members, including an MD and an Emergency Room nurse. Bob is currently traveling around the world developing a plan to bring what TMC has learned to the greater wellness community.

The story of TMC is but one example of how successful wellness practitioners often have a duty, and a higher calling, to become teachers and trainers to their chosen profession within the wellness industry.

Fitness Education—Training an Army of Wellness Professionals

If you've ever spoken with a Personal Trainer, you've already been touched by Peter and Kathie Davis, founders of IDEA and ACE, who built an army of 20,000 fitness professionals and brought professionalism, standards, and education to the fitness industry. Their story is an inspiration to every wellness entrepreneur for every aspect of the emerging $1 trillion wellness industry.

Peter and Kathie Davis met when they both attended a tennis camp at age 13. Their meeting turned into an eventual courtship and marriage and had a profound impact on the health and wellness of the world.

"Fitness and sports have been a part of our lives ever since we were kids," says Peter. "We both competed in basketball and tennis throughout our teen years. We attended San Diego State University (SDSU) to play on the women's and men's tennis teams." After graduating college in 1979 and 1980, Kathie started teaching aerobic dance and training other instructors, and Peter coached the men's tennis team at UCSD.

Kathie immediately recognized the need for aerobics instructors to exchange information. And Peter, a business graduate from SDSU, often talked about starting a fitness-oriented business. But it took them a few years to turn their talking into reality. Their membership organization, IDEA Health and Fitness Association, was born modestly in 1982.

"We were just out of college," Peter recalls. "IDEA was our first real job. The whole thing was operated out of our spare bedroom. It took us quite a while to have enough revenue to move into an office space. We did everything ourselves—opened the mail, answered the telephone, did the marketing."

While most people today recognize the importance of fitness, in 1982 things were different. Consumers were much less aware of how to safely and effectively exercise, and fitness professionals had few, if any, professional tools and resources. For example, to provide music for a class, instructors frequently played a stack of 45 rpm records on a turntable. Classes were often taught in stocking feet, since the importance of proper footwear was not yet understood and shoes for high-impact aerobics did not exist. Personal training was mostly reserved for celebrities and competitive athletes; it had not yet arrived for the general consumer.

The goal of IDEA then was to help fitness instructors gain access to reliable professional information. "We started by sending the first IDEA newsletter to a membership of 300, and later we created the not-for-profit IDEA Foundation [now the American Council on Exercise, or ACE] to offer the industry's first certification," says Kathie. "In addition, IDEA introduced the industry's first Code of Ethics and the first awards to recognize professional excellence in the fitness field." In 1989 the organization hosted the first conference for personal trainers and the following year a newsletter was created for trainers which later turned into a magazine. Now personal training has become IDEA's largest membership category, with 11,000 members.

Since 1982, IDEA has provided health and fitness professionals with unbiased data, pertinent information, educational resources, career development, and industry leadership. IDEA's membership includes personal trainers, mind-body professionals, program and fitness directors, business owners and managers, and group fitness instructors. It is focused on providing practical resources that are based on science.

The company today has more than 20,000 members in over 80 countries. The original newsletter has grown into *IDEA Fitness Journal,* the most respected publication for fitness professionals. Attendance at IDEA's annual World Fitness Convention has grown to over 5,000, making it the world's largest educational event for health and fitness professionals. Another 2,500 professionals attend the IDEA Fitness Fusion, and IDEA Personal Trainer education conferences. IDEA's purpose is to "Inspire the World to Fitness" and motivate its members to reach sedentary populations. Training and certification programs are constantly being added for new areas such as mind-body fitness, wellness, yoga, Pilates, and Gyrotonic integrated fitness.

The skyrocketing growth of IDEA did not come without tireless work and dedication, and the couple's mutual respect for each other's areas of expertise. As executive director, Kathie is responsible for content, industry, and educational issues, and overseeing information presented at conventions and in IDEA publications. She also works with public relations and the media. As chief executive officer, Peter handles business and the strategic-planning aspects, sales and marketing, financing, and relationships with manufacturers.

While today they are respected, competent business leaders, they struggled to learn in the early days. "The biggest obstacle was starting a company (2 years out of college) with no experience in publishing or event planning," says Peter. "We made mistakes and learned as we went but whatever was in front of us was no match for our unbridled enthusiasm and passion."

Peter and Kathie always followed an important business tenet: listen to your customers. For almost 25 years they have continually reached out to IDEA members and industry leaders to keep their fingers on the pulse of the fitness industry. They have also listened to the needs of the customers of their customers—consumers who are increasingly inactive, overweight, and overwhelmed by misinformation about fitness and wellness.

The Davises are very excited about the organization's next evolutionary path: exploring the inner connection between mind, body, and spirit in a quest toward optimal wellness. They have created resources such as the Inner IDEA conference to help professionals explore the exciting new science and benefits of holistic mind-body-spirit practices.

Peter and Kathie feel so strongly about the importance of body-mind-spirit that they are starting a wellness program for their staff. "We have always encouraged our staff to walk or run during the day by having showers available," says Kathie. "However, now we will also be having a wellness room for meditation, yoga or other quiet activities as well as wellness lectures, inspirational films and outside activities including social and volunteer opportunities."

"We now know that if someone is deconditioned and sedentary, it is important to focus on what is happening inside the person as well as on the outside," says Peter. "To get the greatest results, health professionals should use a holistic approach to help people achieve wellness."

What's the future of IDEA and wellness? "We believe that there will be some form of mindfulness in all forms of exercise in the next five years," Peter forecasts. "We look forward to sharing more of our enthusiasm and passion for holistic wellness with our members, and the world."

The Davises really light up when they talk about the recent involvement of their children (Jason, 22, and Kelli, 18) in their business. "Jason and Kelli have caught the passion to make fitness happen because they see a tremendous need to help unhealthy people," says Kathie. As the world becomes connected through the Internet, the kids have the vision to take IDEA and Inner IDEA to a younger generation.

Peter and Kathie cofounded IDEA in 1982 on one basic premise: to help millions of people lead healthier, happier lives by fostering professionalism in the health and fitness industry. They are extremely grateful for what they, their 35 staff members, and their 20,000 professional members—who touch millions of lives every day—have accomplished. But, sadly, they recognize that despite their collective accomplishments, much more remains to be done today to bring wellness to the world than when they started out back in 1982.

Each specialty and subspecialty within the wellness industry will eventually require the same professionalism, standards, and continuing education that Peter and Kathie Davis have brought to personal fitness.

Staking Your Claim in Wellness Finance

For financially oriented individuals, the entrepreneurial opportunity to convert households from sickness to wellness-oriented health insurance is as great an opportunity as is the entire wellness business itself. This opportunity today parallels the opportunity seized 25 years ago by Art L. Williams, an ordinary person who changed the face of the life insurance industry and is now worth an estimated $400 million.[4]

The son of a high school football coach, Art L. Williams was born in Waycross, Georgia, and grew up following in his father's footsteps. Tragically, while Art was in college studying to be a football coach his father died of a heart attack, leaving his family penniless and with very little life insurance. Later on, after marrying his high school sweetheart and starting his own family, Williams was determined not to make the same mistake.

When he went out as an ordinary customer to purchase life insurance, Art Williams was surprised to find how much the consumer was then being taken advantage of by the life insurance industry.

Between 1950 and 1980, major life insurance companies sold mostly whole life policies, primarily to working-class men and women. In those days, life insurance companies recruited individuals to sell their product in each local or ethnic community to their friends and neighbors. Rather then selling their whole life product on its financial merits, agents were taught to go for the emotional sale— which meant sitting down at the prospect's kitchen table and telling the spouse: "If he loves you, he'll sign right here to protect you and the children if something were to happen to him." What the agent didn't tell the prospect was that the same or better coverage could be had for a fraction of the cost elsewhere and that the agent was earning a commission equal to or greater than the first full year of payments.

A whole life insurance policy is, in effect, an ordinary term insurance policy with a mandatory low-interest savings account. For example, a $100,000 death-benefit term or ordinary life insurance policy for a healthy male, age 30, might cost about $1,400 per year. A whole life policy for this same amount ($100,000) typically costs about $5,000 per year—$1,400 for the term or death-benefit portion and $3,600 for the "whole" portion, which partially accrued in the cash value of the policy. Theoretically, the insured would pay $5,000 per year and receive the $1,400 per annum worth of term insurance ($100,000 death benefit) on dying, plus a "cash value increase" each year on the $3,600 extra payment for each year they lived. Eventually, after 25 years, the cash value amount of the policy would accrue to $100,000 and the policy would self-fund—meaning that the insured would not have to pay any further annual premiums and would simply receive their own $100,000 in cash value when they died.

That's the theory. In reality, (1) there was typically no cash value increase the first one or two years since the insurance company would pay $3,600 to $7,200 in commission to the salesperson; (2) only a percentage of the $3,600 would be applied to the cash value increase each year after that; and (3) a very low amount of interest would be paid on the accruing cash value (typically 2 to 3 percent). What the insurance salespeople never told the unsuspecting prospect (and may not have known themselves) is that the prospect could purchase the same amount of term or straight life insurance from the same company for $1,400 per year and deposit the same $3,600 in a federally insured bank account—and that by doing this, the same $5,000 per year would have grown to almost $200,000 in 25 years, guaranteed by the U.S. federal government, versus only $100,000 in 25 years guaranteed by a private insurance company.*

When a cousin explained this to Art L. Williams, he not only became a smart customer by purchasing a term policy and investing the difference, he started selling term insurance part-time to his friends and neighbors.

Williams developed a straight-talking "buy term and invest the difference" approach to educate his customers. It worked so well that

---

*Depositing $300 per month ($3,600 per hear) in a federally insured 5.25 percent interest savings account would yield a balance of $185,474.03 in 25 years. At an interest rate of 7 percent, which might equal the rate of long-term bonds issued by the same insurance company, the balance would be $243,021.51—far more than the $100,000 paid back by the life insurance company on a whole life policy.

soon he quit his job as a high school football coach and became a full-time insurance salesperson.

In 1977, along with 85 like-minded insurance agents, he started A.L. Williams & Associates to promote his "buy term and invest the difference" philosophy. They quickly recruited thousands of accountants, lawyers, and financial planners as their agents.

By 1990, Williams & Associates had a sales force of 225,000 and was the largest seller of individual life insurance in the United States—more than twice the size of his two nearest competitors (New York Life and Prudential) combined.

Eventually, the major life insurance companies were forced to end their misleading sales practices and offer products financially competitive to those of A.L. Williams. With more than $300 billion of life insurance in force, Williams sold his company to Primerica in 1990.[5]

A.L. Williams was successful because the numbers clearly demonstrated the superiority of the "buy term and invest the difference" approach—even in cases where the prospect had to pay penalties or lose cash value by terminating an existing whole life insurance policy. Another reason A.L. Williams agents were successful is that after their clients saw how much money they could save each year, this money was typically invested in annuities and other products sold by Williams & Associates—products that often paid higher commissions than ordinary term life insurance.

As illustrated in Chapter 7, a similar opportunity exists for you to convert your wellness customers from traditional sickness-only health insurance to wellness-oriented high deductible health insurance, using the slogan "Buy High-Deductible Health Insurance and invest the difference in your wellness."

Today, when consumers save up to $3,000 per year on their High-Deductible Health Insurance, they get to invest the $3,000 difference in something much more important to their family than just money—their continued wellness. Wellness product distributors can introduce High-Deductible Health Insurance to their healthy clients and then explain how they can invest all or part of the annual savings in wellness products and services to stay well.

The opportunity to educate consumers about "Buy High-Deductible Health Insurance and invest the difference" is not being seized by the existing insurance brokerage community. Rather, new insurance distribution mechanisms or companies, like www.zaneben.com or www.payforchiro.com, are emerging to distribute this product.

The reason for this is that in most cases, when a new technology comes along, it is often resisted by status quo companies with much to lose—in an often-futile attempt to stop their losses, they bury their heads in the sand until it's too late. Many insurance agents selling $5,000 premium, low-deductible health insurance policies that pay a $1,000 commission will try to avoid switching clients to $2,000 premium High-Deductible Health Insurance policies that pay only a $400 commission. Eventually, they will pay the price for their shortsightedness when their misled customers take all their insurance business—health, life, auto, and homeowner's—elsewhere.

This opportunity to "Buy High-Deductible Health Insurance and invest the difference" may be seized by wellness product distributors outside of the insurance industry that don't even get paid for their efforts, because only licensed insurance agents are allowed to receive or share commissions.

Wellness distributors can profit simply by teaching their customers about wellness-oriented health insurance—because the customer switching to High-Deductible Health Insurance has up to $3,000 per annum more disposable income with which to purchase his or her wellness products and services.

Getting Started

By now you should have noticed a pattern in the career of each wellness entrepreneur mentioned thus far. Each had different educational backgrounds, work experiences, and personal encounters before everything in their lives came together and launched their wellness careers. However, and more important,

Most wellness entrepreneurs started their businesses after first being a customer and finding that their wellness needs were not being met.

Steve Demos couldn't find good-tasting vegetarian protein products, so he started to make tofu and run a vegetarian delicatessen before discovering his fortune making SILK soymilk from the same raw material. Paul Wenner's vegetarian restaurant flopped, and he founded Gardenburger, Inc. only when his former customers could no longer get their vegetarian burgers at his restaurant. Dr. Tod Cooperman founded a company to evaluate consumer healthcare plans, which led him to founding ConsumerLab.com to evaluate nutritional supplements. Dr. Frank Yanowitz had his own personal wellness crisis before committing himself to The Fitness Institute. As a top athlete, Jill Kinney knew what she wanted in a fitness club *before* she began opening individual public fitness clubs and then stumbled into her fortune in managing private fitness clubs for large employers.

In the software industry during the past two decades, many of the fortunes were made by businesspeople who originally started out to create a computerized operating system for their own companies and then found out they could make more money by selling operating systems to their competitors than they could running their original business. Similarly, many of the fortunes in wellness will be made by wellness customers who, on finding that their particular wellness need is not being met by the marketplace, start a company to serve that need for others with the same problem—just as A. L. Williams did for cost-effective life insurance.

The important thing is to get started now in almost any area of the wellness industry and see where your past experiences and knowledge take you.

It may actually be easier than you think, since you already have a headstart based on what you've been doing up until today, as wellness opportunities permeate almost every profession, from A to Z.

Where All Professions and the Wellness Revolution Meet

An *accountant* or a *banker* could combine a wellness distribution business with the opportunity to convert customers to HSAs, HDHP and wellness-oriented health insurance, or just distribute wellness-oriented health insurance as a vehicle to obtain more clients for his or her accounting/banking business (as explained in Chapter 7).

A *cook* might learn how to make healthy versions of popular foods and then open a wellness restaurant, start a wellness catering company, or become a wellness food manufacturer.

Dentists could focus on wellness opportunities to sell more services within their own profession—dentists are already ahead of the medical industry because much of their practice is already focused on prevention.

An *economist,* like me, might focus on identifying trends in the emerging $1 trillion wellness industry, and then market this knowledge to other wellness professionals.

Farmers, or even *home gardeners,* as noted in Chapter 4, should start growing healthier foods like edamame and teaching their customers how to use them.

Hairdressers could start using healthier products in their practice, then start a wellness distribution business to sell these products to their customers.

Insurance agents could follow the example of Art Williams by leading their customers to wellness-oriented health insurance and then market other, more profitable insurance products (e.g., auto, home, life) once they've earned the trust of their customers.

A *journalist* could focus on wellness products or wellness companies, becoming known for expert reporting on the industry that people will want to hear about the most in the coming decade.

Lawyers might similarly focus on any one of hundreds of separate aspects of the wellness or wellness finance industries, developing expertise that will bring them new clients.

Massage therapists are in the ideal position to teach wellness and to begin distributing wellness products to their customers.

Nurses could reorient their practice toward preventing disease instead of treating the symptoms of disease, and combine their reoriented practice with a wellness distribution or wellness consulting business.

An *optician* could similarly focus more on treating the effects of aging and failing eyesight before they occur, and use this new focus to obtain new customers or to start a related wellness distribution business.

Physicians are obviously in an excellent position to retool themselves for almost any area of the wellness industry—starting with proactively seeking healthy people and teaching them how to avoid becoming patients.

Salespeople can either distribute wellness products themselves or just become versed in the latest wellness technology, since that's what will be of most interest to their clients—successful selling in every field starts with building credibility in the eyes of the client.

Teachers similarly need to know what is of most importance to their students—and, as explained in Chapter 8, because of the recent shift from physical distribution to intellectual distribution, teachers may be especially qualified for careers in wellness distribution.

Finally, *veterinarians* are in a unique position to promote human wellness to their customers and animal wellness to their patients. In fact, veterinarians are often more qualified than physicians when it comes to nutrition and supplementation. Unlike medical schools, veterinary schools of medicine have always taught the importance of nutrition, and veterinary schools pioneered the research in many of the human supplements we use today (e.g., glucosamine, major minerals).

Become an Investor in Wellness

The best advice I can give you about becoming an investor in wellness is to first become a customer of any company in which you are considering making an investment.

There is simply no substitute for using the products yourself when it comes to evaluating the long-term potential for a company. Once you have made an investment in a company whose products you like, you should also inspect competitive products on a periodic basis. Technology changes so fast that today's Wal-Mart is often tomorrow's W. T. Grant.[6]

If you are a physician, a wellness distributor, an insurance agent, or involved in any aspect of the wellness industry, you should continuously underwrite and evaluate the products of the companies within your specific industry. Based on what you actually do within the wellness industry, you will often be the first to know when a company is about to get into trouble and the first to know when a company has an important new product.

Suppose you are an ophthalmologist performing LASIK eye surgery for your patients. Not only should you always be in the market for better lasers for your patients, you should keep an active file on every laser made and what you think about the company that makes it—from the quality of their products to their sales performance and service. In doing so, you will be the first to know which companies in your field are poised for growth and which ones will fail, either because of poor management or new competition. If you are not capable of underwriting these companies yourself, you should team up with an investment professional more capable of using your firsthand customer experience to evaluate the stock value of the company. Keep in mind that the fact that you like a product is not by itself enough reason to invest in the company that makes it. The product you enjoy may be only a small percentage of the company's sales and thus have little bearing on the overall performance of the company.

One of my hobbies is personal computer software and hardware—I love to tinker with my computers and purchase a new PC or peripheral accessory almost weekly. I especially enjoy researching the "latest and greatest" new PC gadget and then finding it at the best available price. One venture capital firm invites me to speak to their investment professionals about what new PC toys I have recently purchased, why I bought each particular item or brand, and where I had purchased it. They told me that my firsthand product and purchasing experiences are sometimes more valuable to them than research done by their analysts.

As an economist, it is always amazing to me how hard lawyers, doctors, dentists, engineers, scientists, and other professionals work to make money in their chosen profession—only to see much of it lost when they blindly turn it over to an "investment professional" who claims to "know" which stocks are going to increase in price. If there were such a person who actually knew which stocks to purchase, why wouldn't that person be investing solely for themselves, and why would they dilute their efforts by sharing their information with you?

The Wharton Secret

However, I didn't have this belief back in 1973 when, as an undergraduate physics student, I decided to study business in order to become rich. Upon graduation, I entered the prestigious Wharton Graduate School of Business to get my MBA. When I arrived at Wharton, I heard that a course called Speculative Markets was the place to learn about the stock market and a surefire scientific method for getting rich very quickly. It was such a popular course that you had to wait until your last semester before graduation to get into the class.

On my first day of class in Speculative Markets, the professor asked us not to tell anyone what I am about to tell you—a secret I kept to myself for 26 years. First, he explained that there was absolutely no

Days at work	Number of clients	Value of their $1,000 potential investment if they had followed your advice
1	10,000	$ 1,000
2	5,000	$ 2,000
3	2,500	$ 4,000
4	1,250	$ 8,000
5	625	$ 16,000
6	312	$ 32,000
7	156	$ 64,000
8	78	$128,000

way to get rich very quickly by picking stocks unless you were willing to violate criminal-penalty insider trading laws. But, he continued, when we graduated from Wharton, many wealthy people outside of Wall Street would wrongly believe that people like us, with a Wharton degree, did know which stocks to purchase to quickly get rich. He then explained how we could individually take advantage of this situation to get rich as new stockbrokers on Wall Street.

On your first day of work as a stockbroker, you purchase a list of 10,000 wealthy people along with their fax numbers. You send 5,000 people a fax stating: "I'm John Doe, and I know that General Motors (GM) stock is going *up* tomorrow, so I recommend you take $1,000 and purchase the following option." Simultaneously, you send the other 5,000 people a fax stating that the opposite will occur: "I'm John Doe, and I know that GM is going *down* tomorrow, so I recommend you take $1,000 and purchase the following option." At the end of the next day, depending on which direction GM went, you rip up the list of the 5,000 people who got the wrong advice.

Then you send 2,500 people on your remaining list of 5,000 the following fax: "I'm John Doe. If you took my advice yesterday regarding GM your $1,000 investment would now be worth $2,000. I know that Ford is going *up* tomorrow, so I recommend you take your $2,000 and purchase the following option." You send the other 2,500 people a fax stating that Ford is going *down*. Again, the next day, you send 1,250 of the 2,500 people who received the correct advice a fax stating: "I'm John Doe. If you took my advice yesterday regarding Ford, your $2,000 investment would now be worth $4,000. I know that Chrysler is going *up* tomorrow, so I recommend you take your $4,000 and purchase the following option." The other 1,250 people get a fax stating that Chrysler is going *down*. And so on, and so on, until you have remaining 78 individuals who have irrefutable proof that you "know" which stocks to purchase. Then you start making appointments for lunch and figure out what you want to do with 78 high-net-worth people who think you are the smartest person on Wall Street that ever lived—and who are probably willing to mortgage their homes and give you their life savings on almost any basis if you will agree to invest it for them.

The moral of this story, as my professor explained, is that when you meet someone who can demonstrate to you that he or she knows which stocks to pick to quickly get rich, you are merely one of the 78 out of 10,000 people (less than 1 percent) at the end of a similar chain of events. To make money on Wall Street, there is simply no substitute for taking a long-term position based on good research about a company—its management team, its capitalization structure, and, most important, its products. And the best way to know about those products is to invest within a field in which you already have great product knowledge—your own chosen profession.

Staking Your Claim through Your Religion

Some readers may desire to stake their claim outside of the business arena. Perhaps they wish to spread wellness through their church, mosque, or synagogue. These readers need to understand that wellness has always been part of our great religions and how wellness is already being embraced by some congregations. Readers, clergypersons, and church officers need to understand the connection between wellness and religion.

> **All wellness entrepreneurs need to understand the connection between wellness and religion in order to better motivate their customers to choose and stick to a wellness lifestyle. Additionally, some wellness entrepreneurs may want to combine spreading wellness through their church with their profit-making wellness business enterprise.**

The great religions of the world became great partly by addressing the secular needs of their congregants. Today, although living a wellness lifestyle of diet and exercise is a great secular need, it is ignored by most religions and religious organizations. This is because the concept of becoming closer to God by having a fit and healthy body fell out of favor in the Middle Ages as a reaction to the emphasis placed on physical appearance and beauty by Greek and Roman persecutors. Yet the founding documents of most religions demonstrate that God wants us to be well.

The story in the Bible most common to all religions—the Garden of Eden—speaks of how God made "every tree that is pleasant to the sight, and good for food."[7] This reference goes beyond just aesthetic significance—the kinds and variety of foods prescribed in the Bible contain all the vitamins, minerals, and proteins necessary for wellness.

In our time, we keep discovering "new" age-old natural remedies—from gingko to improve our memories to Saint-John's-wort to alleviate depression. These discoveries continually illuminate the famous cabalistic statement: "God creates the cure before he sends the malady."[8]

Moses Maimonides, a twelfth-century rabbi and physician in Moorish Spain, is esteemed by Jews, Christians, and Muslims alike as one of the greatest theologians of all time. Maimonides reconciled Greek philosophy with the Old and New Testaments and concluded that our obligation to be healthy was a religious obligation, a first order of priority we must undertake before we begin to know our Creator.[9]

Some religious institutions teach congregants how to control their diet. One program, the Weigh Down Diet, is based on the philosophy that overeating and gluttony are sins. Today there are many similar programs, mostly in U.S. churches, making a real difference in the lives of millions of participants.[10]

The Weigh Down Diet and similar programs stress the negative or sinful aspects of overeating. Although these programs have achieved good results, I believe the wellness answer for the majority of Americans will lie in a more positive approach.

I was raised in a Jewish family that observed religious dietary laws. We were not allowed to eat unkosher foods such as lobster, shrimp, or pork—rules I quickly abandoned when I left home for college. It wasn't until years later, when I started spending time in Israel, that I came to understand what I had missed growing up. To my observant Israeli relatives, the requirement to eat only the foods prescribed by biblical law is not seen as deprivation, but as one of God's greatest gifts. They thank God for this knowledge in prayers before and after every meal. For them, eating kosher food is one of life's greatest *mitzvahs* (good deeds).

Just as I in my youth misunderstood the purpose of keeping kosher, many people today wrongly imagine that a wellness lifestyle involves constantly saying no to things they enjoy. But wellness-oriented individuals have learned to cherish and appreciate God for their knowledge of how to take care of themselves. Through the small and reasonable disciplines of daily eating, a wellness-oriented individual, an orthodox Jew, and a practicing Muslim all experience a sense of distinction, specialness, and closeness to God.

Religious faith is the highest motivating force in the world. Wellness entrepreneurs can combine their religion with their wellness business—motivating their customers through faith to adopt and stick to a wellness lifestyle of eating healthy foods and performing regular exercise.

Visual Wellness—Affordably Eliminating Preventable Blindness

Some readers may desire to stake their claim as a nonprofit—doing incredible good solely for the sake of doing incredible good. One such wellness revolutionary is Dr. Geoff Tabin, who has set for himself a personal goal to eliminate preventable blindness in his lifetime.

In the world today, 37 million people are blind. An additional 100 million suffer from low vision, where they have difficulty performing daily tasks or living or working most jobs. The saddest thing about this statistic is that 85 percent of this blindness is preventable or treatable.

Half of these 137 million people suffer from curable cataracts—the number one cause of blindness in the world today. A cataract is a clouding of the crystalline lens in the eye that affects every human being if they live long enough. The cure for cataracts is having surgery to remove the clouded lens and replace it with an intraocular lens.

In developed nations, cataract surgery is the most frequently performed surgery, with two million operations performed each year in the United States alone. More than 90 percent of people who have cataract surgery regain very good vision, typically 20/20 or 20/40. Many patients report having better vision after surgery than they had before they developed a cataract. The cost of cataract surgery in the U.S. is about $3,500 per eye and is covered by Medicare or most private health insurance.

Cataract surgery is perhaps the most successful antiaging or wellness treatment known to mankind.

Sadly, this enormously successful wellness treatment, which instantaneously fixes one of the worst symptoms of aging since biblical times, is denied to tens of millions of people worldwide because of its cost. While total blindness due to cataracts has been virtually eliminated in the developed world, in places with intense ultraviolet exposure, poor diet, and lack of clean water, cataracts cripple almost 69 million people and often progress to the point where they block all vision.

Dr. Geoff Tabin was born in Chicago, the son of first generation Eastern European immigrants. He graduated from Harvard Medical School and originally set out to be an orthopedic surgeon, but took a detour to follow his passion for rock climbing. In 1990 he became the fourth person in the world to climb the highest peak on all seven continents, including the first ascent of the East Face of Mt. Everest.* His passion for climbing, often in third-world countries, led him to work as a general doctor in Zaire and Nepal, where he witnessed first-hand the "miracle" of cataract surgery.

"In the village where I was working it was expected that a person gets old, their hair turns white, and their eye turns white, and then they die," he recalls. "No one had been cured of blindness in the region. Cataracts were a death sentence. There were no external support systems. A blind family member was a great burden on families. After a short operation under local anesthesia people were restored to life. Older people resumed traditional family roles and younger patients returned to work."

Tabin was inspired and returned to America to become an ophthalmologist. After completing his residency at Brown University, Dr. Tabin returned to Nepal to work with Dr. Sanduk Ruit, a Nepali ophthalmologist skilled at finding lower technology (i.e., affordable) solutions that provided the same quality of care delivered in the West but at far less cost.

Tabin adopted Ruit's methods for delivering high quality cataract surgery and they began teaching other Nepali ophthalmologists. Tabin and Ruit trained the first Tibetan surgeon to perform microscopic cataract surgery, and refined their method of skills transfer via high-volume cataract camps. Tabin and Ruit vowed to add their own efforts to those of the other existing eye care programs, with a goal of overcoming treatable and preventable blindness in the Himalayan region in their lifetime.

---

*Dr. Tabin's mountaineering adventures are told in his (climbing) autobiography, *Blind Corners: Adventures on Seven Continents* (ICS Books, 1993).

Tabin realized that solving the problem of blindness in the developing world required a two-pronged approach: create tertiary centers of excellence in ophthalmologic service and establish primary regional clinics staffed by technicians specifically trained in eye care. Moreover, Dr. Tabin concluded that these solutions could only be achieved by educating and empowering local doctors. Dr. Ruit established the Tilganga Eye Centre in 1994 as the first outpatient cataract surgery facility in the Himalayan region. In 1995 Ruit and Tabin formally began the Himalayan Cataract Project (www .cureblindness.org) as a charitable foundation to support their work.

They developed a system of high-quality, high-volume, and low-cost cataract surgery. An intraocular lens factory in Kathmandu and the utilization of local pharmaceuticals and instruments has allowed them to bring the cost of one cataract surgery down to under twenty dollars! They have performed over 50,000 sight-restoring surgeries. The results have been dramatic toward meeting their goal. In 1994, only 1,500 cataract surgeries were performed in the entire country of Nepal utilizing replacement lens implants to restore quality vision. In 2005, over 150,000 people had quality cataract surgery with lens implants.

Tabin and Ruit are delivering today for $20 per surgery the most popular wellness surgery in the world—an intraocular lens replacement which costs 175 times this amount ($3,500) in the United States.

Tabin and Ruit have trained more than 100 doctors from more than a dozen countries, and many more nurses and technicians. They coordinate eye care programs in Tibet, China, India, Bhutan and Pakistan, and added Ghana and North Korea to the list in 2006. In addition, they provide training for doctors from Bangladesh, Myanmar, Cambodia, and Ethiopia. Dr. Tabin spends three months per year teaching in Asia or Africa, and has become the director of the Himalayan Cataract Project.

Dr. Tabin has several suggestions for how a person can reduce his or her chance of developing eye diseases.

1. Stop, or never start, smoking. Smoking is correlated with cataract formation and age-related macular degeneration.
2. Consume a diet rich in antioxidants and omega-3 fatty acids. Fish oils can also reduce the risk of macular degeneration and

cataracts. Wearing sunglasses that block UVA and UVB light also reduces the risk of these diseases.

3. Visit an eye physician for regular checks to detect potentially blinding conditions, such as glaucoma. With early detection vision loss can usually be prevented.

Dr. Tabin is also involved in testing nutritional supplements and eyedrops that may be able to delay or even reverse cataracts.

Drs. Tabin and Ruit will go down in history not as the inventors of the world's most popular wellness surgery, but as pioneers who made this sight-restoring surgery affordable to millions of blind people. As the wellness revolution enters its next stage, there are similar opportunities to make all type of wellness products and services affordable to the masses, just as Henry Ford did with the automobile.

Unlimited Wellness

"How sad it is!" murmured Dorian Gray with his eyes still fixed upon his own portrait. "How sad it is! I shall grow old, and horrible, and dreadful. But this picture will remain always young. If it were only the other way! If it were I who was to be always young, and the picture that was to grow old! For that—for that—I would give everything! Yes, there is nothing in the whole world I would not give! I would give my soul for that!"
—OSCAR WILDE, *The Picture of Dorian Gray* (1891)

Why Wellness Is Unlimited

The individual cells in our body are constantly dying and replacing themselves.* On a cellular level, the biochemical objective of most wellness activity is to ensure that these individual cells receive the raw materials—proteins, vitamins, and minerals—necessary to remanufacture themselves at the optimal level.

But at some point in a person's life, something tells each cell in each bodily organ to stop reproducing itself (except stem cells, as you'll see in a moment). This causes normal aging, illness, and eventually, death. Sometimes, even when a cell or organ does not suffer from a biochemical deficiency, something tells abnormal cells in an organ to uncontrollably multiply until they impair the function of that organ (e.g., cancer). Today we know that this "something" is one of the many and complex instructions in the genetic code for life, commonly referred to as DNA, or deoxyribonucleic acid. DNA is an organic compound found in all cells that contains the genetic code for inherited characteristics and replication.

Our genetic code is a human "textbook" with over 3 billion different letters—written entirely in four characters (A, T, C, and G) with

---

*Our bodies manufacture 200 billion red blood cells each day, replacing all the blood in our body every 120 days. Skin is completely replaced every one to three months. It takes 90 days for old bone to be broken down and replaced by new bone.

no spaces or punctuation. While the actual substance we now call DNA was discovered in 1869, its role in inheritance was demonstrated only in the latter half of the twentieth century, and the complete mapping of the human genome was not completed until the beginning of this century.[1]

Our demand for wellness-based products and services is primarily driven by one function of the genetic code, the one that causes aging—from the wrinkles that appear in our skin to the ultimate breakdown of our bodily organs.

Over the long term, our understanding and eventual manipulation of this genetic code holds the greatest promise for the wellness industry.

By examining a person's DNA, which can be taken from the mouth with just a small swab or scraping device, it is already possible to predict the probability that a person will develop certain diseases.

Soon, based on the recently completed mapping of the human genome, it should be possible to predict every forthcoming disease or condition not caused by external (e.g., diet, exercise) factors.

Scientists expect this type of genetic testing to soon become widespread.[2] In just the next few years, by using this information to predict the probability of developing a certain condition, a wellness distributor could suggest a vitamin- or supplement-based therapy.

For example, a person with a genetic propensity to develop osteoporosis would be directed to take calcium supplements while they were still young, or a person with a genetic propensity for developing prostate problems would be an early candidate to take saw palmetto.

Wellness entrepreneurs who embrace this emerging DNA-based technology first, particularly those in the healthy food and dietary supplement areas, will see their businesses explode with new customers.

Eventually, as technology progresses, vitamins and supplements used in this manner will probably be supplanted by genetic intervention—the actual modification or repair of the problematic gene containing the propensity to develop the disease. Scientists do not expect this type of intervention to become effective in treating the full spectrum of genetically determined diseases for several decades.[3]

For now and in the foreseeable next few decades, our genetic code and the aging it produces will continue to drive the unlimited demand for wellness products and services we experience today. Each breakthrough in genetically based wellness products and services that slow the aging process will simply increase the demand for more wellness, as satisfied customers seek to look and feel even healthier and existing customers live longer to consume more wellness products and services.

Stem Cells—The Heart Surgeon Who is Trying to Make Heart Surgery Obsolete

Another scientific advance that also holds great promise for wellness and antiaging is stem cell research.

Stem cell research has received some bad publicity because certain stem cells are harvested from human embryos. However, there are many other types of stem cells, and most of the research being done has nothing to do with human embryos and is thus not morally controversial.

Stem cells are very special cells, different from any other cells found in living organisms. Unlike all other cells in our body, which eventually stop reproducing themselves (causing aging and death), stem cells can theoretically divide without limit, to replace themselves and replenish other cells. Equally important to being potentially immortal, each new cell after a division has the potential to remain a stem cell or develop into a specialized cell such as a kidney cell, a brain cell, a retina cell, and so on.

Stem cells are classified based on their source (i.e., bone marrow, adult, embryonic, etc.) and all have the following three common characteristics, which qualify them as stem cells:

1. Stem cells are *capable of self-renewal,* meaning they can continue to divide and duplicate themselves for long periods of time without changing their inherent characteristics.

2. Stem cells are *unspecialized,* meaning that they have no tissue-specific or specialized function. They don't beat or pump blood,

like heart cells. They don't conduct information, like brain cells. They don't carry oxygen, like blood cells.

3. Stem cells *give rise to specialized cells* in a process called differentiation, meaning they can become a heart cell, a brain cell, or a blood cell.

Scientists are fascinated by the capacity of a few stem cells in an embryo to develop into a human being. But they are equally fascinated by they way adult stem cells seem to fight injury, cancer, replace damaged tissues, and slow aging. Theoretically, a few stem cells injected into a bad heart or failing kidney could summon the body to grow new heart tissue or new kidney tissue, restoring these damaged organs to normal. Or, even better, a few stem cells could tell an existing organ headed for failure to stop aging and remain strong.

An incredible amount of research is ongoing, involving scientists isolating stem cells from all parts of the human body while preserving their "stemness" and using them to repair injured organs like a failing heart. One of the world leaders in this research is Dr. Russ Reiss, a cardiothoracic surgeon at the University of Utah and Salt Lake City VA Hospital.

Dr. Reiss (Russ) was born in the suburbs of Philadelphia, the son of two successful pediatricians. At an early age Russ was acutely aware that disease could strike anyone, rich or poor, at anytime. The desire and compassion to help sick people was ingrained in him almost from birth.

A light bulb went on when Russ witnessed his first open-heart operation during his third year of medical school at Hahnemann University. He committed himself at that moment to becoming a heart surgeon, and spent the next ten years in residency to rise to the top of his profession. He also completed a three-year research fellowship in immunology and microbiology, where he became fascinated by stem cells. His thesis was an account of how certain adult stem cells taken from the bone marrow could somehow "magically" protect mammals from lethal radiation injury.

At the time, many heart surgeons scoffed at stem cell research. To most, heart surgery was solely about mechanics—when something failed in the heart, you went in and replaced it physically with either a mechanical device or a transplanted organ. Few surgeons were well versed in stem cell biology and understood the implications behind the power of stem cells to heal and protect organs from damage. Just one year after Russ completed his fellowship, researchers at Duke University discovered that stem cells injected into the heart could repair heart damage after a heart attack. Russ's thesis was suddenly validated.

In 1998, Russ was recruited to the University of Utah, the place that had pioneered and implanted the first artificial heart, to complete his training and start up a cardiac stem cell program. Today Russ works with a multidisciplinary, multi-institutional team of researchers who focus on all aspects of stem cell therapy for the heart. Ironically, his goal is to advance stem cell research to the point where artificial hearts, and all types of open-heart surgery, become medically obsolete.

Russ and I have become close friends on the mountain bike trails around Utah and ride together several times a week. Russ has taught me how to appreciate my heart and lungs like a finely tuned race car, and how to modify my breathing and physical activity for optimum performance. When I am working too hard and complain I can't ride that day, Russ drags me from my office telling me "you are no good to others unless you can take care of yourself first. . . . Rest your body, rest your mind, rest your ego."

On many of our rides, Russ is distraught with concern for some of his patients, and he stops frequently to take their calls. He often laments how most of his patients, almost by definition of being a heart patient, have not taken care of their bodies enough to prepare them for what is about to be the most grueling marathon of their life—open-heart surgery. His greatest regret is that many patients whose lives are saved through surgery soon return to the overeating, smoking, drinking, or whatever bad antiwellness behavior caused them to have to meet Russ in the first place. As Russ often says, "there has to be a better way."

"Medications and procedures can be critically important in the management of chronic disease, but they need to be recognized only as adjuncts to one's personal wellness program." *Russ Reiss, MD*

The Opportunity to Do Incredible Good

A few wellness entrepreneurs, like Steve Demos or Jill Kinney, will emerge as the billionaires and media darlings

of our new century. Hundreds of thousands more wellness entrepreneurs will become millionaires—approximately 5 million new U.S. millionaires will be created in
the next five years, many of whom will be making their
fortunes in wellness.[4]

This book has focused on the strategies some of these wellness entrepreneurs are using to become rich, and how you can duplicate
their success. But as you become rich, something more important to
our society than just your bank account will be improving. Economically, we measure our lack of wellness in dollars and population. We
spend $2 trillion in the United States each year on sickness, almost
one-sixth of every dollar we earn. Approximately 90 million Americans, or 30 percent of our population, are clinically obese. And 195
million Americans—65 percent—are overweight and unhealthy.
These numbers have doubled over the last few decades and have
risen 7–10 percent in just the last five years.

The true cost of our need for wellness cannot be measured
in trillions of dollars or in millions of people.

Many of the 90 million individuals who are obese represent a life
misspent. These individuals don't have the energy to fully enjoy their
lives, their work, and their families. They spend a significant portion
of their lives on a medical merry-go-round that treats a minimal
amount of their symptoms—just enough to keep them working and
consuming more unhealthy food and more sickness products and
services.

The 105 million overweight, but not obese, individuals in the
United States are often malnourished to the point of fatigue, nerv-
ousness, headaches, confusion, and muscle weakness. When they
turn to their medical community for help, they are told that these issues are normal symptoms of advancing age.

Until, of course, these unfortunate individuals meet up with you
and your wellness business.

As you go out each day to market your wellness products
and services, you carry a message more important than
the actual product or service you are trying to sell. Underlying the pitch for each wellness product is the notion that

> **your customers can take control of their lives and begin a road to wellness.**

Typically, before consumers purchase a new product or try a new service, they have made the decision to buy it twice before and then forgotten to do so. It typically takes several exposures to the product message to get to each of the three affirmative decisions that lead to eventual purchase. This is why, when launching a new product, advertising agencies tell clients not to expect actual sales until the consumer has had many exposures to the message.

Each time your wellness message reaches a potential wellness consumer, you bring the consumer one step closer to making one of these three affirmative decisions to do something about his or her wellness, even if the consumer does not favorably respond to your individual product or service. In this regard, all wellness entrepreneurs are colleagues, because even when you seemingly fail, you succeed in bringing the potential wellness consumer one step closer to making the decision that could change his or her life.

As we saw in Chapter 2, when you do succeed in getting consumers to try your wellness product and they have a positive wellness experience, they typically become voracious consumers of more wellness products and services—products and services produced or distributed by both you and by your wellness competitors:

- **The single mother who lost 35 pounds now wants to join a fitness club for even more energy.**
- **The boy with more energy from a new vitamin regimen now wants to learn about better nutrition and change his diet.**
- **The father who eliminated pain with magnetic therapy now wants to learn about better vitamins.**
- **The parents of a girl who eliminated colds by taking echinacea now want to learn what's available for their other children.**
- **The former athlete using glucosamine who has returned to bicycling now wants something to improve his memory.**
- **The prostate patient who was cured with saw palmetto now wants to spread his message about naturopathic experiences.**

The Importance of Sticking to Your Plan

It is my hope that you will embark on your particular wellness business today and become one of the leaders in this incredible industry. The sooner you begin, the greater will be your potential reward. But the sooner you begin, the higher the possibility that you might become discouraged if you don't succeed fast enough. Most consumers have yet to have their first positive wellness experience—the one that makes them consumers of more wellness products and services—and thus the universe of wellness customers is just beginning to grow. You might develop a successful product or service, but give up before you realize it because you don't get enough customers right away.

> **Once you have found some initial success with your product or service, it is important that you have the intestinal fortitude and financial resources to keep marketing it to more and more potential customers until you accumulate enough statistics to be able to stand back objectively and make a worthwhile analysis of your results.**

The mathematical concept of *frequency,* that individual events don't follow a set pattern but that many events collectively over time *do* follow a set pattern, is sometimes difficult to understand, particularly for new entrepreneurs. Here's an experiment you can use to better understand frequency or to teach the concept of frequency to your associates.

Flip a coin 10 times and record the result. You may be astonished to find that heads (or tails) appears 80 to 90 percent of the time instead of the expected 50 percent. Then flip the same coin 100 times—when you do this you will almost always record heads or tails appearing 47 to 53 percent of the time. This is why you should never become discouraged with the outcome of a few events. Analyzing *many* events, or *frequency,* is always a better predictor.

> **You might develop a particular strategy for selling your wellness product or service that would eventually succeed with 50 percent of your prospects, but fails with the first 8 or 9 of your 10 initial prospects. Conversely, you might find success on the first few sales calls and then expand too fast, before you understand how you need to refine your strategy.**

Don't be discouraged if you sometimes have trouble explaining frequency to one of your associates who wants to give up. No less a genius than Albert Einstein had the same problem understanding this concept.

Why God Created Frequency

My father was a religious man. He firmly believed in a true and just God who had a reason for everything. Even while he was dying of cancer, he never wavered in his belief that his own medical situation and society's economic problems were both the result of our failure to utilize the tools that God has given us. He firmly believed, to quote Albert Einstein, that "God does not play dice with the universe."

Although my father cherished this quotation, Einstein actually made a great mistake when he said it.[5] Einstein was searching for what came to be known as a *unified field theory,* a theory that would explain the behavior of everything in the universe, from the smallest electron to the largest planet. In conducting this search, Einstein could not accept that individual atomic particles appeared to move at random, like dice, but that when observed with enough frequency, the actions of the particles followed established laws of probability.

Today, the science of quantum mechanics, which is based on this probabilistic behavior of elementary particles, explains everything from nuclear energy to personal computers. What Einstein failed to take into account is that God invented dice, and God gave us the concept of frequency to understand how dice work and to make decisions based on the outcome.[6]

As a manager, a professor, a parent, and a Sunday school teacher, I am often asked by young people why such and such an effort didn't lead to the expected reward. While I try to console them, I, too, am frustrated that although God created a world with rules and order, God also made a world in which those rules are not absolute (i.e., frequency). I believe the reason God did this was to create a world that would constantly challenge, and thus strengthen, our faith. A world where everything doesn't work out *each* time, but a world where everything does work out *over* time—especially for those of us, like Job, with enough faith to follow our plan regardless of how much adversity we experience.

So the LORD blessed the latter end of Job more than his beginning: for he had fourteen thousand sheep, and six thousand camels, and a thousand yoke of oxen, and a thousand she asses. . . . After this lived Job a hundred and forty years, and saw his sons, and his sons' sons, even four generations. So Job died, being old and full of days.[7]

The "Invisible Hand" behind Wellness

In 1996, when I began the research for this book, I was not optimistic that a solution could be found to our need for wellness. Although in my lifetime I had seen the virtual demise of Communism and significant improvements in combating world hunger and racial discrimination, I felt we could not overcome our entrapment in the "sickness" reactionary approach to health.

The reason for my pessimism was that the ill health in our nation is caused by the most powerful force in our society: economics.

John Maynard Keynes once said,

The ideas of economists . . . are more powerful than is commonly understood. Indeed, the world is ruled by little else. Practical men, who believe themselves to be quite exempt from any intellectual influences, are usually the slaves of some defunct economist.[8]

Our obese, overweight, and unhealthy citizens have become slaves to the combined economic interests of the $1.3 trillion food industry and the $2 trillion sickness industry.

In 2002, when I understood how the wellness industry had already reached $200 billion and was headed to $1 trillion by 2012, I could see that the wellness industry was the economic solution to the problem of sickness that economics had largely created.

In 1776, Adam Smith's *The Wealth of Nations* described how the unfettered pursuit by individuals of their own selfish interests leads directly to the increased well-being of society as a whole. The deeper Smith delved into the workings of the economy, the more fascinated he became by what he called "the invisible hand" that guided the actions of individuals toward increased societal wealth. Although Smith, as a progressive scientist in a secular and enlightened era, avoided using the term *God,* it is clear upon reading the original work that Adam Smith knew whose Invisible Hand was at work.

Today, there is no better example of God's hand at work than in the emerging wellness industry and in the positive economic forces behind the wellness revolution that is about to take place.

Fat: What Is It, How Do We Get It, and How Do We Define It?

Suggestion: *Read this appendix once as a consumer; then go back and read it again as a wellness entrepreneur—marking the suggestions that you might want to further analyze as potential wellness business opportunities.*

What Is Fat?

In the Bible the word *fat* is used to describe the most prized parts of the animal—so valuable that they were originally reserved to be burnt at the altar in a sacrifice to God himself. Historically, fat has been used in a figurative sense to describe abundance, exuberance, robustness, fertility, or outward success.

In our time the word *fat* has become almost exclusively pejorative—associated with laziness, disgust, slovenliness, greed, and gluttony.

But what exactly is fat, and why has it come to have such a negative connotation?

Biologically speaking, fats are a subgroup of a category of nutrients called *lipids,* the chemical name for a group of compounds that include fats, oils, and cholesterol. A lipid is generally referred to as a *fat* if it remains solid at room temperature and as an *oil* if it is liquid at room temperature. Fats and oils come from plant and animal products, whereas cholesterol comes *only* from animal products (e.g., meat, poultry, milk, and cheese).

Cholesterol

Cholesterol is an odorless, white, waxy, powdery substance that is found in every cell of our bodies. It is an important building block for cell membranes, hormones, and vitamin D. It also aids in the digestion of fat into caloric energy. When doctors talk about "good" and "bad" cholesterol they are actually speaking about lipoproteins.

A lipoprotein is a combination of fat and protein (lipid plus protein) that wraps around the individual fat and cholesterol molecules in our bodies, transporting them throughout our bodies and aiding the digestion of fat. Two major types of lipoproteins are low-density (LDL) lipoproteins and high-density (HDL) lipoproteins. LDL particles, which carry about 70 percent of the cholesterol in our bodies, are known as "bad" cholesterol because they stick to the walls of our arteries, which can lead to blockages, strokes, and heart attacks. HDL particles are known as "good" cholesterol because they travel throughout the body picking up cholesterol from dying cells and other sources.

The amount of cholesterol in your system is determined by many factors, ranging from your genes to your age to your level of physical activity. For example, smokers have higher cholesterol because smoking weakens the arterial walls and makes the surface membranes more receptive to fat and cholesterol deposits.

But the major determinant of how much bad cholesterol you have is your weight, or more specifically, how much excess fat you have in your system.

Saturated and Unsaturated Fats

There are three major types of fats: *polyunsaturated fat, monounsaturated fat,* and *saturated fat.* For purposes of simplification, we will refer to the first two types collectively as *unsaturated fats.*

Basically, saturated fats (e.g., shortening, lard, butter, meat fats) are the chief culprits in raising blood cholesterol—they are naturally saturated with hydrogen molecules. Saturated fats are typically solid at room temperature, and foods containing saturated fats have a longer shelf life than foods with unsaturated fats.

Unsaturated fats, like olive oil and canola oil, actually lower blood cholesterol. Unsaturated fats are typically liquid at room temperature, but start to solidify when cold, which is why an olive oil-based salad dressing gets cloudy in the refrigerator. Fish contain more unsaturated and less saturated fat than meat, which keeps their bodies from starting to solidify in cold water.

Food manufacturers typically extend the economic shelf life of their products by adding hydrogen to unsaturated fats—a process called *hydrogenation*—which effectively turns unsaturated fats into saturated fats, or good fats into bad fats called *trans-fatty acids*. This is why it is important to avoid hydrogenated oils if you are trying to lower your cholesterol.

There is an immediate business opportunity today in providing foods without hydrogenated oils—particularly to consumers worried about heart disease. These products will have shorter shelf lives, but they could eventually become products of choice for all as consumers learn the difference between saturated and unsaturated fats.

Why We Crave Fats

Fat was prized in biblical times for many reasons. Back then, most humans suffered from a deficiency of fat, and basic calories were scarce. Being plump was often a sign of great wealth. Fat contains the most energy (9 calories per gram) of any of the six nutrient categories—an important consideration for people choosing to store food, either for traveling or for survival between harvests. But probably the main reason fats were so prized then (and still are) is because they taste so good.

We are biologically programmed to love the taste of fat; this programming is now killing us in our world of agricultural abundance.

In contrast to times when fat was prized and scarce, today calling someone "fat" is considered a great insult.

But eating fat does not directly cause you to become fat. Eating more calories than you burn makes you fat—or more correctly, makes you overweight. Eating fat indirectly causes you to become overweight because fat contains more than twice as many calories per gram as proteins or carbohydrates. Aside from containing potentially unnecessary calories, eating too much fat is bad because fats contain artery-clogging cholesterol.

Defining Overweight and Obese

When a person becomes overweight, his or her excess fat, as noted earlier, often appears first in the stomach and upper body on a man and on the thighs and lower body in a woman. Upper-body obesity (*android obesity*) is a male pattern characteristic strongly related to heart disease, hypertension, and diabetes. It is more dangerous than lower-body obesity (*gynecoid obesity*), which is a female characteristic and also dangerous to your health.

How much fat is too much? To answer this question it is first necessary to define the terms *overweight* and *obese*. Although they are often used interchangeably, *overweight* refers to an excess of total body weight (including all bodily tissues), whereas *obese* refers to an excess of body fat only. It is possible to be overweight without being obese, as in the case of a bodybuilder with great muscle mass. It is also possible to be obese without being overweight as in the case of a sedentary person with an excess of body fat and low muscle mass.

Four main concepts are used today to define being overweight or obese: percentage body fat, waist-to-hip ratio, Body Mass Index (BMI), and height-weight tables.

The first and most accurate method is to measure the percentage of your body that is fat. Men should have a percentage body fat between 13 and 25 percent and women should have a percentage body fat between 17 and 29 percent. Anything above these numbers is considered obese and is very dangerous.

Percentage body fat is best measured by comparing a person's weight to his or her weight underwater—this works because fat floats and is less dense than body tissue. Unfortunately, this method is too expensive and complicated and is considered primarily a tool for research.[1] Another method is to use special calipers to measure the skinfold thickness of the triceps and other parts of the body—this can be quite accurate when done by a trained professional because half of a person's fat is stored just under their skin. Bioelectrical impedance (resistance) can also be used to measure percentage body fat.

Another way to measure being overweight and/or obese is by using waist-to-hip ratio, calculated by dividing the number of inches around the waistline by the circumference around the hips. For example, a person with a 30-inch waist and 40-inch hip circumference would have a waist-to-hip ratio of 0.75. Obesity is defined as anything over 0.8 for a woman and 1.0 for a man. This method is obviously good for diagnosing upper body (android) obesity, but can be woefully inaccurate in many cases, particularly for someone with lower body (gynecoid) obesity.

The third method used to measure being overweight and/or obese, the Body Mass Index (BMI), was developed in 1835 by the French mathematician Adolphe Quetelet. Using a statistical model to develop the concept of the *homme moyen,* or average man, he developed the Quetelet Index, which today is better known as the BMI:

$$BMI = \frac{\text{(weight in kilograms)}}{\text{(height in meters)}^2}$$

For example, a person with a weight of 170 pounds and a height of 5 feet 9 inches would have a BMI of about 25, calculated as follows.

First convert 170 pounds into kilograms (2.2 pounds equals 1 kilogram):

$$\frac{170 \text{ lb}}{2.2} = 77.27 \text{ kg}$$

Next convert 5 feet 9 inches (5.75 feet) into meters (3.28 feet equals 1 meter):

$$\frac{5.75}{3.28} = 1.75 \text{ meters}$$

Finally, plug your conversions into the BMI equation:

$$BMI = \frac{77.27 \text{ kg}}{1.75^2} = 25.2$$

Now here's a shortcut you can use. Simply multiply your weight in pounds by 704.5, then divide the result by your height in inches, then divide that result by your height in inches again:

$$BMI = \frac{170 \times \dfrac{704.5}{69}}{69} = 25.2$$

Most countries and public authorities today use BMI as their measurement tool of choice. According to the National Institutes of Health in 2000, 61 percent of the U.S. population is overweight (defined as having a BMI of 25 or greater), and almost 27 percent of the U.S. population is obese (defined as having a BMI of 30 or greater).

While these numbers may be collectively accurate (just walk outside to a public place and count the percent of people who appear to be overweight and obese), they are woefully inaccurate when applied to specific individuals. The BMI formula is the same for both sexes: a 5-foot 9-inch woman weighing 170 pounds is obviously different than a 5-foot 9-inch man weighing the same amount, yet both are considered overweight. The BMI formula is also not adjusted for individual variations. For example, weightlifters have more muscle, which weighs more than fat, and elderly people have lower muscle mass.

Finally, the fourth method, using a height-weight table, is what people are most familiar with since it has been used by the U.S. medical profession for decades. The popular "Desirable Height-Weight Table" was developed by the Metropolitan Life Insurance Company in 1959 and represents the weight and height statistically associated with the lowest incidence of mortality among their insured population (made up mostly of upper- and middle-class white males). The term *desirable* refers to having the lowest incidence of mortality, not the lowest incidence of disease, and was removed from the name of the table in 1983. Although the Height-Weight Table is potentially more accurate than BMI because it is broken down by sex, it has most of the same limitations and should not be considered definitive for any individual circumstance. Additionally, much of the data contained on the current Metropolitan Life Height-Weight Table is arbitrary—the concept of frame size (determined by elbow width) was added with no empirical data to support it.

Regardless of which method we choose to determine the percent of our population that is overweight or obese, it is clear that we have a problem of epidemic proportions.

Shifting from Sickness to Wellness Medical Care*

As explained in Chapter 7, you or your wellness customer may have discovered you can save thousands of dollars each year by purchasing your own individual/family health policy, or you may be ready to switch to high-deductible health insurance, or you may have opened a Health Savings Account (HSA)—or hopefully all of these. Once you do, your healthcare paradigm shifts:

> **You now want to cut down on your healthcare spending since each dollar you save you get to keep—and over the years these dollars could add up to hundreds of thousands of dollars in your HSA.**
>
> **You must learn to balance your new financial incentive to save on healthcare costs against the legitimate healthcare needs of your family. You have a new incentive to eat better, exercise more, and invest in wellness care to improve your health—since staying healthy is the best way to save on your healthcare costs.**

In this Appendix we examine three things you should do to save on your healthcare costs:

1. Stop taking maintenance drugs.

2. Change your lifestyle (diet and exercise) before it's too late.

3. Ask your doctors to spend your money as if it were their money.

*Adapted from *The New Health Insurance Solution* (Wiley, 2005/2007)

Stop Taking Maintenance Drugs That Treat Symptoms, Not Causes

There is one very important idea missing from the section of Chapter 7, "Help Your Customers Save 10 to 75 Percent on Their Prescription Drugs." The idea is that you can save 100 percent on your maintenance drugs (heartburn medicine like Prilosec, antidepressants like Zoloft, heart disease drugs like Lipitor, etc.). These drugs treat your symptoms, not the causes of your illness, which in many cases can be traced to diet, lifestyle, and lack of exercise.

The way to save 100 percent on these drugs is to stop taking them altogether—by finding a doctor or other medical professional who understands the dangers of prescription drugs and will work with you to change your diet or lifestyle.

The prescription drug business was founded by people like Dr. Jonas Salk, who developed the first vaccine for polio, and Dr. Alexander Fleming, who discovered penicillin. The products these dedicated doctors developed prevented diseases from developing in the first place or cured diseases over a relatively short period of time.

Sadly, as healthcare moved away from the work of medical professionals and became the most profitable sector of our economy, the prescription drug industry shifted from making products that prevented or cured diseases to making products that merely treated the symptoms of diseases.

> **Today about 95 percent of the prescription drugs sold are *maintenance drugs*—drugs that treat only the symptoms of a disease, and that you are expected to take for the rest of your life.**

From an economic/business perspective, at least, it's easy to understand why this is so, and you need to understand this if you are taking any prescription drugs on a regular basis. I'll put the answer in the form of a question: If you were the CEO of a major pharmaceutical firm, would you spend your R&D dollars to make a pill that a consumer would only take once (e.g., a vaccine) or for only a short period of time (e.g., an antibiotic), or would you spend your R&D dollars on creating products that consumers would take every day, or two or three times a day, for the rest of their lives?

> **For the past three decades, the majority of private R&D dollars in the pharmaceutical industry have been spent on**

> products that treat merely the symptoms of disease rather
> than cure or prevent disease—thus creating customers
> for life.

If you were a businessperson developing a new health product to sell to your customers, wouldn't you like to have all Americans indirectly pay a tax subsidizing 50 percent of your retail price, even if they had no interest in taking your product? If drugs like Viagra or Levitra were sold over the counter, employers would have to give employees almost $2 in order for those employees to have $1 left after FICA and income taxes to buy the drugs—but because these drugs are prescription only, employers are forced to pay 100 percent of the cost through their group health plans as a tax-free benefit to employees.

> **Today many of the prescription drugs sold do not have a
> strong legitimate reason to be prescriptions—they are not
> addictive or controlled substances like morphine. They
> are issued in prescription form partly to get all Americans
> to subsidize 50 percent of their cost through medical tax
> deductions and partly to force employers to pay for them.**

More important than the fact that many prescription drugs were designed to make you a customer for life, and more important than the fact that all Americans end up subsidizing 50 percent of the price of other people's drugs, is the fact that many prescription drugs are indirectly dangerous, over the long run, to your life and health.

I am an economist and businessman, not a medical doctor; however, in conducting the extensive research for this book, I concluded that few of the tens of millions of people taking maintenance drugs should be taking them. Instead, most people taking maintenance drugs should be working with a medical professional to cure the underlying disease—for example, changing their diet instead of taking Nexium for life (to counteract heartburn), losing weight instead of taking Lipitor for life (to lower cholesterol).

> **In addition to preventing you from focusing on the causes
> of your illness rather than on the symptoms, the prescription medicines you take are the number one reason your
> application for individual/family health insurance could
> be rejected or your premium increased (uprated).**

Let's go back and examine more closely the world's five top-selling prescription drugs—Lipitor, Zocor, Nexium, Prevacid, and Zoloft— which account for more than $25 billion in sales in the United States alone. These drugs have the following things in common for most people taking them:

- They do not prevent a disease.
- They treat only the symptoms of a disease.
- They are designed to be taken for the rest of your life.
- They are not narcotic or controlled substances and thus should not be prescription versus over-the-counter medicines.
- They would have less chance of being sold directly to consumers as real products without first coopting trusted physicians as sales agents.
- They are dangerous to your long-term health, because by treating only the symptoms of a deadly disease, they prevent you from modifying your behavior to cure the disease.

Lipitor: Lipitor, the number one selling prescription drug in the world, is prescribed to lower your cholesterol. Every health and medical professional will tell you that the best way to lower your cholesterol is to change your diet and to exercise, which we will examine in a moment. Instead, millions of Americans take this drug for their entire lives—which is dangerous because it prevents them from making the lifestyle changes that they sorely need.

Zocor: Zocor, the number two selling drug in the United States, is functionally the same as Lipitor. It is truly amazing that Americans spend more than $10 billion a year for these two drugs when generics are available for both for about one-third the price (see Chapter 9).

Nexium: Nexium, designed to treat heartburn, is the latest trick perpetrated on consumers by the pharmaceutical companies. The majority of people who have heartburn have it because of what they eat, not because they are genetically disposed to acid reflux disease. A bad diet can cause depression, heart disease, cancer, and heartburn. Yet when their body screams out in pain for help, millions of people take this little purple pill to stop their body's natural alarm system (i.e., heartburn) from functioning, so they can keep eating unhealthy foods.

Prevacid: Prevacid is functionally the same as Nexium. If Prevacid and Nexium were over-the-counter medicines instead of prescriptions, their advertising would have to inform consumers that the best way to cure heartburn is to stop eating the food that is causing the heartburn. But because they are prescriptions, in addition to getting a 50 percent medical tax subsidy, their national, direct-to-the-public advertising is exempt from normal truth-in-advertising regulations. Prescription drug advertising targeted to consumers should be prohibited since, in the real world, "ask your doctor" often means "change your doctor" if he or she won't give you whatever prescription drug you request.

Zoloft: Zoloft is the number one selling drug in the world for depression and anxiety—more than 28 million Americans (1 in 10) have taken Zoloft or its functional equivalents Prozac and Paxil. According to its own web site (www.zoloft.com), one of the major side effects of taking Zoloft, Prozac, and Paxil is that 2 to 4 percent of people under 18 taking these drugs have suicidal thoughts.[1] In addition to being expensive, drugs for depression are dangerous because they prevent people from dealing with the causes of their depression (including their diets). In psychiatric cases requiring chemical intervention, there are much cheaper alternatives like St. John's wort, which outsells Prozac 25 to 1 in Germany. According to a recent study at Harvard Medical School, antidepressant drugs should not be used in 75 percent of the cases where they are prescribed.[2]

If you take any prescription drugs on a regular basis, find a medical professional and develop a plan to get off your prescriptions: ***Do not attempt to do this without the advice of a medical professional.***

To find a medical professional to help you, start by telling your current doctor: "I currently take [prescription drug] on a regular basis and am looking for a medical professional to work with me to stop." If your doctor can't help you, he or she may be able to recommend a wellness-oriented MD who can, or refer you to a wellness health professional such as an osteopath (DO), naturopath (ND), or chiropractor (DC).

The best way to develop a plan to stop taking prescription drugs is to find an MD-type medical professional who works together with a wellness health professional. For example, in Dover, Ohio, a cardiologist noticed that two of her patients with high cholesterol had good results after attending a Creating Wellness center run by chiropractor Dr. Shawn Kapper. The cardiologist was so impressed that she sent 40 of her patients with heart disease to Dr. Kapper, and the two doctors (chiropractor and cardiologist) developed a non-drug program to lower cholesterol for the betterment of their mutual patients.

Change Your Lifestyle (Diet and Exercise) to Dramatically Cut Your Lifetime Healthcare Expenses— Before It's Too Late

There's a lot you can do to improve your health and cut your healthcare costs, but first let's look at why we spend so much on healthcare.

Why Americans Spend So Much on Healthcare

The United States spends far more per person on healthcare than any other country—about twice as much as other developed nations. Yet people in the United States don't appear to be getting their money's worth. The United States lags far behind other developed countries on almost every important medical statistic—life expectancy, infant mortality, cancer, diabetes, heart disease, and so forth.

So, what is the problem with American healthcare?

Is it our inefficient medical bureaucracy, where 2 to 3 million Americans are employed by medical providers and insurance carriers—not to deliver healthcare, but merely to pass the buck for that care to someone else?[3]

Is it the cost of medical malpractice insurance, which adds more than $27 billion a year to the cost of providing healthcare—enough to annually pay a high-deductible insurance premium for more than half of the 45 million Americans without health insurance?[4]

Is it our employer-based system, whereby the ultimate providers of healthcare for most people (employers) have little incentive to spend even $1 today on wellness and preventive care in order to save $100 tomorrow—because the odds are that the employee will be long gone or receiving Medicare by the time serious diseases like cancer and heart disease develop?

The partial answer is yes to all of these questions, but the main reason Americans spend two times what they should on healthcare is not because of something wrong with American healthcare.

The main reason Americans spend two to three times what they should on healthcare is because Americans

> **(along with Australians and Britons) are two to three times more unhealthy than people in most other nations, primarily because of their diet and a lack of exercise.**

Today, more than 65 percent of Americans are overweight or medically obese—a figure that has doubled since the 1980s. Being overweight is just one of the symptoms of having a terrible diet—most Americans are also deficient in the basic vitamins and minerals necessary to keep their minds sharp and avoid major diseases like cancer. If you are overweight or obese, please get immediate help in changing your lifestyle. Already, 59 million Americans have diabetes or prediabetes, mostly due to being overweight—if you are one of them, you have a 65 percent chance of dying from heart disease or stroke. Moreover, before you die, if you are obese, you will likely consume much of your estate in medical expenses and will needlessly and selfishly be torturing yourself and those you love the most.

The Effect of Diet and Exercise on Your Prescription Drugs

Refer back to the list of the five most popular prescription drugs. Most people taking these drugs can eliminate or reduce their consumption through diet and/or exercise. The primary cause of high cholesterol (Lipitor, Zocor) is your diet and lack of exercise. The primary cause of heartburn (Nexium, Prevacid) is also the foods you eat—although many people do have a genetic predisposition to acid reflex disease requiring long-term medication. And, when it comes to depression (Zoloft), I am convinced that diet and/or lack of exercise is a cause of depression and that a lifestyle change can yield amazing results, particularly for young people.

> **If you have a child experiencing either depression or hyperactive behavior, try changing his or her diet—specifically, eliminate fast foods and processed foods containing preservatives and salt, cut down on dairy products, and add large quantities of fruits and vegetables. As a parent of four and as a teacher of college freshmen for 21 years, I have seen amazing improvements in behavior from changes in lifestyle, diet, and exercise.**

Speak to Your Doctor about Spending Your Money as if It Were His or Her Own Money

I've found that in many cases, doctors already know how to spend your money as if it were their money. They are just too busy to take the time to do so, or they may be prohibited from doing so by the owners of their medical practice or by their malpractice insurance carriers. Here's how to get them to do it.

Prescriptions

Ever since our family switched our health insurance in 1999, when a doctor writes out a prescription, I say: "We have high-deductible insurance." Twice, I've seen the doctor rip up the prescription and write a new one stating, "This drug is cheaper and is really the same thing anyway."

Don't wait for your doctor to prescribe something and then ask for a cheaper equivalent—tell your doctor up front that you have a Health Savings Account and high-deductible health insurance. You'll be surprised how many doctors already know about HSAs and how to save money on healthcare.

One reason doctors don't prescribe cheaper equivalent drugs is that doctors and their medical practices have enormous financial incentives to prescribe certain brands of drugs. The pharmaceutical companies have armies of lawyers figuring out the latest "barely legal" way to compensate medical doctors who prescribe their brand-name products.

Many times doctors don't prescribe cheaper equivalent generics or therapeutic substitutes out of ignorance. There are equivalent generics or therapeutic substitutes for almost all popular drugs if you take the time to search for them. When you politely tell doctors about these generics, most doctors are pleased to learn about less expensive equivalent therapies. They don't teach economics in medical school, and you should not expect doctors to know the price of the things they prescribe. Unlike you, they rarely see the inside of a pharmacy. Doctors get many of their own prescriptions for free, as samples from pharmaceutical representatives.

Medical Tests

Unnecessary medical tests are another area where doctors can waste hundreds or thousands of your dollars. There are obviously some medical tests you should never skip—like having an annual mammogram or taking a biopsy of an unusual growth. But many tests are simply a waste of money. When doctors tell you they want to send you, or a sample of your fluids, for a medical test, here are some questions you should ask them:

- Why do you want this test?
- What are the likely results from the test, and what is the recommended action for each outcome?
- If the therapy is the same regardless of the result, could we skip the test and just begin the therapy?
- Are there any different tests that we should consider?
- How much does the test cost, and is there any way to get it done less expensively?
- If you were spending your own money, would you take this test?

You may be surprised by the responses you get, particularly to the last question. Many tests and medical procedures are not even sanctioned by the doctors who prescribe them—they are forced to do so for liability reasons by their medical malpractice insurance carriers. Ask again, "Would you take this test with your own money?" If the candid answer is no, ask whether you can sign a waiver instead, stating that your doctor advised you to take the test but that you refused against medical advice (AMA).

Surgery

Check your wallet when a doctor starts talking about surgery—then get a second or third opinion. Make sure you receive advice from at least one doctor who is not a candidate to perform the surgery. Doctors often have an enormous financial conflict of interest when it comes to recommending a surgery they might perform themselves. Be particularly careful when your doctor has already leased or purchased expensive equipment (e.g., LASIK tools) that they need to keep busy. Do not hesitate to ask, "What do you get personally if I choose to do, or not to do, the surgery?" Doctors are not subject to the same conflict-of-interest standards that have become commonplace for lawyers, public officials, and other professionals.

Preface: The Revolution Continues: What's New in *The New Wellness Revolution*

1. In a letter to Robert Hooke, 5 February, 1675/6, quoted in *The Concise Oxford Dictionary of Quotations,* new ed. (London: Oxford University Press, 1986), 176.
2. In a letter to Robert Hooke, 5 February, 1675/6, quoted in *The Concise Oxford Dictionary of Quotations,* new ed. (London: Oxford University Press, 1986), 176.

Introduction: Why Wellness Is the Next Big Thing

1. *Merriam-Webster's Collegiate Dictionary.* Springfield, MA: Zane Publishing, Inc., and Merriam-Webster, Inc., 1996.
2. Ibid.
3. "Putting America on Wheels," *The Economist,* 31 December 1999.
4. Walkman is a registered trademark of the Sony Corporation.

Chapter 1: Why We Need a Revolution

1. *Merriam-Webster's Collegiate Dictionary,* 10th ed. Springfield, MA: Zane Publishing, Inc., and Merriam-Webster, Inc., 1996.
2. *Encyclopaedia Britannica,* www.Britannica.com.
3. Ibid.
4. Ibid.
5. *Prevalence of Overweight and Obesity Among Adults: United States, 1999,* National Center for Health Statistics, Centers for Disease Control (CDC).
6. Hostess Twinkies, Oreo, and McDonald's Happy Meals are registered trademarks, respectively, of the Interstate Bakeries Corporation, Nabisco, Inc., and McDonald's Corporation.
7. Oreo, Ritz, and Life Savers are trademarks of Nabsico Holdings, Inc.
8. Oscar Mayer bacon and Philadelphia brand cream cheese are trademarks of Kraft Foods, Inc.
9. In 2006, the U.S. Government launched Medicare Part D Prescription Drug Coverage which basically covers the first $900 a year of prescription drugs and most prescription drug costs over $5,000 a year—but leaves the majority of seniors consuming between $75 and $450 a month to still pay themselves for their prescription drugs.

10. Diller, Lawrence H., MD, "Just Say Yes to Ritalin! Parents Are Being Pressured by Schools to Medicate Their Kids—or Else," *New York Times,* September 24, 2000.

11. There is so much overlap between the different categories that I have deliberately not listed current sales figures for each. For example, the vitamin industry claims current sales of $70 billion—although a close examination of this number yields the fact that it includes vitamins and supplements added to ordinary foods. Similarly, the $12 billion in fitness club revenues does not isolate amounts paid to the clubs themselves for the use of their trainers.

12. Witkower Press, Inc., of Hartford, Connecticut, had published *Arthritis and Common Sense* and claimed in their advertisements that it would help arthritic and rheumatoid sufferers. In 1954 the FTC ordered the Witkower Press to "forthwith cease and desist from representing, directly or indirectly, that their book was adequate, effective, and reliable in giving relief to arthritic and rheumatoid sufferers." Witkower Press accepted the ruling and did not appeal the case. In a similar case against Prentice Hall, the large publisher agreed to the FTC action because they did not want to enter into costly litigation with the federal government. (Pilzer, Paul Zane, "Rodale Press versus the Federal Trade Commission: A Comprehensive Analysis," senior thesis, Lehigh University, Bethlehem, PA, May 21, 1974.)

13. Ibid.

14. Ibid.

15. Later research identified that there are 13 such critical substances and that they are not all ammonia-based substances, but the term *vitamins,* with a changed spelling in recognition of this research, has remained.

16. The story of Edward Jenner's discovery of the cowpox vaccine to prevent smallpox is well known. But it is not well known that the actual process of inoculation itself (deliberately infecting someone with a disease to prevent that same disease from occurring) was developed in the East hundreds of years earlier and that this was well known in Jenner's time.

17. Behe, Michael J., *Darwin's Black Box: The Biochemical Challenge to Evolution.* The Free Press, 1996, p. 10.

Chapter 2: The Baby Boom Generation: Understanding and Controlling the Demand for Wellness

1. *Retro*—"relating to, reviving, or being the styles or esp. the fashions of the past : fashionably nostalgic or old-fashioned 'a retro look'." © 1996 Zane Publishing, Inc., and Merriam-Webster, Inc.

2. Russell, Cheryl, *The Baby Boom: Americans Aged 35 to 54,* 2nd ed., New Strategist Publications, Inc., 1999, 2000, Foreword.

3. U.S. Department of Commerce, Bureau of the Census, *Statistical Abstract of the United States: 1991* (Washington: Government Printing Office, 1991), pp. 1272, 1275.
4. Today, this terrible disease has been almost completely eradicated through the addition of vitamin D to commonly consumed foods.
5. The cause of beriberi was discovered by Casimir Funk in 1912. It has been eradicated through the addition of vitamin B_1, or thiamine, to dehusked grains.
6. Our bodies age or decay over time due to molecules called *free radicals,* which cause them to oxidate or "rust." Certain vitamins may be able to slow or retard oxidation.

Chapter 3: What You Need to Know about Food and Diet

1. Genesis 2:9 (King James Bible).
2. Data compiled from Healthstatus.com (http://www.healthstatus.com).
3. "Forward into the Past: Eating as Our Ancestors Did," *Eating for Health,* www.obesity.com.
4. Genesis 2:9 (King James Bible).
5. Pasteurization is the application of heat to "destroy pathogenic enzymes, and to reduce or destroy spoilage microorganisms" ("Food Preservation," *Encyclopaedia Britannica,* 2000), www.britannica.com.
6. "Betcha Can't Eat Just One" is the name of a television commercial for Lay's potato chips, re-released starring baseball great Cal Ripken (www.ripkenbaseball.com/pr_frito_lay.shtml) on April 2, 2001.
7. McDonald's Corporation, www.mcdonalds.com.
8. Schlosser, Eric, *Fast Food Nation: The Dark Side of the All-American Meal,* New York: Houghton Mifflin Company, p. 6.
9. Lin, Biing-Hwan, Joanne Guthrie, and Elizabeth Frazao, "Nutrient Contribution of Food Away from Home," *America's Eating Habits: Changes and Consequences.* Edited by Elizabeth Frazao, Food and Rural Economics Division, Economic Research Service, U.S. Department of Agriculture. Agriculture Information Bulletin No. 750 (AIB-750), www.ers.usda.gov.

Chapter 4: Making Your Fortune in Food

1. The traditional seven deadly sins are (1) vainglory, or pride; (2) covetousness; (3) lust, understood as inordinate or illicit sexual desire; (4) envy; (5) gluttony, which usually included drunkenness; (6) anger; and (7) sloth. They were identified during the early history of Christian monasticism and grouped together in the sixth century by St. Gregory the Great. (*Merriam-Webster's Encyclopedia of Literature,* Zane Publishing, Inc., and Merriam-Webster, Inc., 1996.)

2. This $55 billion includes approximately $25 billion paid through USDA price support programs to tens of thousands of farmers for not farming. None of this $55 billion is included in the $1.3 trillion total, as it is all either exported or is a subcomponent of the other categories.

3. As of 7/11/06 the National Restaurant Association expected 2006 sales in the nation's 925,000 restaurants to be $511.1 billion (http://www.restaurant.org/research/). This number is estimated to increase 7 percent to $547 billion in 2007.

4. Approximately half of this $100 billion is in products sold to food processors and thus may be double counted.

5. These are 2005 state population figures. *Statistical Abstract of the United States,* 2006.

6. Becker, Elizabeth, "Corporate Welfare Fuels Big Farms," *New York Times,* May 14, 2001.

7. *Merriam-Webster's Collegiate Dictionary,* © 1996 Zane Publishing, Inc., and Merriam-Webster, Inc.

8. Soy-beverage marketers petitioned the FDA to use the term *soymilk* three years prior to NMPF's complaint. The FDA decided not to rule on the petition, which allowed soymilk producers to operate under an umbrella of protection as long as they don't deceive the public in their labeling or advertising. (Frank, Paula, "Soy's Evolution," www.foodproductdesign.com).

9. Fiscal years ending March 31.

10. Author interview with Steve Demos, July 19, 2006

11. Adamy, Janet, "Behind a food giant's success: An unlikely soy-milk alliance," *The Wall St. Journal,* February 1, 2005, page 1.

12. The original Gardenburger didn't contain soy because Wenner didn't like the taste and thought that many consumers had a negative view of soy-based products. Today, most Gardenburger varieties (except for the original style) contain 12 to 14 grams of soy protein per patty.

13. Wenner, Paul, *Garden Cuisine: Heal Yourself Through Low-Fat Meatless Eating,* Fireside, New York, 1998.

14. The original company Wenner founded was called Wholesome and Hearty Foods, Inc. The name was changed to Gardenburger, Inc., when it went public in 1992.

15. As a result of its share price on Nasdaq remaining below $5 for several months.

16. http://www.gardenburger.com/restructure.shtml, July 11, 2006.

17. Restaurant Industry Forecast, National Restaurant Association (www.restaurant.org).

18. In 1999, average household spending on food away from home was approximately $2,583 for persons 35 to 54 versus $1,245 for persons 65 and older. (Restaurant Industry Forecast, National Restaurant Association, www.restaurant.org).

Chapter 5: Making Your Fortune in Medicine

1. Behe, Michael J., *Darwin's Black Box: The Biochemical Challenge to Evolution,* The Free Press, 1996.
2. Trepanned skulls from prehistoric times have been found in Britain, France, and other parts of Europe and in Peru—many of them showing evidence of healing and, presumably, of the patient's survival. The practice still exists among primitive people in parts of Algeria and in Melanesia (www.britannica.com).
3. Although Hippocrates is said to have been born in 460 B.C. and a great many books bear his name, modern scholars attribute this collection of books to several individuals writing under this same name over several lifetimes.
4. Behe, Michael J., *Darwin's Black Box: The Biochemical Challenge to Evolution,* The Free Press, 1996.
5. Behe, Michael J., *Darwin's Black Box: The Biochemical Challenge to Evolution,* The Free Press, 1996, p. 10.
6. Personal interview with Carl S. (Sam) Rehnborg, PhD, son of Carl F. Rehnborg, September 7, 2001.
7. Telephone interview between author and Dr. Tod Cooperman on August 10, 2001, follow-up interview on July 13, 2006.
8. An *intrapreneur* is an entrepreneur working within a large organization.
9. *Executive Health Program,* brochure, The Fitness Institute at LDS hospital, Salt Lake City, UT.
10. Adams, Fisher, Hansen, and Yanowitz, *Maintaining the Miracle: An Owner's Manual for the Human Body.*
11. Dr. Yanowitz also lights up when he talks about being a performing jazz pianist—having recorded an LP and several CDs, not only of standard jazz pieces but of his original compositions.
12. "Physical Activity and Public Health," *Journal of the American Medical Association,* February 1, 1995, vol. 273, no. 5.
13. Wee, Christina C., MD, MPH, "Physical Activity Counseling in Primary Care," *Journal of the American Medical Association,* August 8, 2001, vol. 286, no. 6.
14. "Jill Stevens Kinney—America's #1 Female Club Entrepreneur," *Club Insider News,* May 1999, vol. VI, no. 5.

Chapter 6: What You Must Know about Health Insurance

1. Pilzer, Paul Zane, *The New Health Insurance Solution* (Wiley, 2005/2007).
2. Some states limit the ability of insurance carriers to raise premiums for "small employers" (generally 50 employees or less) due to high-loss

experience, or they limit the size of such premium increases to be within predefined "rating bands" for small employee groups.

3. Himmelstein, David, Elizabeth Warren, Deborah Thorne, and Steffie Woolhandler, "MarketWatch: Illness and Injury as Contributors to Bankruptcy," *Health Affairs,* 2 February 2005, 5 May 2005.

4. In some cases, employees are allowed to continue their employer-sponsored health insurance for 18 to 36 months after termination, at their own expense. This short-term coverage, called COBRA, cost terminated employees approximately $616/month for individuals and $1,450/month for families.

5. In a health maintenance organization (HMO) the provider is paid a flat annual amount per patient instead of being paid for each service rendered.

6. Approximately 20 percent of healthcare insurance premiums go toward overhead.

7. In some cases, employees are allowed to continue their employer-sponsored health insurance for 18 to 36 months after termination at their own expense. This short-term coverage, called COBRA, in 2006 costs ex-employees approximately $616/month for individuals and $1,450/month for families.

A self-employed individual (as defined in Code Sec. 401[c][1]) may deduct as a business expense a statutory percentage of the amount paid for medical insurance on himself, his spouse, and his dependents (Code Sec. 162[l][1]).

Chapter 8: Making Your Fortune Distributing Wellness

1. At this point I also ask the class about the economic implications of inviting a passing ship of 50 destitute foreigners to come live on our island and share our newly developed wealth. During the ensuing debate the students realize themselves that they, and the new immigrants, will both become even richer when the newcomers are welcomed with open arms into our island society.

2. Readers of my prior books may note that I estimated distribution costs in 1990 at 80 percent (versus 70 percent today). This is because distribution costs as a percentage of retail sales fell throughout the 1990s due to the advent of the Internet (or real-time information sharing), but the same advent of the Internet lowered manufacturing costs at an even greater pace.

3. Not every department store owner was asleep at the switch. The century-old Dayton-Hudson Corporation (i.e., Marshall Field, Mervyn's, Dayton Hudson), successfully retooled its existing department stores toward more fashionable merchandise while simultaneously building Target stores from scratch in 1962 into one of the largest mass merchandisers. In fact, they were so successful that the Target division exceeded 78 per-

cent of their $33 billion in sales in 1999, and the company changed its name to Target Corporation in 2000.

4. Home Depot has since "institutionalized" such innovation by requiring existing vendors to submit a plan annually on how they will lower costs, or increase quality, by 20 percent per annum. If the existing vendor cannot meet these guidelines, their entire relationship is opened to competitive bidding by other vendors. This forces the manufacturers to innovate on a continual rather than on a when-it's-almost-too-late basis.

5. Kaufman, Leslie, "As Biggest Business, Wal-Mart Propels Changes Elsewhere," *New York Times,* October 22, 2000.

Chapter 9: Direct Selling— How to Get Started

1. Direct Selling Association (www.dsa.org).

Chapter 10: Staking Your Claim: The Next Millionaires

1. *Merriam-Webster's Collegiate Dictionary,* 10th ed. Springfield, MA: Zane Publishing, Inc., and Merriam-Webster, Inc., 1996.

2. Henry Wells worked as a freight-forwarding agent in Albany, New York, before cofounding Livingston Wells, and Pomeroy's Express in 1843 to handle freight between Buffalo and Albany, and hiring George Fargo as an agent.

3. Telephone interview between author and Dr. Bob Hoffman on August 10, 2006.

4. Cronan, Carl, "Art the Revelator," *The Business Journal of Tampa Bay,* September 28, 1998.

5. Since then he has been active as a philanthropist and a backseat coach: In 1998, Williams purchased the Tampa Bay Lightning hockey team for $117 million and donated $70 million to Liberty University. (Cronan, Carl, "Art the Revelator," *The Business Journal of Tampa Bay,* September 28, 1998.)

6. In the 1960s Sam Walton (the founder of Wal-Mart) often spoke of how he admired W. T. Grant—then the largest department store chain in the United States and a model for efficiency and growth. In 1975, when W. T. Grant filed bankruptcy, 1,073 stores were closed, 80,000 people were thrown out of work, and creditors had to write off approximately $334 million in bad debts and loans. The repercussions of this major failure were felt by communities and small businesses worldwide for years to come.

7. Genesis 2:9 (King James Bible).

8. Zohar I, 196A.

9. "Since by keeping the body in health and vigor one walks in the ways of God—it being impossible during sickness to have any understanding or knowledge of the Creator—it is a man's duty to avoid whatever is injurious to the body, and cultivate habits conducive to health and vigor." (Moses Maimonides (1136–1204), Mishnah Torah.)
10. Mead, Rebecca, "Slim for Him: God Is Watching What You're Eating," *The New Yorker,* January 15, 2001.

Epilogue: Unlimited Wellness

1. Watson and Crick received the Nobel Prize for discovering DNA in 1953, and Dr. J. Craig Venter of the Celera Corporation announced that they had completed mapping the human genome on April 6, 2000.
2. Robert Bazell, "Scientists Map Human Chromosome," December 1, 1999, *NBC Nightly News.*
3. Ibid.
4. In 2000 there were approximately 5 million U.S. households with a total net worth exceeding $1 million, and this number was projected to grow approximately 50 percent by 2005.
5. This mistake as a young man led to "a fruitless quest that occupied the rest of his life." (Albert Einstein, *Encyclopaedia Britannica,* 2000.)
6. Although Einstein's discoveries as a physicist may have been fruitless from this point forward, Einstein certainly more than distinguished himself in his later years as a statesman and champion of world peace. Einstein was professionally ostracized by other leading physicists because of his refusal to accept probabilistic laws of quantum mechanics—although they later successfully used his fame and political connections during World War II. Einstein was called upon by them to get President Roosevelt to endorse the Manhattan Project to build the atomic bomb, but then Einstein was kept in the dark about their progress until the bomb was actually detonated over Hiroshima.
7. My friend and colleague Norman Beil disagrees with me that Einstein was incorrect on this point. Beil contends that statistics are used to make decisions only when we do not have the right answer—as in meteorology, where we use statistical data to predict a "28 percent chance of rain" even though whether or not it will rain is a binary outcome. Beil feels that Einstein was saying we should not give up searching for a unified field theory and rely on statistics, but rather that we should keep searching, and rely on statistics only when we have given up all hope of finding the correct answer.
8. Job 42:12–17 (King James Bible).
9. Keynes, John Maynard, *The General Theory of Employment, Interest, and Money* (San Diego: Harcourt Brace Jovanovich, 1964), p. 383. Keynes's great work was first published in England in 1936.

Appendix A: Fat: What Is It, How Do We Get It, and How Can We Define It?

1. In addition to simply weighing underwater and dry, adjustments must be made for the amount of water displaced (Archimedes' principle), water temperature, water density, and lung capacity (using helium).

Appendix B: Shifting from Sickness to Wellness Medical Care

1. "This analysis showed an increased risk of suicidal thoughts and behavior from 2% to 4% in people under 18," *About Zoloft: Common Questions,* 2005, Pfizer Inc., 9 May, 2005, www.zoloft.com/zoloft/zoloft.portal?_nfpb=true&_pageLabel=common_questions.
2. Glenmullen, Joseph, "Prozac Backlash: Overcoming the Dangers of Prozac, Zoloft, Paxil, and Other Antidepressants with Safe, Effective Alternatives," *Dr. Joseph Mercola Online,* 2005, 9 May 2005, www.mercola.com/2000/apr/9/prozac_backlash.htm.
3. Krugman, Paul, "Passing the Buck," *New York Times Online,* 22 April 2005, 9 May 2005, www.nytimes.com.
4. Americans spend more than $27 billion a year on medical malpractice, according to the Congressional Budget Office. The average individual health insurance premium for a healthy individual is $92 per month, or $1,104 per year ($27 billion per year divided by $1,104 per year equals 24.5 million), U.S. Congressional Budget Office, *Limiting Tort Liability for Medical Malpractice,* 8 January, 2004, 9 May, 2005, www.cbo.gov/showdoc.cfm?index=4968&sequence=0.

Alternative Medicine: The Definitive Guide. Puyallup, WA: Future Medicine Publishing, Inc., 1993.

Anders, George. *Health Against Wealth: HMOs and the Breakdown of Medical Trust.* New York: Houghton Mifflin Company, 1996.

Andrews, Charles. *Profit Fever: The Drive to Corporatize Healthcare and How to Stop It.* Monroe, ME: Common Courage Press, 1995.

Andrews, Sam S., MD, Luis A. Balart, MD, Morrison C. Bethea, MD, and H. Leighton Steward. *Sugar Busters!: Cut Sugar to Trim Fat.* New York: Ballantine Books, 1998.

Bailey, Covert. *The New Fit or Fat.* Boston: Houghton Mifflin Company, 1991.

Balch, James F., MD, and Phyllis A. Balch, CNC. *Prescription for Nutritional Healing.* Garden City Park, NY: Avery Publishing Group Inc., 1990.

Behe, Michael J. *Darwin's Black Box: The Biochemical Challenge to Evolution.* New York: Simon & Schuster, 1998.

Berman, Louis A. *Vegetarianism and the Jewish Tradition.* New York: Ktav Publishing House, Inc., 1982.

Binzel, Phillip E., Jr., MD. *Alive and Well: One Doctor's Experience with Nutrition in the Treatment of Cancer Patients.* Westlake Village, CA: American Media, 1994.

Brown, Montague, Everett A. Johnson, and Richard L. Johnson. *The Economic Era of Healthcare: A Revolution in Organized Delivery Systems.* San Francisco: Jossey-Bass, Inc., 1996.

Castro, Janice. *The American Way of Health: How Medicine Is Changing and What It Means to You.* New York: Little Brown and Company, 1994.

Dauner, C. Duane, with Michael Bowker. *The Healthcare Solution: Understanding the Crisis and the Cure.* Sacramento, CA: Vision Publishing, 1994.

Diamond, Harvey, and Marilyn Diamond. *Fit for Life.* New York: Warner Books, Inc., 1985.

———. *Fit for Life II: Living Health.* New York: Warner Books, 1989.

Eddy, Mary Baker. *Science and Health with Key to the Scriptures.* Washington, DC: Office of the Librarian of Congress, 1934.

Follard, Sherman, Allen C. Goodman, and Miron Stano. *The Economics of Health and Healthcare.* Upper Saddle River, NJ: Prentice-Hall, Inc., 1997.

Fraser, Laura. *Losing It: America's Obsession with Weight and the Industry That Feeds on It.* New York: Penguin Books USA Inc., 1997.

Frech, H. E., III. *Competition and Monopoly in Healthcare.* La Vergne, TN: American Enterprise Press, 1996.

Gaesser, Glenn A. *Big Fat Lies: The Truth About Your Weight and Your Health.* New York: Fawcett Columbine, 1996.

Herzlinger, Regina. *Market Driven Healthcare: Who Wins, Who Loses in the Transformation of America's Largest Service Industry.* Reading, MA: Addison-Wesley Publishing Company, 1997.

Kalechofsky, Roberta, PhD. *Vegetarian Judaism: A Guide for Everyone.* Marblehead, MA: Micah Publications, Inc., 1998.

Katahn, Martin, PhD. *The T-Factor Diet: Lose Weight Safely and Quickly Without Cutting Calories—or Even Counting Them!* New York: W. W. Norton & Company, Inc., 1989.

Kunnes, Richard, M.D. *Your Money or Your Life: Rx for the Medical Market Place.* New York: The Cornwall Press, Inc., 1971.

Millenson, Michael L. *Demanding Medical Excellence: Doctors and Accountability in the Information Age.* Chicago: The University of Chicago Press, 1997.

Morreim, E. Haavi. *Balancing Act: The New Medical Ethics of Medicine's New Economics.* Washington, DC: Georgetown University Press, 1995.

Muller, H. G., and G. Tobin. *Nutrition and Food Processing.* Westport, CT: The Avi Publishing Company, Inc., 1980.

Ornish, Dean. *Dr. Dean Ornish's Program for Reversing Heart Disease.* New York: Random House, Inc., 1990.

Osmani, S. R. *Nutrition and Poverty.* New York: Oxford University Press, Inc., 1992.

Pilzer, Paul Zane. *God Wants You to Be Rich: The Theology of Economics.* New York: Simon & Schuster/Fireside, 1995/1997.

———. *The Next Millionaires.* Dallas, TX: VideoPlus, Inc., 2005.

———. *The Next Trillion: Why the Wellness Industry Will Exceed the $1 Trillion Healthcare (Sickness) Industry in the Next Ten Years.* Dallas, TX: VideoPlus, Inc., 2001.

———. *Unlimited Wealth: The Theory and Practice of Economic Alchemy.* New York: Crown Publishers, 1990/1994.

Pilzer, Paul Zane, with Robert Dietz. *Other People's Money: The Inside Story of the S&L Crisis.* New York: Simon & Schuster, 1989.

Porter, Roy. *The Greatest Benefit to Mankind: A Medical History of Humanity.* New York: W. W. Norton & Company, Inc., 1997.

Powter, Susan. *Stop the Insanity: Change the Way You Look and Feel—Forever.* New York: Simon & Schuster, 1993.

Reid, Daniel P. *The Tao of Health, Sex, and Longevity: A Modern Practical Guide to the Ancient Way.* New York: Fireside, 1989.

Roberts, Marc. J., with Alexandra T. Clyde. *Your Money or Your Life: The Healthcare Crisis Explained.* New York: Doubleday, 1993.

Rodwin, Marc A. *Medicine, Money and Morals: Physicians' Conflicts of Interest.* New York: Oxford University Press, 1993.

Schlosser, Eric. *Fast Food Nation: The Dark Side of the All-American Meal.* New York: Houghton-Mifflin, 2001.

Shaouli, Rabbi Moshe Cohen, and Rabbi Yaakov Fisher. *Nature's Wealth: Health and Healing Plants Recommended by Professors of Science and Medicine.* English edition edited by Ruth Steinberg. Copyright Rabbi Jacob Fisher, 1999.

Simon, Julian L. *The State of Humanity.* Cambridge, MA: Blackwell Publishers, Inc., 1995.

Skidelsky, Robert. *John Maynard Keynes: The Economist as Savior, 1920– 1937.* Harmondsworth, Middlesex, England: Penguin Books, 1994.

———. *John Maynard Keynes: Hopes Betrayed, 1883–1920.* Harmondsworth, Middlesex, England: Penguin Books, 1986.

Starr, Paul. *The Social Transformation of American Medicine: The Rise of a Sovereign Profession and the Making of a Vast Industry.* New York: Basic Books, 1982.

The PDR Family Guide to Prescription Drugs. New York: Crown Trade Paperbacks, 1996.

Tips, Jack, ND, PhD. *The Pro Vita! Plan: Your Foundation for Optimal Nutrition.* Austin, TX: Apple-A-Day Press, 1993.

Weil, Andrew, MD. *Eating Well for Optimum Health: The Essential Guide to Food, Diet, and Nutrition.* New York: Alfred A. Knopf, 2000.

Weiss, Lawrence D. *Private Medicine and Public Health: Profit, Politics, and Prejudice in the American Healthcare Enterprise.* Boulder, CO: Westview Press, 1997.

Wyke, Alexandra. *21st-Century Miracle Medicine: RoboSurgery, Wonder Cures, and the Quest for Immortality.* New York: Plenum Press, 1997.

My first acknowledgment goes to the wellness revolutionaries profiled in this book, and the many more whom I have learned about since 2002. I wish I had the space to tell all of your stories, and the great impact you are having on the lives of your clients, patients, and customers. You are *The New Wellness Revolution* and I salute you— Viva la Revolution!

The next acknowledgment goes to my editor, Richard Narramore. As the editor of *The New Health Insurance Solution* (2005/2007), Richard realized the importance of my prior book, *The Wellness Revolution* (2002), and that it should be revised and updated.

Next are the numerous friends, family members, and colleagues who have supported me through thick and thin the past 53 years. Unlike the acknowledgments in my previous seven books, I am deliberately not going to list you here out of respect for my readers and for fear of leaving someone out—you know who you are and how much you mean to me.

And finally, and most of all, is the immense love and gratitude I feel to my wife, Lisa, and to our four children, Miriam, Maxwell, Michael, and Mark.

Paul Zane Pilzer is a world-renowned economist, a multimillionaire software entrepreneur, an adjunct professor, and the author of seven bestselling books.

Pilzer completed college in three years and received his MBA from Wharton in fifteen months at age 22. At age 24, he was appointed an adjunct professor at New York University, where he has taught for 20 consecutive years. While employed as Citibank's youngest officer at 22 and its youngest vice president at 25, Pilzer started several entrepreneurial businesses—earning his first $1 million before age 26 and his first $10 million before age 30. Over the past 30 years, he has started and/or taken public five companies in the areas of software, education, and financial services. He is the founder of the nation's two leading suppliers of individualized health benefits to corporate America.

He was an appointed economic advisor in two presidential administrations and warned of the impending $200 billion savings and loan crisis years before official Washington was willing to listen—a story that he later told in *Other People's Money* (Simon & Schuster, 1989) which was critically acclaimed by the *New York Times* and *The Economist* magazine.

Pilzer's *Unlimited Wealth* (Crown Publishers, 1990) explained how we live in a world of unlimited physical resources because of rapidly advancing technology. After reading *Unlimited Wealth,* the late Sam Walton, founder of Wal-Mart, said that he was "amazed at Pilzer's business capacity" and his "ability to put it into layman's terms."

Pilzer's *God Wants You to Be Rich* (Simon & Schuster, 1995/1997) explained how the foundation of our economic system is based on our Judeo-Christian heritage. This *New York Times* business bestseller was featured on the front page of *The Wall Street Journal* and on television shows ranging from *60 Minutes* to *First Person with Maria Shriver.* It has been published in 18 languages.

And now, in *The New Wellness Revolution,* Pilzer identifies the newly emerging "wellness" business and explains how wellness entrepreneurs can find their fortunes in this soon-to-be $1 trillion industry.

Pilzer, a former commentator on National Public Radio and CNN, has appeared three times on the *Larry King Live!* television program and on the cover of several national magazines. He speaks live each year to approximately 250,000 people, and more than 12 million audiotapes of his speeches have been sold.

He lives in Utah with his wife and four children, where they are all avid snowboarders, mountain bikers, and chess players.

For more information please visit www.paulzanepilzer.com.